The
Loving
Dominant

The Loving Dominant

third edition

by John and Libby Warren

greenery press

Cover photo by Barbara Nitke, *www.barbaranitke.com*

Published in the United States by Greenery Press. Distributed by SCB Distributors, Gardena, CA.

Contents

Acknowledgments

I will never forget the advice and help I received from Len Dworkin. He will always live in my memory, as will the memory of his lovely submissive, Michelle.

While all the mistakes in this book are my fault, there would be many more if not for the efforts of M.M. of San Francisco, Ally of Florida, and Kevin Damore of Oakland, whose editing skills and tact made the book readable and preserved the author's ego.

Many thanks go to Mistress Margo, Lady J, Mistress Kay, Goddess Sia, Jack McGeorge, Frank Rinella, and Travis for providing an invaluable insight into functioning of female dominant-male submissive relationships. Tatu, a natural fiber rope enthusiast, has done a wonderful section on that specialized area of bondage that explains it better than I could have done

Others, without whom this book might never have been written, the posters on the Prodigy electronic bulletin board, the newsgroups soc.subculture.bondage-bdsm and alt.torture, the CollarMe website, the members of The Boston Dungeon Society, TES, Nashville PEP, SPICE and Threshold.

Warning and Disclaimer: Readers should understand that all BDSM carries an inherent risk of physical injury, emotional injury, injury to relationships, and other types of harm. While we believe that the guidelines set forth in this book will help you reduce that risk to a reasonable level, the writer and publisher encourage you to understand that you are choosing to take some risk when you decide to engage in these activities, and to accept personal responsibility for that risk.

While we have diligently researched the information we put in this book, it may nonethless be incomplete, inaccurate, or out of date. Thefore, in acting on the information in this book, you agree to accept its contents "as is" and "with all faults." Please notify us of any errors so that we may address them in future printings.

The information in this book should not be used as medical or therapeutic advice. Neither the author, the publisher nor anyone else associated with the creation or sale of this book is liable for any damage caused by your participating in the activities described herein.

Foreword to the Third Edition

Those of you who have read the edition of *The Loving Dominant* that was published by Masquerade Books or its second edition from Greenery Press won't find many surprises in these pages, although I do appreciate the additional royalties.

There are several new sections and I've greatly expanded a few existing ones. For example, the section on electricity is much much larger than it was in either of the previous versions.

The biggest change is on how to find partners. The original Loving Dominant was written at a time when the Internet was largely a thing of corporations, governments and universities. BDSM, when it was mentioned, was a thing of whispers and giggles. Today, we can be much more open and the Internet has changed the world almost beyond imagination.

References to S&M or Domination and Submission have been largely replaced by BDSM, an umbrella term combining the words Bondage, Discipline, Domination, Submission, Sadism and Masochism. While I have some discomfort with "sadism," I feel it is a more inclusive umbrella and a more accurate representation than simply domination and submission. The shift in terminology has created a bit of a problem in language. To avoid labored constructions, I've retained "dominant" or "submissive" where it was appropriate even though the reference could apply equally to a "top" or a "bottom." I attempted various semantic tricks like "dominant/top," "dominant or top" and even the generic "player." All of them did more violence to the flow than I was comfortable with.

I'll also be spending more time talking about pure sensation players since I admit giving their interests an undeserved short shrift in the original version.

The happiest change from the original volume is that the DSM IIIr, the learned tome that branded what we do as pathologically nuts, has been supplanted by the DSM IV, which takes a lot more understanding view of us whip-swinging perverts.

Aside from those modifications, most of the changes are either fine tuning on my part or a recognition that time has marched on, leaving some parts of the old book more useful as a historical archive than as a guide to what is happening currently.

Foreword to the First Edition

What is "domination and submission?" It is a form of erotic play that takes place when one voluntarily gives up some or all of his or her power and freedom to another for the purpose of sensual excitement. For most practitioners, it is a kind of chocolate frosting on the conventional sexuality cake, an enhancement and expansion rather than a substitute for the genital sex.

To many who indulge in its pleasures, it is a cathartic sexual game based on fantasy, a sensual psychodrama. Moreover, the term describes both activities and relationships. People, who take part in BDSM games at anything more than the most surface level usually discover that these activities intensify the emotional connections between themselves and their partners.

There are only two universals in the practice of BDSM. First, there must be a power transfer between or among the parties in the relationship. Second, all activities must be consensual.

In the transfer, one person gives up a certain amount of power, and another person or persons accept it. The individual who gives up power is the submissive, and the one who accepts it is the dominant. The amount of power given up by the submissive varies widely among couples and may be different at different times for the same couple. At one end of the spectrum, the submissive can agree to remain absolutely still and passive while the other reads a story or describes a fantasy. At the other end, the submissive can display rigorous restraint while enduring (and enjoying) the application of intense and varied stimuli.

This transfer of power doesn't have to be at the physical level of, "You must do this," and, "You can't do that." It can be on a much deeper spiritual level. A casual play partner showed me an ancient Hindu drawing of a couple making love with curved and straight lines, called chakras, that led from various parts of one body to the comparable parts of the other's. She explained that they represented energy transfers the Hindus believed took place during sex. As I looked at the picture, I realized that during the scene I felt this energy transfer, but I hadn't considered visualizing it in such a way. My partner, in some kind of metaphysical way, seemed to be sending me a force that I returned to her through my actions in the scene.

Consensuality means that not only has the submissive partner consent to the activities, but that the dominant or top also consents. The latter point is often overlooked, but it is very important to understanding the true dynamics of the relationship that underlies the activities.

Other terms that have been applied to these games are "B&D" (bondage and discipline) and "S&M" (sadism and masochism). The former is an accurate description of the activities of some members of the greater BDSM community. However, there are many who revel in forms of BDSM with neither a rope or a whip. Although the term S&M is very popular with many BDSM dominants, I feel that we would be better off cutting our ties with it.

My reasoning is that while masochists make up a significant part of the BDSM community, far from all submissives are masochists and some masochists are far from submissive. Some masochists can be most emphatic about demanding and getting a proper dose of pain during any given session, while others aren't as vocal.

However, what bothers me about the phrase S&M is the S. The Marquis de Sade, as anyone who has read his writings knows, favored unwilling victims for his cruel activities, which were entirely concerned with his own pleasure and not at all concerned with consent. To me, this is a true description of a sadist. Nothing could be farther from the spirit of the typical dominant/top who engages in an erotic dance of power with the submissive. While some dominants choose to proclaim that they are sadists, I have noticed that even they will generally distance themselves from nonconsensual practices.

Since there are pathological sadists in the world, I prefer to leave this term to them and describe us as dominants or tops because the terms are more neutral and less limited. After all, people are confused enough by BDSM play. We don't need to make the distinction more difficult.

Do not be fooled by my choice of the word "play" for what goes on is BDSM. As any mother knows, play is inherently dangerous. Who among us survived through childhood without a cut or painful scrape? For this reason, I will never describe any BDSM activity as "safe." I recently heard of a submissive who suffered a fatal heart attack while cleaning his mistress' toilet, an activity which would have normally been quite safe but was rendered fatal by the intense excitement he felt fulfilling his fantasy. A lady of my acquaintance suffered a dislocated shoulder while combining bondage with a truly mind-blowing orgasm.

Some BDSM undertakings are riskier than others. In this book, I will be taking care to differentiate the risky from the not-so-risky and to explain ways to minimize the risk inherent in any of them.

The truth about most BDSM movies and books is that many things that are shown or talked about are extremely dangerous. True, many movies and a few books have a short legalistic warning against trying to duplicate what is shown, but such a generic warning is little help for someone trying to find out how to do it right.

Previously, I mentioned the terms dominant and top. These are terms to describe two overlapping kinds of play. A dominant may use both physical and psychological components to play with his or her partner. A top applies physical stimulation to the bottom without requiring a complementary submission on the bottom's part.

The best illustration I can provide of a top/bottom scene took place several years ago. I was watching a novice top whipping a bottom I had played with several times. After a few minutes, she pushed herself back from the wall she had been leaning against, turned around and took the whip out of the surprised top's hand, handed it to me and said, "John, show him how I like to be whipped." There was no submission here. It was simply one person applying stimulation to another, a top and a bottom.

I write from my own point of view, that of a male heterosexual dominant. However, I sought assistance from several of my sister dominants and tops and have tried to provide the information women who work with men need. In addition, a number of male and female submissives have provided valuable and, sometimes, vital insights which, I have included.

A good motto for any dominant: NO UNINTENTIONAL PAIN. I hope this book will help you and your partner find exciting and creative things that you can do in an atmosphere of relative safety and complete consensuality. I've been playing BDSM games for almost thirty years and seriously studying the art for more than a decade. This book is the distilled essence of that study and experience.

You will find the vertical pronoun "I" scattered throughout the book. Although an overweening ego may be in some way responsible, my primary intent is to emphasize that many of the comments in this book are my opinion and are fit subject for debate or refutation. I hope others will carry this orderly and ethical approach to the art of BDSM to greater heights than I can manage.

The Loving Dominant is intended for a wide audience. My primary goal is to reach novice dominants, or those who feel they are dominants, and help them overcome the psychological barriers to undertaking such a politically incorrect activity. I also want to show them techniques that can be used to bring pleasure to their submissives and themselves. While some of the activities I write about may not interest tops, much of the technique sections should prove valuable.

Experienced dominants may have largely overcome the discomfort of violating conventional sexual rules and will be familiar with many of the techniques I describe. However, the most experienced of us gets in an occasional rut. Most experienced dominants will find some new ideas here, and reading about what others do in the field may get the old excitement back and inspire new heights.

While I have written this book for dominants, I sincerely hope that submissives and those who feel they might enjoy being submissive read it. They can gain an insight into "how the other half lives," and it may give submissives the courage to act on their needs and desires.

Other individuals may have had the desire to experience BDSM, but lacking the proper words, may have been unable to verbalize or visualize their yearnings.

In addition, I hope that some copies of this book fall into the hands of the general public. Too often their perceptions of BDSM people are shaped by sensationalized media stories and pornography. The truth may not be as shocking, but I hope it is still interesting. To those readers, I am "defending my perversion." In fact, you may feel that some of the anti-BDSM positions I try to refute are extreme, but I assure you they are not strawmen set up by me to be knocked down. Every one of them represents a real point of view, often with a vociferous group behind it.

Although I have included a highly personal and opinionated glossary at the end of this book, I feel this is an appropriate place to go over some confusing terms. For example, throughout the book, I use the word "scene" to mean two different, related things. "The scene" is an umbrella term for all BDSM activities and the people who take part in them. On the other hand, "A scene" is what takes place when a dominant or a top and a submissive or a bottom (or any combination) get together and play. Thus, I might write, "In the scene, it is considered unconscionable to ignore a safeword," referring to the umbrella term, or, "When you are doing a scene, safety is of primary importance," refering to a specific activity. People may also refer to living the scene. This usually means that they attempt to maintain their BDSM persona on a 24-hour-a-day basis, but it can also mean simply that the person is serious about his or her participation in BDSM.

The most important word in the BDSM vocabulary is "safeword." This is a word or phrase that serves as a signal that things have become unbearable. Common safewords are "red light" and "mercy." In general, we do not use words like "stop" or "no" because many submissives increase their enjoyment by play acting that they are not in a voluntary situation. Screaming and begging turns them on. However, in a top/bottom scene, "stop" is a perfectly valid safeword. One can even use Lady Green's, "If you don't stop right now, when I get loose I'm going to rip your balls off." In short any sufficiently unequivocal signal is an acceptable safeword.

All The Colors of Kinkiness

People often talk about BDSM as if it were some sort of monolithic activity, like accounting or poker. (My apologies to accountants or poker players. I know better, but the line was too good to pass up.) In fact, the umbrella of consensual transfer of power covers an astonishing variety of acts, attitudes, degrees of commitment and extremes of kinkiness. BDSM or "The Scene" is like a very liberal Chinese restaurant. You can take as many, or as few, items as you want from Column A, B, and so on.

Each couple can decide which activities bring them the most pleasure. Some couples savor a highly intellectual BDSM that can be so subtle that even someone observing their scenes would be unaware that anything kinky is going on. Others enjoy a level of stimulation sufficient to horrify many observers. Still others appreciate elaborate psychodrama that may or may not include stimulation. The only people who can determine what is right for you and your partner are the two of you. There is no right or wrong way to do BDSM. It is also important to recognize that "intense" is not the same as "good." The two spectrums are unrelated. Two people sitting together and whispering can be having just as satisfying a scene as two others amid slashing whips and full-throated screams. It is what that particular couple wants and needs that determines the appropriateness of a scene.

Individual styles can also vary widely. Some dominants like to project a harsh, stern demeanor and keep the caring sensitivity carefully hidden. Others cherish the role of loving guide and protector. A scene can be as serious as a religious ritual, or it can be a laughing, giggling frolic.

Submissives, too, project a broad range of images to the world. Some, particularly men, like to maintain a passive, stoic image that can be frustrating to a dominant or a top looking for guidance. One female dominant complained in frustration, "How in the hell can I have any fun if I can't tell if he is?" Of course, others value and encourage that sort of a show of unruffled endurance.

Some submissives say they can only really let go when they have intentionally adopted a role. In effect, they create an internal psychodrama in which they are a captured secret agent, molested peasant maid or blackmailed debutante.

Ann, an Atlanta submissive, makes a point of distinguishing her "uppity submissive" from what people in the scene call a SAM (Smart Assed Masochist). While the SAM tries to "top from the bottom," that is, to control all aspects of the scene, Ann's uppity submissive is more likely to signal her eagerness for stimulation by pinching the dominant's bottom in passing or looking up with innocent eyes and asking, "Is that as hard as you can hit?"

Of course, bottoms don't have to make any such distinction. The essence of a top/bottom scene is giving and receiving "pain" and no pretense of unwillingness or reluctance is necessary.

There have been numerous attempts to examine the various approaches to BDSM. One of the most successful of these was detailed by Diana Vera, writing in *The Lesbian S/M Safety Manual*. Based on her experience and observations she described nine levels of submission. These range from a kinky sensualism in which everything revolves around the submissive's needs, through play submission where the submissive gives up control but the stimulation is erotic and pleasing to both. All the way at the other end of the spectrum is consensual slavery where the slave exists solely for the dominant's pleasure. This short piece is intriguing reading for anyone who is interested in thinking about submission as well as actively submitting. However, I caution that while it may look like a hierarchy, it is simply a description of various play styles. One may try several, but one should not think that there is any progression involved. A better way of looking at it would be as little boxes arranged on a tabletop. One can fit in one box or another, but none of the boxes are better than any other.

Another way of looking at conceptualizing the scene comes from my own dear Libby. Instead of considering the severity of the activities or the portion of the day they take up, her approach examines the emotional intensity of the submission and the degree of trust put forward by the submissive. In her section, "A Submissive Looks At Submission," later in this book, she goes into detail about her three levels of submission: fantasy, clarity and transparency.

Inspired by Libby's format, another submissive woman offered her three categories. Unlike Libby's, these are not in a hierarchical structure but, instead, are based on the needs of the submissive. The first is "stimulus driven." Here, the submissive is taking part because he or she is seeking out a specific stimulus, like the pain of whipping or the confinement of bondage.

The second category is "relationship driven." In this, the main desire is for a relationship, often with a particular person. Individuals in this kind of relationship take glory in the multichannel communication between the submissive and the dominant and enjoy the richness of the information flow.

The final category is "fantasy driven" where the submissive seeks to make a fantasy or fantasies real. Sometimes, this is accomplished by living through the fantasy; however, others find satisfaction in finding an individual who shares his or her fantasy and no specific action needs to take place.

However you choose to play, welcome to a land of fantasy in the midst of reality. Here, perhaps more than in any other aspect of your life, you are free to choose your own route to ecstasy.

Are You a Loving Dominant?

Well, are you? It may seem like an easy question to answer, but it can be more difficult than you realize. Sadly, in our society, domination, sadism, cruelty and brutality have become confused and intertwined.

Crude, unrealistic fiction has made the situation worse. Publishers have found that to reach the broadest possible audience, they must include themes that are repugnant to many. Because consensual, loving BDSM in fiction is so rare, those who are interested in these themes must pick through thousands of pages, like looking for jewels in a dungheap, to find sections they find provocative, while other readers wallow in the nonconsensual brutality.

The following is a series of questions that you need only to answer in your own soul. Be honest with yourself and look deeply into those answers to see if this scene is really for you.

Do you get as much pleasure or more from erotically exciting your partner as from your own enjoyment of the sexual act?

If this is true, you are likely to be a good dominant. The essence of this kind of play is to take another's power and then use it for mutual pleasure. If you already seek to maximize your partner's gratification, you have a mindset that will adapt well to BDSM.

Do you want an easy relationship with you as the unquestioned boss?

If yes, then BDSM is unlikely to be for you. A BDSM relationship is more, not less, complex than one that is purely vanilla. This is because BDSM relationships generally have all the components of a vanilla relationship, plus those that are unique to BDSM.

It is common to hear dominants talk about how hard they have to work. This is because in exchange for the power that is given us, we must find ways of using that power for the benefit and pleasure of both participants. At the same time, because of the trust given us, we must be very sure that nothing we do is harmful to anyone in the relationship. This kind of careful balancing act certainly isn't attractive to someone looking for an easy ride.

Have you been in an abusive relationship and would like to "turn the tables" on someone like the person who abused you?

This is another rough start. A significant number of people in BDSM have been in abusive relationships, and some of them consciously use BDSM psychodramas to help them work through the negative feelings that resulted from these experiences.

However, revenge is a poor motivation for such an intimate relationship, and it is likely to result in further damage to your self-esteem.

Why do you want to control another person?

This is a sticky one. Film star Vanessa del Rio once told me one of her earliest fantasies was of having a group of tiny people in the palm of her hand. She loved to imagine that she had complete control of them, but, to me, the key was that she imagined that she would use this power to make them happy.

The desire to help, to enhance or to make others happy is common among dominants. This may be why so many dominants are in the teaching and helping professions: medicine, social work, religion. Other-centered people make good dominants. Self-centered people often find that the strain of the responsibilities inherent in a BDSM relationship is overwhelming.

In a consensual relationship, control applied purely to self-gratification is a self-limiting proposition. Submissives who do not get what they are looking for are unlikely to remain in a relationship for very long.

Do you have fantasies involving nonconsensual activities or harm to another?

This isn't as serious as you may believe. The trick is being able to keep the fantasies inside your head and separate from the scene you are playing with another person. Most of us have large, hairy monsters in the dark corners of our mind. What separates the civilized from the uncivilized is how tight a leash we keep on them.

Having fantasies is all right; acting on them isn't. Aside from being totally against the ethical principles of the scene, such "play" can get you locked up with other people who believe in nonconsensual play, and they may be bigger than you are.

Dig All Those Crazy People

Why? Why do people do this? Why do people love this? Some of us are fascinated with the genesis of these feelings and enjoy searching for the root cause of our desires. Others, myself included, hold with Alexander Pope that, "Like following life though creatures you dissect, you lose it in the moment you detect it."

Sometimes, I suspect that too close an examination can actually destroy the feelings being studied, and I recognize that an understanding of causes is not necessary for enjoyment. I have only the vaguest idea of why chocolate ice cream tastes good, but that ignorance decreases neither my enjoyment nor my consumption.

I'll admit my sexual tastes are more unusual than love for chocolate ice cream. Still, no one has done deep analyses of why some people like chocolate sauce on their pizza. People who love it pack the Hershey's syrup on trips to Pizza Hut, and the rest of us avert our eyes and shudder a bit or maybe borrow a dollop and see how it tastes on the pepperoni. They are simply classified as weird or, if they are rich enough, eccentric.

Psychologists, psychiatrists, social science theorists, theologians and feminists haven't lined up to find answers for this chocolate "perversion," for people carrying handkerchiefs they never use in their coat pockets or for voting Republican. These are simply "trite eccentricities" unworthy of study.

To make the question even more complex, the language of experience is not the same as the language of classification. Race car drivers don't study physics, although they may pick up a good bit of it in passing. They drive. They experience. They don't think about the underlying mechanics but about the feel of the car and the track.

People have studied poems since before Aristotle wrote *Poetics*. Their reactions still come down to "This poem speaks to me."

However, some enjoy sharpening their Aristotelian knives and having at "the search for why." If you tend toward this approach, I dedicate this search for causes to you.

Some give a simple answer to "Why?" "It is fun, enjoyable." "We like to do it." Unfortunately, this kind of simplicity isn't looked upon kindly by the members of the Ivory-Tower Brigade, who glory in philosophical head-knocking and counting dancing-angels.

Unfortunately, all too many of these deep thinkers have largely fixated on sadistic monsters and masochistic victims. Like Shakespeare's Horatio, they have failed to realize that there are more things in heaven and earth than are dreamt of in their philosophy. Neither loving domination or sensual submission is part of the paradigms they develop. To admit that these exist might knock their carefully constructed houses of cards askew. To make matters worse, the competing theories are all different, and most of them, are mutually exclusive.

I was strongly tempted to exclude much of the psychological theory on the grounds that it is inconsequential to the people most actively involved. Unfortunately, I have been repeatedly and forcefully reminded that anyone attempting to discuss BDSM with a learned audience or with doctors is going get presented with these spurious explanations.

I suppose that it is better you encounter them here, amid interpretation and exegesis, than to have them flung into your face with an implication that they are, somehow, revealed truth. Just take a firm grip on your temper and read on.

Theories of sadism and masochism:

In the labeling craze of the 19th century, when scientists still clung to the mystical concept that to label something was to control it, D.R. von Krafft-Ebing came up the terms "sadism" and "masochism" in his book *Psychopathia Sexualis*. This learned tome was a sort of Sears and Roebuck catalog of perversion, listing just about everything that two or more people could do together to get their individual or collective rocks off. Krafft-Ebing must have had a good laugh on thrill-seekers perusing his volume; he put the boring stuff in English and the good parts in Latin.

As most people in the scene know, the term "sadism" came from the writings of the Marquis Donatien Alphonse Francois de Sade and masochism from those of Leopold von Sacher-Masoch. Both de Sade's writings (including *Philosophy in the Bedroom, Justine, Juliet, Twenty Days at Sodom*) and Sacher-Masoch's *Venus in Furs* are still hot-selling items today. A quick glance at any of de Sade's work will show you why many dominants are infuriated when they are accused of being sadists. Nonconsensuality was the order of the day for the Marquis.

Krafft-Ebing got it almost right with submission when he defined masochism as:

> "A peculiar perversion of the psychical sexual life in which the person affected, in sexual feeling and thought, is controlled by the idea of being completely and unconditionally subject to the will of a person of the opposite sex; of being treated by this person as by a master..."

Aside from the near miss of failing to recognize that submission is independent of hetero- or homo-erotic orientation and throwing in the term perversion, he came fairly close to how many submissives would describe themselves. However, after that good start, he ruined it by adding three words, "humiliated and abused," at the end. With just three words, he narrowed the definition to include only the small percentage of submissives who do enjoy humiliation, and convicted the master, a person who is doing what the submissive wants done, of being abusive.

Krafft-Ebing was even less kind to dominants and tops, who he implicitly lumps with sadists.

> "Sadism is the experience of sexually pleasurable sensations (including orgasm) produced by acts of cruelty, bodily punishment inflicted by one's own person or when witnessed in others, be they animals or human beings. It may consist of an innate desire to humiliate, hurt, wound or even destroy the others in order thereby to create sexual pleasure in one's self."

Unfortunately, aside from some amusing – or horrifying – examples (depending on your point of view), Krafft-Ebing is almost useless to anyone looking for insights. Sadism is simply seen as "a pathological intensification of the male sexual character," and females are seen as anxious, irritable and weak. (I wonder how Mistress Mir, Goddess Sia or any of the other myriad dominant women feel about that?)

Freud, the father of modern psychology, took the ball and ran with it. Not one to do things by halves, he came up with three separate and sometimes contradictory theories. In "Three Essays on the Theory of Sexuality," he claimed that sadism is a component part of the sexual instinct, an "instinct for mastery" that is inherently masculine, and masochism is "nothing but inverted sadism." Freud declared that sadism and masochism are interchangeable. Masochism is only sadism that has turned inward upon the self.

Sadists behave as they do, according to this theory, because, during childhood, they were trapped in the anal stage of development, attempting to control the parent figure by releasing and withholding feces. (Does the term "crock of shit" come to mind?)

In his later essay, "A Child Being Beaten," Freud shifted the birth of sadomasochism to the child's first oedipal conflict and linked it with parental punishment and punishment fantasies. His argument was that the child links forbidden, sexual feelings with the fear of punishment. In effect, pain is the payment for pleasure.

With better footwork than a running back, Freud next feinted toward his first theory but then went wide and, in "The Economic Problem of Masochism," hypothesized that masochism, not sadism, is the primary component and linked it with the death instinct. For one thing, masochism, in his eyes, was necessary so that women could endure childbirth.

Eric Fromm, a leading light of the Frankfurt School, a group of German intellectuals who desperately tried to explain the rise of Nazism, moved the discussion of sadism and masochism from the individual, where Freud had staked his claim, to society, or at least to the individual's reaction to society. In *The Fear of Freedom,* Fromm postulated that freedom itself was frightening in that it caused intolerable loneliness and that individuals adopt various strategies to escape from it. He maintained that sadomasochists use control as such an escape hatch.

For example, masochists were described as consciously complaining about being weak, inferior and powerless, while at the same time seeking circumstances where these feelings were intensified.

Fromm argued that the masochists, failing repeatedly at being strong and independent, became even more weak and passive to reduce the conflict between what they want and what they could accomplish, like someone who says, "If I can't play perfect baseball, I'll become the team clown and everyone will think I'm fucking up on purpose."

The sadists, on the other hand, were seen as recognizing their inferiority and powerlessness and seeking to control others to gain an ersatz strength in place of real strength. In effect, he saw us as failed admirals playing with toy boats in the bathtub.

Jean Genet, the author, drew on Freud's third field goal attempt in his philosophical classic, *Being and Nothingness*, where he argued that both sadism and masochism were responses to a fear of mortality, of death. In his play, *The Balcony*, lawyers and other powerful individuals played out masochistic fantasies in a surreal house of domination. The theme implies that they are doing this to strike a psychic balance and atone for their sadistic behavior in the real world. It's as if they were saying, "I hit him; now you hit me, and everyone will be even."

A Swedish psychiatrist, Lars Ullerstam, supported Jean Genet's hypothesis regarding masochism as an exculpatory behavior. However, he pointed out that the presence of powerful, rich men in such BDSM brothels may also be because they, unlike their less powerful counterparts, can afford to pay the fees involved. Thus, it may be that the overwhelming number of lawyers who dominatrixes report seeing as clients, are not expiating sins particular to this profession. They may simply be making an obscene amount of money and, thus, be able to afford the dominatrix's service.

Jessica Benjamin, in her *Powers of Desire*, alleged that both sadistic and masochistic behavior were fueled by a need for recognition. The masochist suffers to be recognized as worthwhile by the sadist while the sadist subjugates another person to force recognition from him or her. Benjamin, on the other hand, gets her recognition by writing books.

During the conference that followed publication of the Playboy Foundation Report in the 1970s, researchers had a chance to differentiate sadism from dominance. W.B. Pomeroy described a segment of a filmed scene which depicted a waxing. He had noticed that the "sadist" was watching, not just the place where the wax was falling, but also the expression on his partner's face. When this sadist detected that she was getting close to the edge, he raised the candle to reduce the intensity of the stimulation. Pomeroy commented, "It suddenly occurred to me that the masochist was almost literally controlling the sadist's hand."

Sadly, a less imaginative colleague pooh-poohed the idea and insisted that "genuine" sadists are not interested in a willing partner. (I'm personally glad this myopic soul was not present at the discovery of penicillin. He probably would have thrown out the moldy bread.)

Working in what is known as the Object Relations School of psychology, Margaret Mahler attempted to explain sadism and masochism by looking at a child's early relationship to objects. Rather than placing the critical age in puberty as did Freud, she held that such desires begin before the age of four.

In sort of a Cliff's Notes explanation, I'll just say that object relations theory says that children go through a series of phases in which they seek either greater independence or greater reassurance. Mahler argued that both masochism and sadism come from a failure to have these needs satisfied at the proper time. In effect, the person is trapped repeating the critical phase in hopes of "doing better this time.'

For example, she believed a sadist may have been unable to form a satisfactory relationship with his or her mother and turns to sadism in an attempt to make a controlled relationship in which he or she can try to recreate that relationship. On the other hand, the masochist was able to form a satisfactory bond but was unable to break it at the appropriate time. Thus, he or she is seeking a relationship from which a clean break is possible.

There has been good news in recent years. When this book was first written in the early 1990s, the primary reference for the American Psychiatric Association was the *DSM IIIr* (Diagnostic Statistical Manual, third edition, revised). This "learned tome" was not at all kind to us, holding that to seek either sexual submission or dominance was a treatable disorder. (Of course, they termed it either Sexual Masochism or Sexual Sadism, bringing in a different kettle of fish.) Interestingly enough, according to *DSM IIIr*, it was all right to simply have these fantasies, but seeking them out that made one a candidate for the place with the latex wallpaper.

A person could dream of going to a loving leather-clad woman. He could burn in his bed each night with unslaked desire for the hug of the rope and the kiss of the whip. However, one trip down to Mistress Harsh's House of Loving Leather made him a potential resident of the laughing academy.

Intent was immaterial. In the view of the authors, someone who pleased his or her lover with a bit of erotic spanking was lumped right along with a creep setting fire to kittens.

Fortunately, through the efforts of kink activists and kink-friendly therapists lead by the author/activist Race Bannon, *DSM IV* presented us in a much better light. Now, to be treatable, we must either be disturbed by our desires or have those desires take over our worlds to the point where they disrupt out daily lives.

Even Madonna has a theory about why we like what we like. In an interview with *Newsweek* magazine, she suggested that her sexuality may stem from her Catholic upbringing and is quoted as saying,"When I was growing up, there were certain things people did for penance; I know people who slept on coat hangers or kneeled on uncooked rice on the floor... and as for me, I think somehow things got really mixed up. There was some ecstasy involved in that.

"And the whole idea of crucifixion – a lot of that, the idea of being tied up. It is surrendering yourself to someone. I'm fascinated by it. I mean, there is a lot of pain-equals-pleasure in the Catholic church, and that is also associated with bondage and S&M."

From the index cards of a 19th century cataloger to the musings of the Material Girl herself, this is a sample from the varied buffet table of psychological explanations of BDSM – or to be more precise, Sadism and Masochism. You are free to pick and choose as it pleases you.

Suggested Reading:
S&M: Studies in Sadomasochism (Thomas Weinberg ed.)
Different Loving (Brame, Brame & Jacobs)

Why would someone want to be submissive?

For myself, I believe that many submissives are strong people who are taking a vacation from their responsibilities. By giving their considerable power to others, they benefit from the aphrodisiac of contrast. To shift, willingly, from powerful to powerless gives their libidos extraordinary jolts.

This erotic nature of contrast may explain why, during the many years I spent in Asia, I never encountered what I considered a truly submissive woman. Most women in Asian cultures are steeped in submission; it is not a choice, nor is it a change. For me, the fire was missing from their submission. They got no more of a sensual charge from their submission than American women get from signaling a cab or buying a meal.

Many of the submissives I have talked to find that their attraction to the scene is based largely on this contrast between having power and control and releasing themselves to simply experience power-lessness at the hands of another whom they trust. Almost everyone knows the sheer joy of coming home after a hard day's work and slip-ping off the wingtips or high heels and putting on a well-worn pair of slippers. Many submissives simply carry it a step further and slip off the entire business-mandated Type A personality to submit to a trusted dominant.

There is a misunderstanding on the part of some wannabe doms and many in the vanilla public about the essence of submission. Part of the fault is our phrasing. We speak of "a submissive person," and that is not precisely correct. A better phrase would be "a person who is submissive to..." This understandable error is created and com-pounded by playacting in the cyber world and misleading plots in pornographic novels.

In the real world the nature of the submissive is often quite different from what is seen in these limited purviews of fiction and fantasy. This is particularly true in the case of submissive women. These ladies are not submissive to just any individual who happens to want to play as a dominant or as a top.

A woman who has elected to give her submissive side permis-sion to play is, in my opinion, stronger and more courageous than those of her vanilla sisters who have that side and do not let it show. Such a woman is not likely to submit herself to anyone who just hap-pens to own a whip.

Far from simply waiting for a dominant or top to appear, these women seek and select the person to whom they will submit. In turning over their power to this individual (or, more rarely, these in-dividuals), the submissive woman forms a bond that is often stronger than that of a conventional sexual dyad.

By the same token, depending on the personal style of both the submissive and the dominant, the submissive woman in such an affiliation may be quite active and aggressive outside of the scene portion of the relationship.

Submissive men are both more complex and simpler than their female counterparts. Either because of the nature of the male/female dichotomy, such as early childhood conditioning and the nature of our society, many male submissives are much less selective of whom they submit to. While a submissive female is a rare sight in the BDSM clubs, submissive males in search of a master or smistress make up the bulk of any given night's attendance.

Some submissives report say that they have chosen their role because they found that the strength and control they have in their vanilla lives interfere with their sensual enjoyment. A number of years ago, I had a relationship with a brilliant and successful psychologist who had to be bound and helpless in order to reach orgasm.

Her explanation was consistent and cogent. Before discovering bondage, she found that, as she approached orgasm during intercourse, an anxiety would appear that would quite overwhelm the building passion. This anxiety did not appear during masturbation. Examining the anxiety in a cool and detached manner as if it were a symptom reported by a client, she concluded that she had been socialized to please and cater to her partner during sex. She concluded that her subconscious mind, recognizing that during climax she would be out of control, was sabotaging the orgasm.

Her solution was to make the desire-to-please irrelevant. Because when she was bound she could not do anything either to please or displease her partner, she found that bondage allowed her, in her own words, "to wallow in sensation." When she was tied, she was able to reach orgasm repeatedly.

An alternate explanation, offered by another member of the psychological community, suggested that the root cause was, instead, a deep-seated guilt about non-marital sex. In effect, her subconscious was punishing her for engaging in "sinful" behavior. In this scenario, the bondage "gave her permission" to enjoy sex because it wasn't her "fault."

A submissive man allowed that guilt did play a significant factor in his love of bondage. As he put it, "It is difficult to get past the Calvinist idea that feeling good isn't enough. There must be some greater purpose, some tangible benefit for society." Being bound and helpless freed him from the need to search for that benefit.

Other submissives have said that they have found, in loving submission and certain pleasure/pain activities, a way of coming to terms with legacies of emotional pain. For example, it is not uncommon for a submissive to be drawn to recreating scenes of abuse or rape with a loving partner acting the part of the aggressor. While, on the surface, this might be seen as counterproductive, those I have spoken to are unanimous in declaring that the psychodrama helped them "get control of the trauma."

The logic seems to be that the original act left the victim with a sense of powerlessness, but reenacting it in an environment of BDSM, where he or she can set the parameters of the action and even abruptly halt the scene with a safeword, gives a feeling of empowerment.

I should note here that these submissive individuals, both male and female, initiated the idea of using a scene psychodrama in this way. I would strongly caution any dominant not to coerce a submissive into such scenes with the thought of providing a sort of home-brew therapy. The dynamics of control seem to indicate that a suggestion of this sort must originate from the individual most directly affected.

Other submissives report that BDSM helps them deal with emotional pain by allowing them to "go away," to escape into the intense sensuality and endorphinin-engendered haze where memories and even rational thought becomes secondary. This is often referred to as "subspace," but, as with much in this world, the criteria vary greatly for what "subspace" actually is and how one gets there.

Of course, this going-away isn't unique to BDSM. I doubt that there are many of us who have not set down an engrossing book to discover we were cramped and ached from the position in which we had been sitting. The book literally took us away from our bodies.

A friend who is active in the arts observes that the first five minutes of a play or musical presentation may be accompanied by coughs and other noises from the audience. Soon, these vanish as the performance lifts the audience from the mundane sensations of their bodies to a higher plane where noises from tickles in the throat and squeaks from uncomfortable chairs cannot follow.

When these submissives talk about their use of BDSM to deal with their pain, it's not clear whether they are describing a benefit or a cause. Did the emotional pain lead the person to choose a submissive role in BDSM play? While this is possible, I could equally persuasively argue that the person was already submissive and was simply using the BDSM scene to deal with the existing pain.

Another need or cause cited by some submissives is that in their early lives they sealed away their emotions. In some cases, this was the result of abuse; in others, it was because the family ignored or concealed emotion. As one submissive woman put it, "By being submissive to my master and relinquishing all control to him, we are slowly tearing down the protective walls I built because of some things which happened in my childhood. For me, BDSM is a way of confronting my fears and allowing myself to grow emotionally. What I find most appealing about BDSM are the emotional and psychological aspects – although the physical is also fun. Would I still find it appealing if my childhood had been different? I don't know, but I doubt it."

Another woman commented that before she took part in BDSM activities she had been very passive and stuck in vanilla relationships. However, after experiencing the intense communications necessary to make a BDSM relationship work, she found herself being more forthright.

Is the increased ability to communicate simply a benefit of the scene, or did the blocking these women experienced cause their submissive feelings? Did the blocking and the feelings have the same original source? Obviously, there isn't any clear, single answer.

Why would someone want to be dominant?

Some individuals take the inverse of my relaxing-from-power explanation of submissive behavior to state that dominants, then, must be weak individuals who need to take the power from others to experience a contrast to their helplessness.

Aside from the kneejerk reaction that this ain't so, the available evidence doesn't seem to fit. Before I took to writing full time, I was the vice president of a successful market research company. Many of my fellow dominants in and out of the major scene organizations hold stressful, high-pressure jobs and do very well.

If our motivation isn't the reverse of the submissive's motivation, what is it? I have come to the conclusion that the essence of what motivates me are two interlocking items. One factor is that I get a tremendous charge from my partner's pleasure. BDSM is a wonderful way to get someone off more intensely than most vanilla people can imagine.

Many teachers and guides say that one of their major rewards is to see someone excited by a new idea or an unexpected vista. Having been a college professor, I know exactly what they mean, and I can see a definite kinship between that feeling and the feeling I get watching a woman in a paroxysm of pleasure. There is a feeling of accomplishment knowing I have helped someone climb higher and go further than he or she could have gone alone.

Another factor in my attraction to the dominant role is that the BDSM situation allows me to be in almost complete control. In today's modern world, this is a situation that is becoming more and more difficult to attain. In fact, the more powerful one becomes, the more it seems that he or she is buffeted by collateral factors and outside forces.

For example, to a naive observer, I may seemed to be in complete control in my office. However, I have to depend on my employees doing their jobs correctly. I have to depend on suppliers to be on the ball. Much of what I seem to control I really "managed," a much less satisfactory situation. In BDSM, I am in complete control, to fail or succeed as my talents and imagination permit. I control every factor, and I do not have to depend on anyone. Any object I depend on (whips, ropes, suspension gear) I can test and retest until I am certain it works. Being in that kind of control pleases me intensely.

This, of course, may not be the true cause of these feelings. No mirror is completely accurate and ego is a subtle distorter of fact. I can only urge you to look into your own hearts and, most importantly, enjoy.

4

Consent and Consensuality

Consent is more than just an ideal for BDSM relationships; it is a touchstone, an axiom, a sacrament. Without full, knowing consent, relationships are in immediate danger of becoming brutal exploitative affairs without beauty or elegance.

Consent can vary from the very specific ("You can do this, this and this, but not that") to a simple knowing acceptance ("I trust that you will do nothing to harm me"). However, it must be constantly present and mutually respected within the relationship.

You don't have to say exactly what you mean

Safewords are central to consent in BDSM. Using these phrases permits the submissive to withdraw consent to a particular activity or terminate the scene at any point without endangering the illusion that the dominant is in complete control.

An acceptable safeword can be "no" or "stop." All that is required is that it be clearly understood as an unequivocal signal that there is a problem and the submissive wants to stop. One of my favorites is "Stop what you are doing right now or when I get loose I'll rip your balls (tits) off and shove them down your throat." It is certainly unequivocal.

However, many submissives enjoy an illusion of nonconsensuality and relish being able to beg for mercy with unrestrained fervor. For these, the use of such blandishments is an inherent part of the trappings of the scene. For them, phrases that would not be used in the heat of the scene are the best safewords. Expressions like "red light" and "give me mercy, mistress" are common. One problem that can be encountered is, that by the time a safeword is needed, the submissive may be so caught up in the excitement of the scene that he or she has forgotten what the safeword was. Another approach is simply to say (yell, scream) "safeword." In any case, the change in tone and body language as a submissive searches for the safeword is usually enough to warn a sensitive dominant that something is wrong.

Some BDSM couples have adjuncts to safewords: "slow words" and "go words." A slow word is a signal to the dominant that, while the activity is not beyond the submissive's tolerance, the limit of tolerance is being approached. It is a signal, not to cease all activities but, to ease off a bit and, perhaps, to take a different route. Those who use "red light" for a safeword often use "yellow light" as a slow word.

A go word is simply a signal to the dominant that everything is all right and he or she can continue and increase the intensity of the stimulation. Again, some couples use phrases like "yes, please" and "more," but others who wish to maintain the illusion of nonconsensuality enjoy the irony of using "no" and "please stop." However, when this latter type of go word is used in a public or semi-public scene, it is advisable to inform at least some of those present that it will be used. Otherwise, an inadvertent termination of the scene by outside influences may result.

A second type of safeword is used by some people who use intense psychological stimuli as well as physical stimulation. This is a emotional safeword. While one word can be used to signal that either physical or psychological limits have been surpassed, some couples prefer to have separate safewords. This allows a submissive to signal, for example, that while the physical chastisement is still enjoyable, the humiliation has reached an unendurable point.

In some scene groups, there is a heated debate about the need for safewords. While the majority seems to concur that they are necessary, a vocal minority deems them contrary to the spirit of BDSM. The most extreme members of this group put forth the concept of irrevocable consent. That is, once a submissive has given consent to a dominant, the dominant is free to do whatever he or she wishes. This outlook seems to be most common among the gay community. During a lecture at a BDSM group, one gay dominant expressed this philosophy succinctly, stating, "If he goes home with me, he's mine until I'm tired of him."

A female dominant reflected a more mutualistic viewpoint, but still rejected the concept of safewords when she said, "If I can't tell when he (the submissive) isn't enjoying it any more, I don't have the right to call myself a dominant."

A less radical outlook is that safewords are acceptable in the early stages of a relationship, but as the relationship matures they become unnecessary and reflect a lack of confidence in the empathic abilities of the dominant.

Interestingly, this desire to drop safewords from a relationship's vocabulary is often voiced by the submissive, who declares he or she wants to demonstrate absolute trust in the dominant.

It is important to recognize that a safeword benefits both parties. Many dominants value the use of a safeword because it allows them to "work closer to the edge" than would otherwise be comfortable. Particularly at the beginning of a relationship, safewords offer reality tests that assure the dominant that they are reading the submissive's responses correctly.

During her initial session, a novice submissive made such a fuss, pleading and begging, when she realized that I intended to shave her pubic region, that I was unsure whether she was going with the fantasy or genuinely objecting. After she had cried, "You can't do this to me," I replied, "Of course I can, unless, that is, you use your safeword." She paused only a moment and then moaned, instead, "I'll do anything you want; just don't do this to me." Reassured, I went on mixing the lather. Safewords don't only work to make the submissive feel safe, they provide a margin of safety for the dominant.

Of course, as the relationship matures, a dominant will become more familiar with the submissive's reactions and safewords become less important. However, they shouldn't ever be discarded. Fatigue, distraction or changes in the submissive's physical or psychological functioning make them an important backup in all BDSM relationships.

Protect us from our "protectors"

Among some groups and individuals outside of the BDSM community, there is a vocal contention that some people are not competent to give their consent. Like most generalizations, this one has a degree of truth. The law recognizes that some individuals are separated from reality to such an extent they constitute a danger to themselves and/or to society at large. They are considered *"non compos mentis,"* not of sound mind.

In the last few decades, exacting rules have been enacted to prevent people from being declared *non compos mentis* at the whim of someone in authority. However, in the past, people have been committed to mental hospitals for such minor idiosyncrasies as failing to bathe or for desiring daily sex from their spouse. In addition, certain groups, such as minors, are considered by law to lack competency and the ability to make trustworthy decisions.

Normally, it takes a pattern of irrational behavior to motivate a court to rule someone incompetent, and this ruling is deemed universally applicable. A person who is found incompetent has all of his or her decisions removed and placed in the hands of another.

However, a few of the previously mentioned groups would both narrow and broaden the definitions of competence and incompetence. For example, some extremists argue that today's society is so male-dominated that a woman cannot truly consent to any form of heterosexual intercourse, whether it is vanilla or in the context of BDSM. In effect, they argue that any act of heterosexual sex is rape, and the only consensual sexual activities a woman can engage in are with other women. Lesbian sex, by their definition, is based on equality.

Although they would hold that a woman who desires heterosexual intercourse is not competent to make that decision because of the domination of society by males, they would not extend it to the point of denying her the right to make contracts, buy property or go into business in that same society. They also fail to see that BDSM relationships thrive between lesbians, as reflected in the rich and growing body of lesbian BDSM fiction.

Others take a more moderate approach. Vanilla sex is considered acceptable as long as both partners mouth the right words about equality and acceptance. However, when someone, usually a woman, engages in BDSM activities as a submissive, it is then taken as prima facie evidence that that person is incapable of giving consent, a classic Catch-22.

It is difficult to argue with these people. Their beliefs have often hardened to such an extent that they are unable to recognize loving, supportive couples even when they meet them in person.

Moreover, there are undoubtedly individuals and couples in the scene who desire or take part in activities which most would find frightening or repulsive. *The Correct Sadist* (a highly overrated and not particularly informative book) describes a man whose cock had been mutilated until it resembled a peeled banana. Michele, a dear friend, told me of a man whose ankle had been pierced to such an extent that he could be literally hung from a meat hook.

However, while we might desire to avert our eyes from what, to us, are "disgusting" activities, taking the approach that the participants in these activities are somehow less sane than ourselves puts us on a slippery slope. If it is possible to reject a person's ability to give consent simply on a basis of a desire for mutilation, could it not be argued that a desire for whipping or bondage would be equally likely to indicate derangement?

Moving it out of the emotionally laden sexual arena, how are we to treat those members of our society who bungee jump, body surf through pilings or race motorcycles? A cherished friend spends her vacations hundreds of meters under the ground, crawling through openings a gopher would reject with disdain. Should I judge her mentally incompetent because of this proclivity?

When we argue that because of a single desire a person lacks the ability to give consent, we are headed for a safe, sane, boring society that will eventually stamp out every scintilla of excitement and adventure.

A Submissive Writes About Submission

This section has been written at my request, by Libby, a lovely and sensual submissive woman who has become my wife, partner and best friend. I'm providing it to give you a first-hand look at how one submissive sees her submission. Her words may not be true for all submissives, but she speaks for many. Throughout the editions, it is the single most-commented-upon section in the book; because it is such an important part, the third edition is carrying both our names as authors.

I was quite squeamish as a kid, so when I told my childhood friends I was going to study biology in college they said, "You? I can't imagine you dealing with bugs, guts and gross things. It used to make you sick to your stomach to see a piece of old spaghetti in the sink." Well, yes, but once I was exposed to the lure of science I just couldn't keep from it. I'm sure I would get a similar or even stronger reaction if I were to share my interest in being a submissive woman.

In my everyday life, I'm a strong, competent and successful woman. Yet, even before I was exposed to the submissive role, I was called to it by my earliest childhood fantasies. My attraction to a sub-missive role is even stronger than the pull I feel toward my chosen professional life, because I was called to it from a place deep within me. I'm not sure how the seeds of submission were planted within me, but I am driven to nurture those seeds into full bloom by "following my bliss," as Joseph Campbell would say.

So, what is submission to me? To me, submission is a desire to be special or significant. My earliest fantasies, and they were when I was very young, always involved being somehow chosen and desired. I will borrow here from the image of the goddess who is a composite of virgin, maiden and crone to describe how these forces, desires and needs coalesce within me as and reach expression through submis-sion. The part of me that is virgin wants to always be able to approach new things in an open-minded and curious way without giving a thought to my own security. The part of me that is maiden seeks to explore passion and creativity. The chance to explore passion, sensual-ity and sexuality within the framework of safety that the virgin enjoys takes freedom onto the path of liberation. The crone is the wisdom part of me that is self-assured enough to look at my dark desires. If the virgin can be safe to enjoy the erotic pleasure that is awakened in the maiden, then crone may risk to surrender herself to the dark side of her soul.

Facing my uncensored soul, without turning away, looking aside or getting preoccupied in divergent energy interferences, I see a desire to surrender completely to another who is that one special person with whom I find mutual love, affection and emotional trust. Being able to do this makes me integrated, complete and whole. As the two of us become absorbed in each other we become increasingly unified and soul mates. There is always the polarity of the dominance and submission to keep our bond alive and vital.

Levels of submission

Philosophically, I have been developing a way of looking at levels of submission. In this model, trust is an integral part. I have categorized three levels of submission: fantasy, clarity and transparency. The fantasy level is where everyone starts out, and for many this is sufficient. The BDSM fantasies are varied and unique as the individuals who create them. Some are mild, like spanking or bondage, while others are what some consider edge play.

There really is no hierarchy of the fantasies, but some are obviously easier to realize than others. While they remain strictly a fantasy, no trust is involved. The fantasy level would also include mind play and some negotiated play or clearly defined and limited scenes during which trust can begin to develop.

In the next level, power transfer begins, and there is great opportunity for trust to develop. I call this level "clarity" because there is a clear understanding of what power is being transferred. This is often stipulated by contracts and limited by the establishment of safewords. The submissive is watchful at first and careful to determine that the dominant is technically competent, as well as caring and comforting. The range of activities is again determined by the mutual fantasies involved.

Because of the range, there is a great deal of diversity among the so-called real dominants. As trust develops, so does the relationship. For some involved in BDSM activities, it is sufficient to have these times set aside for scenes, but for others the trust building helps to develop the relationship outside of the BDSM activities. There is a continuum within this level with functional scenes at one end and real relationships at the other.

In the third level, called transparency, the partners know each other well, and trust for personal safety is well established. Safewords are still operative, but they are not as necessary because the dominant has a sharper awareness of the submissive's limits. Paramount in this level is excellent communication and a willingness for each to trust the other with what is truly within their hearts and souls.

In this level, one begins to establish emotional trust, a kind of, "I trust my body, safety and pleasure to you. Now, may I also trust you with my emotions, hopes and other desires?" It is here, with the passion-desires of the maiden having been met, the fully realized woman, incarnated as goddess, begins to hope and believe her relationship-desires and drive to be special or chosen can be met. Many BDSMers move into this level, but it takes ongoing work to maintain transparent trust.

The experience of submission

Well, what is it like to step across that threshold from fantasy into clarity? I've had BDSM or S&M or B&D fantasies as far back as I can remember. As I came to realize these sexual fantasies, I was a bit ill at ease, thinking I was a masochist. None of the terms to describe what I felt seemed to capture what seemed to me to be very natural, exciting and compelling.

I feared enacting my fantasies for several reasons: that I would not be safe doing so, that I would verify that I was a pervert, and that reality would not be as good as fantasy. I believed that somehow I would be able to negotiate safety and be able to deal with the pervert label if I acted on this desire, but I was very reluctant to give up exciting sexual energy that I derived from the fantasy.

After a while, I knew that I would have to at least have to find out. It actually took more courage to get over being a BDSM virgin than to lose my virginity in the first place. Behind the mask of a computer bulletin board, I felt safe enough to talk about it. I stalked my lover on a national family-oriented bulletin board after I found out he had BDSM interests and experience. I had long thought about answering BDSM or B&D personal advertisements, but an image of a snickering and licentious sadist always prevented me.

This computer bulletin board stalking did allow me to discover things about him outside his BDSM interest which made him seem like a reasonable risk to me. After stalking for a while, I wrote him a private email that said, simply, I shared his interests. He wrote back, and a week later I was on my way to visit him in NYC.

We met on leap-year day. To me this was symbolic of taking a leap into this new and wonderful world. In that twenty-four hours, we did several scenes, went to The Vault where, in spite of my reservations, I did my first public scene. In this first encounter, I felt that the innocence of the virgin and the wisdom of the crone were operative, but the passion of the maiden had not really been released.

For me, reality was muchbetter than fantasy. The world of BDSM is replete with contrasts and polarity, but when I first entered this stage of clarity, I was quite surprised to feel an ambivalence when I reentered my vanilla routine.

When I awoke the first morning back at home, I felt ambivalent about proceeding any further, despite a wonderful rest caused by having had my body sensually satisfied to the point of exhaustion. I wanted to run right back and do it all over again, but I kept asking myself if I wasn't I was dragging my body somewhere my mind was not yet prepared to go. I realized that, in giving BDSM a try, I had been trusting myself and my perceptions about the situation. However, to go any further, I would have to trust my mentor, and this scared the living daylights out of me. I had tapped into my own passion, the lioness within me had roared, and she would not again be silent. The maiden was about to be liberated.

Losing control is a common fear in the trust-building stage of clarity. One submissive who was playing in the fantasy stage asked me how I could give my mind over to someone. My response was that, in the process of submission, my mind does drift off, and it can drift off quite a bit, but this happens in a most pleasant way.

Initially, fear can make it seem like a battle of wills, but as fear is replaced with trust the battle becomes a dance. Often, when someone dances with another person for the first time, they find themselves stepping on each other's feet. Eventually, as each becomes used to the other's style, they begin to move as one. If one listens to the music with the heart and responds with the will it is truly a brand new and exciting dance.

Physically, submission is hard to describe to one who does not have submissive tendencies burning within the soul. I had, long ago, accepted that I must be a masochist. This was not a very pleasant thought, but it was the only term I could find anywhere that described my taste for pain. I knew that I did not like being hurt. In fact, I am a wimp when it comes to what I call real pain, but I and many other submissives can only describe the joy of a whipping or a spanking as increased intensity. The language is truly impoverished in trying to describe the physical feeling.

Because there is clearly a sexual component, and most people recognize the nebulous word "turn-on," perhaps, I should just say that I am turned on by acting on my submissive urges and feeling the physical aspects of submission, such as bondage, whipping, spanking, waxing or needle piercings.

I have always been a spanking enthusiast. It still elicits the strongest sexual response in me. When I am spanked, my vaginal juices flow like a fountain, and sexual tension builds in my clitoris into a tidal wave force that longs to be relieved by an enormous orgasm. Whipping has the added smell and feel of leather, the caress and sting of the leather providing contrast in sensation and in emotion.

Bondage was not initially a primary turn-on for me. I asked some of my submissive friends why bondage is such a turn-on, and typically, the answer was that it made them feel secure or allowed them to be sexual. As I have grown to trust my dominant partner, I have become more willing to be rendered helpless before being disciplined. The symbolic, consensual helplessness heightens the physical response and amplifies the pre-orgasmic sexual tension.

Waxing is something that I had never heard of before becoming involved in BDSM, but I really love the sensation. First, I experience anticipation as I see the wax from the burning candle building up into a small hot puddle. The wax splashing on the skin is somewhat like a hot rain drop, but as it quickly cools, it feels like a point of massage oil. There seems to be a direct line connected to the clitoris, making the sexual response even more intense.

These are just a few examples of how I experience submission physically. To those who still feel you have to ask, "Why do you enjoy pain?" The answer is, I have the strongest and best multiple orgasms this way.

Integrating spirituality and ritual

Looking at the stage of transparency takes me into the arena of deep trust. For many it has a spiritual component. I am called to the reality of BDSM from within what I understand to be my soul. All of my religious upbringing and the faith development that took place in adult life led me to accept this truth.

I can no more deny this call than the Biblical prophets could deny their call. I have seen this in others as well, others who risk more in the way of heart and home than I do by answering the impulse within.

The word soul represents an individual's ideas, feelings, hopes, fears and desires. Everything that shapes us, surrounds us or in any way influences us rests within this soul. When one senses the stirring within one's soul it is nearly impossible to not heed impulses, whatever they may be. For me, the most satisfactory image of soul comes from the ancient Greeks, who viewed the different aspects of the soul with different deities. Psyche, the spirit, was married to Eros, the body. To me, this is why the call is so strong, It is a call to be whole, to be integrated and happy within.

It often comes up that there is a strong similarity between religious experience and BDSM experience. I have been asked, "Do the submissive's feelings in a BDSM relationship compare to other control/surrender situations?" For me, it is more than a similarity. BDSM is part of my spiritual journey. I would call it a faith experience rather than religious. Anyone who experiences the joy of new-found faith is often willing to give up control to God. In mature faith, however, one finds that God speaks to one's heart through the community and through the aching and longings within the heart.

To listen to the spirit that calls beyond what you are takes courage. You know it is a right move spiritually when you feel peace about the decision, and the move is affirmed by the community. Often in new faith and in new BDSM experience people think that they are giving themselves totally. In both cases, preconceptions and "the way it ought to be" mentality are cast aside in order to make room for new fulfillment. But, in neither case, do people abandon who they are at the core of their existence. Instead, they often find that they become more true to themselves.

Rituals within the BDSM scene may seem like a very strange concept, but they can't be discounted. Patriarchal religions have long attempted to separate the holy from the body – especially from the sexual aspects of the body. Yet, if there is one way the almighty could be sure that we would go forth and multiply, it is by a marvelous gift of sexual drive.

I associate the act of submission with ritual. Many of the toys we use in BDSM play are phallic symbols: knives, sticks, candles and needles. The vaginal symbols are more subtle, bowls, water or other liquids that flow such as melted wax. During a scene, beyond the enjoyment of the participants, there is a symbolic reality expressed that says sexuality is part of who and what we are.

My Catholic background makes me think of a BDSM scene as similar to a liturgy, where the actions or props are symbolic of a spiritual truth. For me, the spiritual truth in BDSM is that we are greater together than alone. The polarity of our BDSM roles symbolize the uniqueness of individuals, and we approach the divine by the ecstasy of the scene being acted out.

I often play out in my mind a scene where I symbolically give my gift of submission. It starts with two of us walking to the center of the scene or ritual space. My outer clothing is vanilla, and I have on a priest-like stole, a symbol of authority and power, that is rainbow-colored. This shows that we start out as equals. Pacabel's *Canon* begins softly and slowly grows louder. As the music becomes manifest, I kneel down, bow and then take the stole and remove it from myself and place it on my lover.

He motions me to take off my vanilla outer clothing, and I do. As a symbol of a willingness to become vulnerable, he puts cuffs on me, a symbol that I trust being helpless before him. Here, I would feel the fire. It might be real fire on skin or my skin reddened and warmed by the whip, symbolic of passion. Pachelbel's *Canon* finishes, and Weber's *Music of the Night* begins. This music by itself is symbolic of spiritual journey as it talks of letting fantasies unwind and letting the darker side give in. At this point, there is a waxing, symbolizing fire and light. The fire in the candle is symbolic of the fire in the soul, and the image of light coming into darkness is replete with symbolism.

As the music crescendos, the lyrics ring out, "You alone can make my soul take flight. Help me make the music of the night." We embrace and caress. This, to me, is symbolic of reaching heights in a journey that one could not reach alone. As the music dies down, we move apart. He takes off the stole and holds it out in front of him, draped over his hands. He bows. I return the bow, and, while my head is still submissively bent, he replaces the stole around me as a symbol of power returned. We again embrace and kiss as equals.

While this BDSM ritual is in many ways reminiscent of liturgical dance, it does fit my own fantasies of being exposed and becoming known deeply and intimately by another so it is still a personal expression. When I think of a private scene, it seems like private prayer and as such is open to multitude of diverse expression.

Submission as personal growth

Being a submissive woman has taken me on a journey that has challenged my preconceived ideas, and it has forced me into values clarification. The life force or spirit within me has been strengthened, and continue to be guided by the spirit of Goddess/God in every step of the journey. I have gone beyond pain and pleasure into a world of self-discovery, personal fulfillment and community outreach. I have discovered a side of me that is curious about my previously repressed bisexual nature and a receptivity to open relationships.

At times, I have felt like Abraham in the Old Testament when he was asked to give back to God his son, who was to be the instrument of God's promise. How could I give up the values of my youth or the hard-won advances of the feminists who have gone before me? Listening to that small voice within, I have been abundantly blessed, like Abraham was, when I trusted the spirit within rather than conventional wisdom. At other times, I've felt like I was an unwilling prophet like Noah or Paul. It has seemed that I have been compelled to be a prophet of a new sensuality as they were called to spread the word of God. My early faith development and refinement, even though it was in a very patriarchal religion, has taught me to live through questions. Being submissive may have put chains on my body, but it has removed my soul from bondage.

A Feast of Joy... A Dish of Pain

One of the things that makes discussing BDSM so difficult is the word pain. Submissives don't necessarily seek pain, even though many enjoy many forms of pain as part of the play. What many of us do would seem to be painful, but most dictionary definitions of pain include phrases like, "leading to evasive actions" or "which are avoided." Yet, these stimuli, far from being avoided, are sought. Therefore, BDSM actions cannot be pain. Or, can they?

This conundrum reminds me of a story about a politician, who being asked if he opposed liquor, said, "Are you referring to the demon rum that destroys lives, reduces families to ruin, and is the shame of our cities, or are you referring to the delicious elixir that rejuvenates the tired, gives peace to the troubled, and contributes so much in taxes to our national treasury?"

The problem seems to lie in a failure of the English language. Obviously there seem to be at least two, and perhaps more, kinds of pain. I've never known a submissive who got off on a stomach ache from a bad hotdog. However, many greatly enjoy the very similar pain resulting from an enema. A swat from a closing spring-loaded door is annoying, but one from a leather-clad lover is exciting.

Nor is enjoyment simply situational. More than once I have had to pause during a session to untangle a strap which was pinching my submissive or to ease her leg cramps. Why did these pains bring her down when she was receiving a substantially greater pain from the whipping, strapping or waxing?

The answer could be that the pains are different. Popular myth has it that Eskimos have dozens of different words for snow. We have only one word for pain, which is another interesting shortcoming for English.

As far as I know, psychologists have not examined this terminology shortfall. However, there has been considerable research into stress, which affects the body much like pain. The stress researchers found that there are two kinds of stress, eustress (good stress) and distress (bad stress). Interestingly, the distinction between these two stresses is completely within the soul of the individual. Where one person might see a rollercoaster ride as the high point of her day, another might find it a glimpse into hell.

The same stress can be distress for an individual at one time and eustress at another. We all know individuals who revel in the push and tug of office politics. However, occasionally, even these political animals get fed up and need to get away when the eustress of political infighting becomes distress.

People in BDSM instinctually recognize that there are positive pains and negative pains. Our discussions are laden with indirect references to them. We may talk about something that "gets me off" or "sends me somewhere else," while another activity/toy/person "turns me off" or "brings me down."

Often, at the beginning of a session, we are dealing with a relatively narrow cone of positive pain. Most submissives prefer to begin with some relatively light, sensual, familiar stimulation. As the level of endorphins build and the submissive gets into his or her space, the cone of positive pain widens, and the dominant has a broader range of stimulation to choose from.

This is where experience and sensitivity come in. By riding just short of the edge where positive pain becomes negative, the dominant can take the submissive to heights of pleasure she never knew she could reach. However, crossing over that edge, moving outside the cone of positive pain, can distract the submissive and shatter the spirit of the scene.

This is what creates the intensity of communication between the submissive and the dominant. Body language, tone and timbre of cries, and even odor, provide clues that allow an experienced dominant to bring the submissive right up to the edge without crossing it.

To make matters even more complex, this edge does not lie at a particular point on the submissive's pleasure map, nor is the passage to it analogous to reaching a conventional wall or barrier. The edge varies from day to day and is responsive to the pace, timing of the stimulation and tool employed. In fact, in the non-Euclidian space of BDSM, it is also possible to go beyond the edge without passing it.

For example, a particular submissive may be in sheer heaven with hours of firm measured spanking but may reach the edge rather quickly with a few swats of the cane. Conversely, the cane may produce a marked negative reaction when used early in the session, but it could be welcomed as a scene-ender which drives that particular submissive right into paroxysms of pleasure when preceded by extensive stimulation with other toys.

Another thing that differentiates the kinds of pain is a sense of control and trust. Recently, doctors have been fitting patients with small pumps, which the patients can dose themselves with pain medication. To many people's surprise, the patients used less medication than they would have been given in a typical nurse-supplied situation. It wasn't that doctors and nurses had been overdosing patients; the patients who could control their own pain could tolerate more of it. They were in control of the situation.

This may explain why a twisted strap or cramp can be painful and a whip pleasant. The strap and cramp are unexpected and uncontrolled. There is no assurance that no harm will be done. The whip, on the other hand, is controlled by someone seen as trustworthy, one who would not inflict lasting or gratuitous harm. The submissive recognizes either overtly or covertly that he or she has the overriding say in the scene.

Because the previously mentioned cramp wasn't part of the script between myself and my submissive, it was, therefore, frightening and painful. It was an alien intrusion into this dance of trust and submission. Since I did not control it, my submissive did not even have the indirect control over the stimulation to which she had become accustomed. This created a sense of negative pain, and she used her safeword to bring the situation once again under control.

This sense of control over the outer parameters of the scene may also explain why experienced submissives playing with unfamiliar dominants are unable to tolerate the same degree of stimulation they would enjoy with familiar partners.

It is the development of this trust that is the test of a true dominant. It is fragile, easily broken and can rarely be mended seamlessly. However, it is a treasure beyond price and the key that opens fantasy to reality.

Stalking the Wild Submissive

The single most common question in BDSM is, "How do I find a submissive?" (I'm also asked, "How do I find a dominant?" but that's another book.) Occasionally, it is spoken with an air of angry frustration as if there should be a branch of Subs R Us on every corner. More often, the tone is one of frustration and disappointment.

I won't sugarcoat the truth. It is difficult and frustrating for both sides in this eternal dance. If you are seeking a male submissive, remember that you are asking him to admit to desires contrary to every precept he was brought up to hold. If you are seeking a female submissive, keep in mind that by admitting her desires, she could be seen to be rejecting gains that women have slowly and painfully made over the last twenty, fifty, one hundred years. Is it any wonder the streets are not filled with people wearing buttons reading "I'm Submissive; Take Me"?

There are basically two routes to your goal. One is to attract an individual who has already made up his or her mind that submission is the desired path. The other is to help a potentially submissive person liberate his or her feelings. Neither is easy.

Let's look at the first path. On the surface, it looks smooth. We have a group of submissives looking for dominants and a group of dominants looking for submissives. Put them together and all will be well. In an ideal world, this would be true. Unfortunately, you're not looking for just "a submissive." You want someone whose needs and desires complement your own.

To make things harder, within each group, there is a smaller group of people who are not what they seem. Each group includes mindfuckers, blackmailers and outright confidence tricksters. Removing them from the mix sometimes seems like an overwhelming task. (I should note here that there is also a kind of play called "mindfucking." The kind of lowlife I'm referring to has no relation to that.) We'll talk more about these people in a few pages.

Submissives are looking for someone strong in spirit and confident, someone to whom they can entrust their safety. A seemingly frenzied search does not present these qualities to the onlooker.

Perhaps, the best approach for a dominant to take is presented, somewhat tongue in cheek, in this short parable written on Prodigy by a Midwestern dominant.

Somewhere in the stormy North Atlantic, aboard the USS Dominance:

"Captain... our sonar shows subs lurking in the area."

"Easy, Mr. Libido. We'll let them come to us."

"Begging your pardon, Captain, but shouldn't we be seeking them out?"

"Mr. Libido, you obviously don't know how the USS Dominance retains its control over the high seas."

A klaxon horn goes off, and an urgent voice blares from the loudspeaker. "Sub sighted off the starboard bow!"

"All hands, this is Mr. Libido! Man your battle stations! Full speed ahead!"

"Mr. Libido! You will rescind those orders and never dare to overstep your authority on my ship again!"

"Captain, the USS Dominance is a dominant ship!"

"Exactly, Mr. Libido. And as a dominant ship under my command she will stay her course while the sub approaches. Stand down from battle stations. Steady as she goes."

"Captain, as Executive Officer on this ship I must protest your extraordinarily passive behavior in the presence of a sub."

"Mr. Libido, protest if you will, but the sub will be handled my way, or it will not be handled at all."

"Sir, do you mean we will capture it by projecting a calm, secure image on the rough seas?"

"Mr. Libido, continue to learn. One day you will be a captain of a dominant ship yourself."

Rose, a New York submissive, phrased it this way: "I like a guy who respects himself. He is more likely to respect me and my gift to him. He is more likely to take care of himself, and by extension of me. I like a guy who understands that trust of this depth can only evolve if we take our time.

"Some guys always overdrive their headlights, no matter how rotten the driving conditions. That doesn't mean that I don't like to travel fast – only that there is a time and place for that and the beginning is figuring out where all the buttons are and what they do.

"Finally, since this is all about domination and submission, shaping behaviors and pleasing each other, I like a guy who understands at least the rudiments of shaping behavior. Some people are natural-born dominants, masters or trainers, but that doesn't mean the skills can't be learned. And there are lots of rules about shaping behavior that apply, no matter whom you're shaping."

Making contact

There are various media outlets for avowed dominants and submissives to seek each other out: newspapers, magazines, the Internet, clubs and associations.

Whatever the medium, the method is to give and gain trust, for a dominant must earn the trust of a submissive by being trusting, while keeping alert for those who are flying false colors. Submissives look for this trust in an attempt to separate us from the nonconsensual sadists and those who would do them harm. Unfortunately, there are those among them who would use this trust to hurt us.

Because of this danger, it is a good idea not to reveal too much about yourself during initial contacts. This, naturally, is directly at odds with the need to give trust. It is a delicate balance, not susceptible to easy solution.

It's also good to keep a sense of humor. This may not seem easy when you feel as if your beating heart has been ripped from your chest by some bastard or bitch, but life goes on. It's important to keep both the victories and defeats in proportion.

Without going into details, I'll draw an illustration from my own life when things looked extremely black, so black in fact that I was sitting on my porch looking at a shotgun and debating using it to end the pain. As I sat there, I realized I needed to take a piss. At first, it enraged me that so physical a feeling should be intruding on the depth of despair I was feeling. But, then I really, really needed to take a piss. It hurt. Suddenly, I realized just how shallow a person I was to let a thing like a full bladder encroach on a moment of metaphysical torment. I broke out laughing, I pissed, and I went on with my life.

Contact at a distance

This is the section of *Loving Dominant* which has undergone the most "sea changes" as one edition follows another. Part of the changes have been due to advances in technology. When the first edition was being written, the Internet was still mostly a thing of corporations, universities and governments. Most people who had online lives did so with thirty-baud dial-up modems and connected directly to bulletin board systems, which could be as huge as Prodigy or CompuServe or as small as a home computer in someone's spare room. Now, high speed lines connect homes to an information superhighway, and the web's potential has increased exponentially. But one thing remains the same. People want to meet people, and computers provide powerful tools to do so.

Before the Internet, magazine and newspaper advertisements were the preferred way to cast a wide, but impersonal, net over a large population. There were kink-dedicated, kink-friendly publications like *Latent Image*, or swinging magazines where you could spell out exactly what you wanted. More difficult were vanilla publications where a kind of code was prevalent. Submissives would talk about "wanting to surrender to an assertive man/woman" or "give up control." Dominants would mention seeking someone "restrained" or "passive." Often, literary references supplied the clues. "I loved reading *Exit to Eden/Story of O/Venus in Furs*"… with the writer hoping the minimum-wage toiler on the advertising desk wouldn't be able to pick up the reference.

It is interesting that this same sort of subterfuge was necessary on some online systems in the early days. Prodigy, for one, was initially very anti-BDSM and would refuse to post messages referring to any sort of scene play. The kinky folks quickly found that they could gather in the literature section and post comments about Anne Rice's *Beauty* books that were, in reality, thinly disguised description of their interests and activities.

Now most of these magazines are things of the past, and computers are the modern way to meet others who share your interests. During a class at The Boston Dungeon Society, one female instructor casually commented, "I don't know how anyone can be serious about their sex life if they don't have a computer." It got a big laugh, but the point was serious. As the computer came of age, people realized that they had a very powerful tool for communicating as well as calculating. By linking the computers to other computers, people have created thousands of networks both large and small, which can help people of similar interests find each other.

One of the most attractive facets of most computer systems is anonymity. Most systems allow you to choose a name that serves as both an identification and as a mailing address. Your true name is a closely guarded secret.

This is both a positive and a negative thing.

The anonymity permits you and the other people to have frank, honest discussions on subjects which might be impossible to broach if your true identity were online. Many, dominant and submissive, male and female, feel they might be in danger of social condemnation if our vanilla friends and colleagues learned of kinky interests. Online, we can let our hair down and be ourselves, protected by the shield of anonymity.

The dark side of the "cyber mask" is that it plays into the hands of those whom believe "honesty" is just a word in the dictionary.

If you spend any significant amount of time in the scene, particularly online, you will encounter mindfuckers and confidence tricksters. Although they are most prevalent online, drawn there by the anonymity of the exchanges, they aren't a creation of the computer age. Back, as Libby often puts it, "when dinosaurs roamed the Earth," people in the scene often made contact through classified advertisements. One knowledgeable individual from that era put the percentage of fake advertisements at more than ninety percent.

One fuel for this engine of deception was the reply mechanism. You were expected to send a letter in a sealed envelope with the advertiser's code number written in pencil on the outside. This was supposed to be accompanied by a fee and a loose stamp. Since the publishers made money from both selling the advertisement and forwarding the reply, many succumbed to the temptation to create false advertisements and simply pocketed the reply fees (and the unattached stamp). Some recent lawsuits indicate that online dating services may be following a similar strategy to run up their numbers, increase advertising fees and tempt more people into becoming paying members.

As Alphonse Karr put it in 1849, "*Plus ça change, plus c'est la même chose,*" or "The more things change the more they stay the same."

A common form of deception is often called "the mindfucker." Some of these mindfuckers seem have no malevolent intent, but they are simply confused or terrified by what they want. Others are just intentionally cruel. The most common encounter of this type begins with the exchange of a series of passionate notes or phone calls, in which she or he seems to be everything you ever wanted and more. You get hotter and hotter – and suddenly the contact is broken off. A crueler scenario could have you traveling hundreds and perhaps thousands of miles to have no one waiting for you when you arrive.

There is really no perfect defense from these people. The old saying, "If it seems too good to be real, it is," applies. Getting as much information about the submissive as possible before committing to any major inconvenience or making any significant commitment is key. However, many genuine submissives are reluctant to give out much information to a relative stranger because there are nuts masquerading as dominants, too. Therefore, you must strike a balance between what you perceive as a risk and what you have as a need.

The same rule applies to the confidence tricksters. However, they generally reveal themselves in their single-minded search for money. The scenario goes like this – she (males are most often the victims here) seems to be your dream partner. There is an exchange of letters and, perhaps, phone calls. She informs you that she wishes to fly to your arms and dungeon, but she doesn't have the price of a plane ticket. Would you...?

This is not to say that there are no dominants and submissives who are short on traveling money. However, such a request should send up warning flags. Other clues are typed rather than written letters and an inability or unwillingness to phone you. Again, some people find it easier to type personal letters than to write them, and a small percentage truly lacks the ability to send and receive calls. However, caution is called for.

Fortunately, most tricksters who sink to this kind of work are woefully lacking in skill and intelligence. If they were smarter, wouldn't they have been running an oil company? I have received "personal" letters that were photocopied, unsigned computer-generated letters and "personal" photographs that had been photocopied from bondage magazines. I don't really object to them trying to trick me. I just wish they had a higher opinion of my intelligence.

These sort of scams have become so common that some online matching services have posted warnings that email asking for money or originating in certain countries, like Nigeria, are to be looked at skeptically.

Blackmailers are more difficult to deal with. Fortunately, the numbing of the American mind has made this a vanishing breed, except when political figures and socialites are the targets. If you don't fit into either category, you probably have little to fear. In more than forty years in the scene, every single one of the "blackmail" efforts with which I've come in contact has been a byproduct of a personal dispute within the scene. Most have come out of divorces where one spouse tries to paint the other as some kind of a perverted monster either for custody reasons or to gain a monetary advantage. Less often, they have been like the flake whose loony behavior in a private club got him banned and set him on a letter writing campaign to get "even" with the club.

These scoundrels generally constitute a minor threat. However, you run a much, much greater risk going online from the place where you work. Many people have gotten used to running quick web searches and even making online purchases on company time without a problem, and this emboldens them to do other, personal things when they are at work. The logic is, "If the company hasn't blocked the website or mentioned the other stuff, they must not be watching." That may not be true.

Many companies monitor which websites their computers access. Some go further and watch each keystroke made on all the company computers. However, bosses are human and likely to ignore minor infractions of the rules as long as the work flow isn't interfered with. They may ignore an occasional purchase or visit to a joke website, but things can get very different when sex is involved. Even if the boss is willing to let things slide, do you really want some pimple-faced IT drone looking electronically over your shoulder while you type? A good rule-of-thumb is, keep it at home and on your personal computer.

Like anonymity, the Internet's international reach is both a positive and a negative thing. It's positive because you can be in contact with literally thousands of people, which significantly increases the chances of your finding a perfect match. On the other hand, your perfect match could be 3,000 miles away.

When this book came out, I tried to provide a comprehensive list of websites. At the time it seemed do-able. Now, with hindsight, it was like trying to count the snowflakes while standing in the middle of the damned blizzard.

While I was rewriting this section of *Loving Dominant*, I did a few quick Google and Yahoo searches just on BDSM. They both returned more than twenty two million hits. That's no longer a blizzard – that's an ice age.

You know how to conduct a websearch, but I'll just add a few hints. Because the search engines use information from inside the website, there isn't a perfect formula for finding anything. Just try to think up terms that you think would be in the kind of page you are looking for and experiment, experiment, experiment. For example, if I were looking for a BDSM group in south Florida I might offer "BDSM," "group" and "southeast Florida," and I might get some hits.

Or I might not, because a lot of sites don't have "southeast Florida" specifically in their description. I could go wider and look for "BDSM" "group" and "Florida." This would yield a lot more sites, but many that would be too far away to be of interest. Another approach would be to try "BDSM" "group" and "Boynton Beach," "BDSM" "group" and "Delray Beach" or "BDSM" "group" and "Palm Beach." There would be fewer hits, but the ones I got should be more likely to be of interest.

Some websites are purely one way. They have information that you can see. These are the books and the advertisements of the Internet, but other sites allow you to interact with other viewers. Message areas allow you to leave a message, much like pinning a note up on a wall. Anyone who comes by can read it, and if they want, comment on it by adding other messages linked to it. Chat areas are just what they sound like. You are in a room with other people and can chat back and forth by typing messages.

Chat rooms are really nothing new. I first encountered chat rooms when I was a graduate student at Ohio State University in the mid-'70s. A local company, CompuServe, was looking for subscribers and I joined using 110-baud teletype (kids, ask your grandfather about those). One exciting aspect was what CS called "CB Simulator." Just as it sounds, it was a chat room that worked like the contemporary Citizen's Band radios. After searching a bit, I found one channel that catered to people with BDSM interests. Let's just say there was a lot of paper at the end of each day to throw away and the introduction of a CRT screen was a blessing.

Look at chat sites as if they are scene clubs, and message sites as if they were magazines carrying classified advertisements, and things become a lot clearer. In fact, a chat room can have an advantage over a scene club. In a scene club, there are a lot of factors coming into play that may be less than helpful for the average person. Because people can see each other, they often favor the beautiful people over the interesting people. Since ninety percent of the population isn't beautiful, we tend to get the short end of the stick in such an environment. In chat, you only see the other person's words. That can be a big advantage in getting to know him or her. Also, online, you don't have to contend with the blasting music that some clubs substitute for ambiance. Some people like the challenge inherent in trying to lip-read whether the person they've just met is mouthing "You're cute; I like you" or "You've backed into a candle and your jacket is on fire." I don't.

The chat sites also combine an air of intimacy with a certain psychological distance. I know one male submissive who had a great deal of difficulty with the club scene because when his advances were rejected he tended to become so embarrassed that he would leave. When his offers were rejected in a chat he found that it didn't quite have the same impact.

Also, in a club, people are often thinking, "Who can I go home with tonight?" This doesn't help when you are looking for a relationship. This attitude also tends to keep a significant portion of the scene population out of these places. In a chat room, things can move at a more sedate pace. People know you aren't going leap through the screen at them so they can be more forthright about what they want and how they want it.

In a message area, you can just leave a classified advertisement if the rules allow it, but this would be the equivalent of buying a Lotus to drive to the corner store. Usually on these message boards, series of messages appear, discussing all sorts of matters from whipping techniques to levels of submission. If you start replying to messages and expressing your opinion or asking questions, you can quickly develop a reputation on the board as a thoughtful, intelligent person, and you may well find that you are being approached by someone whose interests complement your own.

I make it a point to post helpful hints regularly on the message centers where I have accounts. I also respond to requests for information. The posts can be as simple as a list of BDSM books I have found enjoyable or as technical as scene design and execution. In fact, many of the sections of this book first appeared as messages on Prodigy between 1989 and 1991 as informational posts.

These notes allow cautious submissives to evaluate me as a dominant without even revealing their presence. They can get an idea of what my level of skill is and how closely my philosophy of BDSM matches what they are looking for.

By the time they contact me, the "hook" is firmly set. All that is necessary is for me to decide the extent of involvement I will permit. In many cases, it is limited to guidance and advice; in others, the involvement can become much more intense. However, the computer has permitted each of us to exercise control in an area that was appropriate.

The most successful of these attempts yielded a short email on February 19, 1992. The full text of the message was "I think we share some interests in common." The message was from Libby, the woman who has become my world... and my wife.

What are you looking for?

In my opinion, one of the major, self-imposed impediments both dominants and submissives bring to the search for a partner is a long list of requirements. Now this doesn't mean that we need to drop back to the level of a teen-aged boy, whose only requirements in a sex partner is she needs to be alive and breathing. Compatibility is important even in a casual scene. (And if you don't believe me, try watching the outcome of a scene between a pain-play bottom and a pony/control-play top.) In a long-term relationship, it's vital, but just what does it take to make "compatibility?"

Each time you add another "must have" requirement to your list, you are shaving the list of candidates by a greater or lesser degree. Ask yourself, "Is hair color really that important?" Most people, upon reflection, will agree it isn't. How about weight? Age? Sex? Species? Ok, maybe I'm going a little far here, but at least, you're thinking, and that's the important thing. Look at your list and strike out anything that's "nice to have" but isn't a "must."

Writing an advertisement

There are many sites that specifically exist so people can post advertisements in addition to chatting or leaving messages, but advertisements can be tricky. You don't want to write a book. That gives a sense of desperation that does not reflect the calm and controlled demeanor that attracts a submissive.

On the other hand, advertisements like "Are you submissive? Write me" are unlikely to attract a high quality group of submissives, but they are likely to be the natural feeding ground for the unsavory groups I've mentioned. Keep in mind this is the first step of a seduction. Outright commands ("Drop to your knees and write") can attract a certain group of fantasy players, but to attract people who seek a long-term submission and concomitant relationship, a more informative advertisement is needed.

The best approach is to think seriously about what kind of a submissive you want and what he or she would want to read. Be as realistic as possible. Fantasy at this stage is counterproductive.

You should also try to project a confident, assured air. The world can be very disappointing for anyone seeking to make a kinky match. After all, we have all compatibility needs, and we also need someone whose kinky needs and desires complement our own. However, showing frustration isn't the best way to find a submissive. Relax for a moment and try to put yourself in the mindset of someone looking for a dominant partner. How would you react to lines like, "I know most of you people are phonies," or, "I'm getting so tired of liars and bullshitters?" They may be honest indications of how you are feeling, but that isn't the goal of the advertisement.

Your advertisement should include information about yourself, but lying is a serious mistake. Some lies will be discovered almost immediately. One wannabe dominant, who described himself as "tall and imposing," was quite successful at meeting submissives, but the meetings rarely went beyond that. He couldn't understand why. A glance in the mirror might have helped: he was five-feet six and weighed less than 120 pounds. You can imagine the suspicions submissives might have felt about any other information he had given them.

Other lies may take a while to come out. Marital status, amount of experience, group membership and such are difficult to lie about consistently. Every person is different, but the intensity of trust necessary for a BDSM relationship rarely survives such falsehoods.

Honesty is the best policy

In general, the approach in seeking male submissives can be a bit more abrupt than that in seeking females. Speaking more plainly, what will scare the bejesus out of a novice female may be just right to attract a novice male. Of course, the perfect strategy is a matter of hot debate among those who use this approach. I have noticed that of my female dominant friends who run the worship-at-my-feet-while-I-whip-your-ass type of advertisement do tend to get more responses than their more sedate colleagues. However, they also tend to attract a greater percentage of mindfuckers and no-shows. All in all, it seems to even out in regard to the number of male submissives who actually appear.

When writing my advertisements, I acted on the assumption that submissive women are not looking for someone who will declare dominance. Almost all men will loudly claim that they are dominant; most are wrong. In any case, the simple declaration of dominance is not enough to motivate most submissive women. They are not looking for declarations of brutality or strength. Almost anyone can swing a whip or a paddle. Nature has made most men stronger, at least in their torso and shoulders, than most women.

What they are seeking is some evidence that the person behind the advertisement is trustworthy and sensitive to their needs. Writing an advertisement that reflects these qualities is much harder than simply announcing dominance. Rather than providing a set of catch phrases or sample advertisements that anyone could copy, I suggest that you look deep inside yourself. If you still cannot convey the requisite sensitivity in words, you may not be ready to hang a riding crop from the left side of your belt.

When you get a response to your advertisement, don't be surprised if a submissive, particularly a female submissive, is forthright in demanding more information about you. After all, the submissive is the one who must feel secure in giving up freedom. There may be a few maniacal axe-wielding submissives around, but I haven't heard of them. The Ted Bundys of the world have made submissives understandably nervous.

The most extreme example of demanding information I ever encountered was M, a thirty-year-old female submissive, who was a top-level executive in a nationwide store chain. She began with a standardized, thirty-minute interview probing into details of the potential master's experience and background. As she put it, "I look at it as if I were hiring a vice president. After all, I am going to have to put my safety into his hands. I want to know if he can handle it." She went through more than fifty candidates before settling on one. They are quite happy together.

Going from online to face-to-face

One of the big questions on everyone's mind when they think they have clicked with someone online is, "When should we meet?"

As with so much in the Scene, there is no hard and fast rule. One big factor is the distance between the correspondents. Obviously, except for a wealthy, leisure-class minority, the cost, both in money and time lost from work, is a significant factor. It's a lot easier to make a trip to the local mall food court than to schlep yourself across the continental US. It's only human, and realistic, to have in the back of your mind, "What if she/he isn't right for me?" Writing off a few gallons of gas is a lot easier than doing the same for a three-figure plane ticket.

My personal advice is to meet as soon as both parties are comfortable that there's a real possibility of something there. With a carefully planned, public meeting, the worst that can happen is you discover, "this ain't gonna work."

A basic axiom of life is that until (and sometimes not even then) you meet someone face to face, you don't know them. Just what should a dominant or submissive find out about a potential partner before making that big step? What you should know about another person before you meet is largely up to you and your comfort level.

I've seen lists of questions in web pages that go far beyond what most people would need for comfort and, in fact, become unacceptably intrusive. For example, let's say you ask for a social security number? Now, what could you do with such a number to assure yourself that the person is safe enough to meet with? It's not the most convenient of factoids. Think of what kind of harm someone could do with your social security number should they prove to be malevolent. This is a case where the downside is much greater than the upside.

It's not so much what you ask, but what you confirm. I've known people who before meeting another asked about the person's home and cell phone number, his date of birth, his place of employment and where he lived and then blissfully went off on the date, thinking they knew him, only to learn later that not one thing they had been told was accurate.

I have a paperweight that was given to me by the staff of the student newspaper at the University of Southern Mississippi that reads "If your mother tells you she loves you, check it out with an independent source," a phrase I had pounded into their heads about checking out every detail one is given. You may think you "know" something, but until you confirm it you've only been "told" it.

With telephone numbers, I advise to call him or her on them. As for addresses, I say send a nice vanilla card to the address and then ask him or her if it's been received and a question or two to see if it really has been. Until you've confirmed information of a given fact, you don't really know it.

Some people put considerable stock in references. I have mixed feelings about them. One big problem about the online scene is that most people only know someone from his or her chat, postings and emails. X may be completely sure that Y is a wonderful person, but X isn't going to be putting his or her ass on the line; you are. If you ask for a reference about someone, be sure to ask just how the referrer knows the person. If it is purely online, then it's unlikely they really know much more than you do.

Any online reference should be treated with reasonable skepticism if you don't really know the referrer. It's not all that difficult for someone to create a "sock puppet" identify for the sole purpose of validating and praising his or her primary identity.

Finally, beware of "friendly warnings" from online sources. It's far from unheard of for someone to spawn a campaign of vilification out of a desire for revenge. Quite often, "this person isn't a real submissive," or, "she's a lying tease," translates to "she said 'no' to me." Multiple sources giving the same information shouldn't increase the credibility because, as noted before, some people have "sock puppet" identities, and other people simply pass on warnings in an unquestioning belief that negative news is more credible.

Many in the scene use "safe calls" or "silent alarms" for the first few meetings. These, in their simplest form, mean contacting a friend, telling him or her where you'll be and who you will be with. At a prearranged time, you call your friend and let him or her know you are all right. Some people arrange an innocent-seeming code to signal a problem without needing to come right out and say it. The explicit arrangement is that, if you miss the call or signal there is a problem, the friend should come over or contact the police.

It's a good idea, if you do it properly. I've heard of situations where the couple simply lost track of time only to be reminded of it when the cops came banging on the door. Other times, nothing happened because the contact person didn't consider it significant that the call was not made.

To me, the real value of a safe call is the reaction of the other person when you mention one is in play. Anyone with a clear conscience will just nod or might suggest that the two of you set an alarm clock so you won't miss the call. A big, flashing red light would be raising a fuss or even refusing to go through with the meeting.

An extreme example of a safe call working, although not exactly as the individuals intended, was the case of a Texas psychologist, who wanted to meet with a guy she'd met online. She called a man, Travis, who is as well known for his proficiency with a singletail as for his skill in in handling social issues, and she asked him to be her safe call. The man she was expecting to meet was John Edward Robinson Sr., who used the screen name of "Slavemaster." When he heard about the safe call, Robinson became outraged and beat the woman before releasing her. She contacted Travis. They contacted the police in Kansas where Robinson lived. The investigation that ensued eventually uncovered dead, tortured bodies in oil drums on his property. He was later convicted in 2003 of multiple murders.

Fortunately, the number of "Slavemasters" in this world is incredibly small. By and far, almost all of the meetings I know of which that have gone bad happened because of ignorance or over expectations on the part of the individuals involved. However, there are some bad people out there, and a safe call is one reasonable precaution to take for an initial and maybe the next few meetings.

At the very least, leave information about the person you are meeting somewhere. That can be as dramatic as giving a friend a sealed envelope with the request "If you don't hear from me by Thursday, open this" or as simple as leaving the same information on your refrigerator door or on your bed.

I strongly recommend that you don't meet with the intention of having a scene. The first meeting is a time to exchange a lot of information, and it is hard to keep someone's attention when she or he is worrying or looking forward to what will be happening in the next few minutes. It also gives you a chance to digest what you've learned after the intense emotional flux of the initial meeting has receded.

Some people may read these suggestions, thinking, "This stuff is fine for submissives/women, but I'm a dominant/guy. I don't need this sort of stuff." Maybe you don't, but in this world, no one is completely safe. It's important to know what's available so you can model the situation such that you are comfortable and your safety needs are being met.

Public clubs, organizations and ovents

For the purposes of this book, I am using the word "club" in the sense of "nightclub," a commercial establishment. We'll get to member-run not-for-profit organizations in a few pages.

Public clubs

To many who have not experienced them, public clubs sound like nirvana. Hundreds of leather-clad dominants and submissives mixing in an erotically charged atmosphere. Your perfect submissive could be waiting on bended knees for you to grasp the collar and drag him or her off to your lair. In real life, they are fun and exciting. However, as is so often the case, the reality is not quite the same as fantasy.

There are two types of clubs: scene and non-scene. At a scene club, you can actually whip, spank, or otherwise play with your submissive. Non-scene clubs are places where you can show off your gear, talk to potential partners and relax with others in the scene, but no actual discipline can take place, at least overtly.

As at most non-scene clubs, most of the activity consists of meeting and talking with other members of the scene. If two or more people hit it off, they go elsewhere for their more serious amusements.

Both scene and non-scene clubs can be very exciting places to be. However, there are some problems that prevent them from being the answers to a dominant's dream.

Both attract throngs of tourists. Either because of a deep-seated fear or through simple bad manners, some of the tourists may behave rudely and inappropriately. For example, you will never hear anyone in the scene shouting, "Hit her again, harder," during someone's scene. Some clubs try to minimize the tourist trade by imposing a strict dress code. To enter, you must be dressed in leather, latex or other fetish gear or you must be a transvestite or transsexual in drag. Alligator-polo-shirt-wearing frat rats usually don't get past the door.

Strict dress codes are the rule in most of the London clubs I'm familiar with. Many of them use the premises of more conventional clubs when kinkiness is not in session. For example, The Pussycat Club in Hendon clearly spelled out their stand in the advertisements, writing, "Strict dress code. Leather, Rubber, Bondage, PVC and TV. No Denim, No Fur, No Cameras. No Swingers." Severin's Kiss in Soho took a similar stand.

In most scene clubs and non-scene clubs, leather and black clothing is standard wear, but conventional street clothing is acceptable. However, you will probably want to dress up a bit to fit in and distinguish yourself from the tourists to get into the flow of the scene. After all, as one psychologist who was talking to a scene member, delightedly exclaimed, "You get to have Halloween every weekend."

This doesn't mean you have to go out and buy a full leather rig. For men, black pants and a black shirt does the job. Women have a wider range of options – from riding clothes to, well... one dominant often shows up in a Victorian school-teacher's outfit, complete with cameo at her throat.

Even the part of the crowd that is made up of scene members, like the scene itself, is disproportionately male. The vast majority consists of male submissives – much to the pleasure of the female dominants. Female dominants and male dominants are present in almost equal numbers. However, unescorted female submissives seem almost nonexistent.

This is not to say that male dominants should avoid these clubs. They provide a useful place to meet others in the scene and to make one's reputation. Word of mouth is highly respected in the scene, and if the escorted submissive women come to like and trust you, you can be certain that their unattached sisters will soon learn about it.

Naturally, male dominants should treat escorted women with the greatest respect and courtesy. There are few greater sins than being dominating or rude to another dominant's submissive. The nicest thing that will happen, if you fail to obey this unwritten rule, is that you will get the cold shoulder. You should make sure to include the lady's dominant in any conversation, doing otherwise is extremely rude.

Another reason that unattached male dominants choose to visit these clubs is that a significant number of the "female dominants" are actually submissives dressing in dominant fashions so they can visit the club without being inundated by the attentions from wannabe doms.

Female dominants have an easier time, but clubs create problems for them too. Far too many of apparently submissive men are actually SAMs (Smart Assed Masochists), who are intent on using them, or any other woman, as a prop in their fantasies. Far from being submissive, these men can be very uncooperative with anyone who does not look or behave in a manner precisely fitting into their fantasy.

I was with Ace, an attractive female dominant, at Paddles one night when a man approached her and said, "Mistress, may I worship your boots?"

With appropriate courtesy, Ace gave him permission. But then, after a few minutes, the man said, "Mistress, may I take off your boots and worship your feet?"

It had been a long evening, and Ace was tired. In a gentle voice, she told him that she had been standing all evening and felt that her feet were swollen and, if she took them out of her boots, she would be unable to get the boots on again. However, she said he could continue to worship the boots.

He simply dropped the leg he was holding, looked at Ace and said, "That's no fun," then, he turned and walked away. While this man was far from being representative of all male submissives, his kind is unfortunately common in the club scene.

Female dominants will have a considerably easier time than males in finding someone to play with at public clubs. However, those who are seeking more than a simple bit of play may be just as disappointed at first as their male counterparts. The solution is to use the same strategy employed by male dominants in search of a submissive. Mingle, get to know the regulars, both male and female, dominant and submissive; plug into the grape vine, and eventually you are likely to have good luck.

Scene organizations

Another way of meeting submissives already in the scene is through organizations. Some, like TES, People Exchanging Power, New England Dungeon Society and Black Rose, are organizations with officers, by-laws and dues. Not all that different from the Rotary or a ham-radio society. However, the scene has its own, peculiar set of organizations known as munches.

According to most scene historians, the first munch took place in Palo Alto, California, in the early '90s, when a group of people who had gotten to know each other on the newsgroup alt.sex.bondage decided to meet each other at a burger joint. The regular meeting grew and adopted the name "Burgermunch," which was soon shortened to "munch."

Munches quickly spread across the country and overseas until it became relatively rare for a metropolitan area not to have one. Of course in the anarchistic world of BDSM, munches vary widely. Some have changed until there is little to differentiate them from conventional organizations, while others maintain the casual, show-up-if-you-can attitude of the original Burgermunch.

Generally, you'll find them in some sort of eating establishment. For example, in New England many of the munches are in mall food courts where on a given day or days of the month a group of individuals appear, push tables together and chat for a while.

One of the big bonuses of the open-style munch is that a nervous newcomer can grab a table nearby and "scope out the crowd" before approaching and asking, "Is this the munch?"

It's difficult to overstate how valuable that sort of openness can be. At one time when I attended TES, it gathered in the basement of a church. All too often, I detected the sound of someone descending the stairs outside the closed door, followed shortly by the sounds of someone reluctantly ascending. It was an ordinary wooden door, but for someone insecure and scared of his or her own needs, it might have been an iron-bound oak portal set in a granite arch with "All Hope Abandon, Ye Who Enter Here" carved above it. How much easier it is to sample a plate of kung-pao chicken while observing from ten or so yards?

When you are looking to meet people, it's a good idea to view munches much like a consignment store. Because going to the munch is very much an occasional thing for a lot of people, if you don't see something you like on your first visit, don't give up. It may be there the next time, or the time after that. Also keep in mind, like at a consignment store, the good stuff doesn't stay on the shelf for long.

While each munch makes its own rules, generally the more public the munch's venue, the more discreetly guests are expected to behave. This generally means wearing vanilla clothing, not displaying toys, and keeping your voice down, particularly when discussing scene matters.

Like munches, organizations are run by and for the members. The vast majority hold public meetings, but they also have some members-only activities. Most organizations are quite inexpensive to join, and even if you live too far away to attend meetings, their newsletters and other publications can be a valuable source of information and guidance.

For me, the most valuable reason for belonging is the joy of being with people who share my needs and desires. There is a feeling of family that can be infinitely comforting to someone whose desires are looked upon by the rest of the world with distaste and sometimes hostility.

If there is such an organization near enough for you to visit, by all means, do so. For the first meeting, sit, listen and observe. Get a feel for the dynamics. Many people's reaction when I bring up organizations or munches is to say, "Oh, I'm a very private individual; I couldn't risk that."

This is a completely understandable reaction. However, the risk is really a lot less than you may think. While "outing" does take place, in my experience it almost always takes place independent of a person's organizational memberships. Almost all of the outing cases I can recall in over forty years of playing have been directly related to divorce proceedings, where one spouse is trying to blackmail the other into a more favorable settlement or to paint him or her as unfit to have custody.

A common question is, "What if someone I know sees me at the meeting/class/party?" You could arrive at the munch, take off your coat, sit down and suddenly realize that one of the people at the table is Jim from accounting. You must fight the sudden urge to throw your coat over your head and run from the room. Guess what Jim is thinking right now? Exactly, the same thing you are. Borrowing a phrase from the Cold War, scene people refer to this phenomenon as "Mutually Assured Embarrassment."

As a dominant, you may feel compelled to make your presence known immediately upon arriving in a new group. Don't! Dominant means strong and secure. If you come across as pushy and insensitive, you could earn a reputation that will stay with you for a long time.

I recall the close of a TES meeting. As was customary, everyone was putting away chairs. One man, whom I had not seen before, motioned to a woman, whose collar and cuffs clearly indicated her status. He told her in an imperious tone to put away his chair. When she looked at him in amazement, he informed her that he was dominant. She turned around and walked away. This exchange had not gone unnoticed by others, and this particular "dominant" soon stopped coming to meetings.

Talking to people is perfectly OK, but you should be careful not to angle your attention only at submissives of the opposite sex. Not only is this rude, but it gives an impression of a single-minded pursuit that is most undominant. There are no hard and fast rules on how to act, but erring on the side of caution is probably a good idea.

I do not know of a single organization that pays much attention to clothing at their meetings. After all, many people will be coming directly from work, and few corporate organizations include black leather in their dress codes. On the other hand, some members come in full scene gear. What you wear is entirely up to you. However, a bit of black and a bit of leather will probably send the message that you are not entirely ignorant of the ways of the scene.

If, as is common, there is a point where those in attendance identify themselves according to their orientation and interests, take advantage of it to make yourself known in the most favorable terms possible. Just remember, as with advertisements, lying is inadvisable. Most lies will eventually be found out and may do irreparable damage to your reputation.

With organizations as well as at clubs, it is a mistake for a male dominant to expect to make contact with a female submissive immediately. It usually takes some time to build up a reputation to the point that your approaches will be welcomed. A female dominant may face the opposite problem because of the abundance of male submissives. She may be faced with the pleasant difficulty of having to pick and choose.

Conventions and events

One of the results of the expansion of the scene and the new openness engendered by the Internet has been the appearance of regional and national events like Thunder in the Mountains and Folsom Street Fair. These vary in size from a few hundred people to thousands and usually combine classes, play parties, socials and vending. While the events can be daunting, they offer people a wonderful opportunity to see the depth and breadth of the scene in a single weekend.

They are also perfect for people concerned about being recognized by friends and co-workers since they can select one being held hundreds of miles away, and who knows, once having been exposed to the pleasures of being surrounded by like-minded individuals, even the reserved person may opt to take the chance and begin attending local events.

Searching outside the scene

For one reason or another, a dominant may be willing or unable to avail herself or himself of advertisements, clubs or associations. Still, it is good to remember that the vast majority of the submissives have not yet declared themselves or have not even realized the full range of their desires and, therefore, cannot be reached through conventional routes.

Although there is some overlap between the techniques for identifying and seducing submissive men and women, there are enough differences to justify taking each group separately.

Identifying a potentially submissive woman is a situation fraught with peril. Not only is a direct question inappropriate, but many women have repressed their submissive tendencies because of embarrassment or because they have been taught that such feelings are evil or a betrayal of their fellow women.

I look for intelligent, strong, self-assured women. Frightened little mice do not have the courage to accept and act on their needs. Also, a woman who feels inferior can be manipulated into a submissive role against her will. This is ethically indefensible. With them, I tend to use a technique that I cause "plausible deniability," a method that allows me to back off with no loss of face in the event of rejection.

During the dating process, I put the woman in situations where she is lightly restrained. For example, I hold her hands behind her back during a kiss or kiss her while she is still entangled in clothing she has been removing. If she panics or withdraws, I apologize and "admit" to having been overcome with enthusiasm. If she reacts with passion, I try a bit harder. The trick is to keep it light and playful.

During sex, I watch for her to do things like grabbing sheets with wide-spread arms because it is a position often adopted by people who are fantasizing that they are being restrained. I also try holding her hands above her head or "accidentally" tangling them in the sheets when I am on top or holding them against her thighs or behind her back when she is on top.

Conversational probing can be as subtle as the physical testing. Literature is a good ice breaker. If she has read *The Story of O* or books by A.N. Roquelaure, it gives me a chance to discuss the situation in a suitably abstract, nonthreatening atmosphere. If she brings up de Sade's writings, it gives me an opportunity to compare his writings with reality by saying something like, "Yeah, I've read some of his stuff, but what I hear about people who do bondage and stuff like that is that they are nothing like characters in his books. They seem to really care about consent and sensuality instead of just pain for pain's sake."

It is amazing what people will discuss in the abstract that would be extremely threatening to discuss on a personal level. I use such abstract discussions to get a feeling on "where a woman is" on a subject. Even a violent reaction to any kind of BDSM literature is not necessarily a negative sign. Many women, as I have noted above, are fighting a great deal of social pressure to defeat what they have been taught to believe are bad feelings. I pay more attention to gut-level feelings, perhaps based on subliminal body language, which come out of the discussion.

Of course, the danger here is that my desires may interfere with my judgment. The partial solution is a lot of introspection on my part.

If the discussion turns from abstract to specific, I do not deny my impulses, but avoid all terms like "domination," "submission," "sadism," "masochism," "bondage" or "discipline." These are emotionally laden terms that are defined slightly differently by every individual. Nor do I speak in terms of my needs and desires. Instead, I tell her what I enjoy doing for my partner, while stressing the sensuality and respect. As in the initial stages of all BDSM relationships, I try to earn the degree of trust that will allow her to submit to me.

Despite the teachings of certain psychological schools, my experience is that not all women are submissive and only a relatively small percentage of them can act on submissive tendencies. However, through these approaches, I have been able to make some wonderful friendships and build a number of lasting relationships.

These techniques can also be used by dominant women to find a submissive man who has not yet declared, or perhaps even realized, his submissive nature. For example, the sensual bondage scenes in *Basic Instinct* or *Exit to Eden* are a sure conversation starter. Also, because of fashion, women are able to send more overt signals than men about their orientation. A man wearing a kinky leather outfit with a whip earring will probably be taken as gay by many women. A woman in similar regalia will certainly rate a second look from most men, even those who haven't explored their submissive desires.

The greater latitude for accessories is also a factor. Outside of the punk rock scene, handcuffs aren't a common accessory for men. However, a woman can casually dismiss one hanging from her belt with "The chrome sets off my black dress."

The differences in body language between men and women can also work for the dominant woman on the prowl. While a man would be unwise to assume anything about a woman who dropped her eyes in the face of an appraising stare, a woman who gets that reaction from a man would be wise to press her advantage.

A word of warning, novice dominant: women often restrict their search to men who are overtly submissive and/or effeminate. Experienced ones report that they find their most satisfactory conquests among aggressive, masculine men. It is unwise to dismiss any specific "type" from consideration. Submissives are everywhere. They just need to be found.

7

Winning Over the Vanilla Lover or Spouse

A common situation in marriages or long-term relationships is one member discovering or finally admitting to a BDSM orientation, leading to the problem of convincing the other to join in these activities. If you are in that situation and hoping to convince your partner to submit to you, you may have a difficult task.

As I've written previously, even when submissive feelings are strong, admitting to them is a traumatic experience. For someone who does not have these feelings, being asked to act the submissive role is intimidating and humiliating. If, on the other hand, you have discovered deep submissive drives within yourself, there is a short section addressed to your specific needs at the end of this chapter.

When you suggest the possibility of trying BDSM games, never use the terms S&M or B&D. Even the less familiar BDSM should stay in the closet for a while. Perhaps your major problem is that most people think they know what these things are all about; the mere fact that they are dead wrong doesn't alter the situation.

Sit down and think. What turns you on? Everything? Come on. Scat? Golden showers? Blood sports? Let's cut it down to the bone. What is it that you want? If you don't know what you want, you can't get it.

You, as a dominant, should practice putting yourself "in the submissive's head." Put yourself in the place of a vanilla person whose spouse has admitted a liking for sadism. Do images of Ted Bundy or The Blond Bitch of Buchenwald leap to mind? They should.

If you stir up these fears, the only people who will benefit are divorce lawyers. What you need to put in your lover's head is the image of your true desires. You also need to stir the emotions your lover may have repressed. There are several ways to do this and none of them are mutually exclusive. They can be combined as you see fit. After all, you are strongly attached to his person. Who could know him or her better than you?

One approach is the direct one. If bondage is your turn on, bring to bed a scarf or the belt from a bathrobe. Don't charge right in; mix a lot of horseplay with play bondage. Normally, a scarf is terrible for serious bondage, but we are talking light play right now. Share the fun; let him or her have a go at tying you up.

Stimulation is trickier on a direct approach. You must be certain it is recognized both consciously and unconsciously as sexual and not punitive. Spanking is probably the best "entry level" stimulation. It is familiar and doesn't involve instruments that might evoke a negative response. ("Where in hell did you get that?")

One approach I have used when dating overtly vanilla women is to exclaim during sex, "You bad girl! You scratched me with your fingernail." No woman, even the most dedicated nail-biter, will feel entirely comfortable claiming innocence. "You should be punished for that." Then, I pull her over my lap and give her a few swats with one hand, while keeping her well excited with the other. Spanking can also combined with intercourse positions. Just put him or her on top and swing away.

When converting a vanilla lover, as with seeking out a submissive lover, talking about books and movies is a good way to lead to conversation to your own desires. Before I got into a relationship with a romance author, I had always dismissed romance novels as chaste escapism. They may be escapism, but they are not chaste. A husband who discovers dominant tendencies and whose wife reads authors like Rosemary Rogers, Jayne Krentz and Sandra Brown is halfway to heaven. Read a few of her romance books. Then let her "catch" you doing it. Suggest that some of the scenes in them are "interesting." It is a wonderful duel that both of you can win.

Otherwise, bring home a few books to leave where she can find them. As I noted before, writing by Anne Rice, A.N. Roquelaure, Anne Rampling are a nice start to introducing someone to BDSM fantasies.

The original *Joy of Sex* has a nice section on bondage; unfortunately, later printings have watered it down. Madonna, the lady who made sleaze nice, has several books where she sings the praises of BDSM.

Vanilla videotapes abound with BDSM scenes. Bring some home for an evening of watching. A casual comment while watching *Bull Durham* like, "Wow, doesn't Susan Sarandon look like she is having fun," or, "I bet he enjoys that," can begin an illuminating conversation. Avoid X-rated BDSM DVDs. They are so intense they can be threatening. Remember, you want to keep it fun and non-threatening. Some vanilla films that have good bondage scenes are *Bull Durham*, *The Collector* and *The Nightcomers*. Spanking fans have particularly recommended John Wayne's *McClintock*. *Secretary* is a wonderful exploration of the world of dominance and submission. Some dominants may be a bit put off by the presentation of the male dominant, but if they are honest with themselves, they'll recognize the hesitance and fear that's behind his actions.

Generally, the only reason most television talk shows have BDSM subjects is to attack them. Don't watch them live with your spouse. First, tape them and consider how effective each would be as a recruiting tool. Casually slip the good ones into your evening viewing.

Always keep it light and move slowly and patiently. There is a, probably apocryphal, story in the scene about a man who greeted his wife while dressed completely in leather, wearing a leather mask and carrying a bullwhip. While she stood there in shock, he proclaimed, "You are now my slave. I am your master. Your only thought is to please me." She recovered from her shock, place kicked his balls up to about his neck and went back to cooking dinner.

As I said, slowly and carefully.

Bringing out the dominance in your spouse

A submissive approaching a vanilla spouse for domination faces a somewhat less complex, but more confusing, situation.

Right now, some of you are probably thinking, "This is a book for dominants. Why is this here?" The answer is simple. Submissives may buy this book to give their vanilla lovers. Why cheat them of an opportunity for happiness? – Besides, including them is a way for me to boost my royalties.

First, I'll speak to the novice submissive. Before you approach your significant other you need to narrow things down to specifics in your own mind. It isn't enough to admit to a desire to be dominated. What one person calls hot play can be either lukewarm tapioca or unthinking brutality to another.

Look into your own fantasies and decide where you really want to start. The two of you will be beginning a journey of exploration and having a firm starting point will make things easier later on. You need to decide what your absolute turn offs are.

One danger in broaching this subject is that you may initially agree to do some things that you really don't feel comfortable with or absolutely turn you off. If you backtrack later, this can be confusing to your partner, who may take it as a rejection or betrayal. You are probably both quite insecure right now. Consistency is the best course for the beginner. However, there is nothing wrong with admitting some things both attract and frighten you and telling your partner that you might like to try these later. It is also OK to find that you really don't like something. That is what safewords are for.

Give this section to your lover and ask him or her to read it if you think it's appropriate.

You're probably a bit confused at this point. Someone you thought you knew pretty well has admitted to a passion you may not even have suspected. But, think about it; you have been given a profound compliment. A lot of trust has gone into making this disclosure.

First, let me explain what your lover is taking about is not really that abnormal. I've written this book to help you. I'd like you to look the whole thing over later, but right now, you're going to need a little guidance as to what your lover meant. Fiction and the media have probably given you a very distorted idea of what it means to be a dominant or a submissive. First, and most important, it means sharing love and trust. You've already got that or your lover wouldn't have put this book in your hands.

Your life isn't going be turned upside down. You won't have to don leather garments or carry a bullwhip, but you can if you want to. Your lover won't be showing up at the PTA wearing nothing but chains and handcuffs. All that is going to happen is that the two of you will embark on a sensual dance, begin playing an erotic game that thousands enjoy every day.

You aren't going to be called on to be brutal or insensitive. On the contrary, you will discover that playing the dominant role will multiply your present sensitivity to your partner many times over. At the same time, it will allow you to experience sensual pleasures that you may not have dreamed of.

Your lover will not become weak or passive. Think about the strength and courage it has taken for him or her to admit to having these feelings. That strength and courage isn't going to disappear. In fact, by joining with him or her in this game, you will be adding to that strength and nurturing a level of confidence you haven't seen before.

For the moment, the best thing is for the two of you to talk it over. To a large extent, BDSM is communication. Your lover has fantasies he or she wants you to enter. You need to hear these fantasies for yourself to make up your mind.

In the previous chapter you can find some techniques for exploring fantasies near the end of the *First Scene* chapter. You may want to use these somewhat erotic techniques or just sit down with your lover and talk. The only important things to do are to recognize how stressful this is for both of you and to not make any judgments while the two of you are talking.

Afterwards, take what you have learned, and using your imagination, turn it into something that the two of you can act out. It need not be anywhere near as complex as the fantasies you have heard. You aren't DeNiro, and you don't need a cast of thousands. Look at the basics. Is there bondage? Stimulation with a whip or other instrument? Fantasy characters? Humiliation? You don't need to try them all at once. Break out one or two major ingredients and create something you can do. The rest of this book is just chock full of ideas.

Some individuals instinctively have the ability to do an amazing alchemy and turn what most people would call pain into pleasure. Others can learn to do this. Still, others, as much as they may desire to do it, cannot make the change. For example, if the fantasy includes whipping or spanking, start slowly, give five or ten relatively gentle strokes of the whip and then pause for reassurance; include a lot of feedback, including go words as well as safewords.

One novice couple came to me with a fantasy in which she was captured by a pirate and whipped on her breasts. We developed a scenario in which he demanded that she perform fellatio. By staying in her role as a well-brought-up young lady, she, of course, refused. He, then, whipped her breasts, stopping every few strokes to renew his demand. By refusing haughtily, she signaled him that all was well and she was enjoying what was going on. When the intensity of the sensation approached her limits, she "submitted" to his demands.

With men, the fantasy often revolves around humiliation. This is a delicate road to tread for both of you. Some people cannot engage in humiliation without feeling considerable discomfort even when they recognize that it is based in fantasy and play. It can result in a negative image of the person being humiliated, in a negative self image on the part of the humiliator, or the other way around.

Remember, too, that BDSM is based on consensuality. This goes in both directions. If you are not happy, or at least at peace with what you are being asked to do, sit down and discuss your feelings. It is just as wrong for someone to make you, as a dominant, do something you do not wish to do as it would be for you to force an unwilling submissive to do something.

However, if everything works, you will be amazed at the new dimensions that are opened up for both of you. BDSM doesn't replace vanilla sex; it simply adds new vistas of which most people are not even aware.

Suggested Reading
When Someone You Love Is Kinky, Dossie Easton & Catherine A. Liszt, Greenery Press

The First Scene

So you've done what once seemed impossible: found a submissive who's eager to play with you. It's now up to you to put together a scene that accommodates both of your fantasies and desires, but steers clear of anything that's beyond the physical or emotional limits of this particular partner – or, for that matter, beyond *your* physical or emotioanl limits.

In order to build this scene you're going to have to do some talking. These initial discussions should be quite detailed, but they can also be a mini-scene in their own right. The conversation can be played as a job interview with a young person attempting to get a well-paying job with a dominating, powerful person of the opposite sex, a medical examination, a Catholic-type confession before a priest or mother-superior, or a respondent to a Kinsey-type sex survey. Some sample questions are in the appendix which contains a questionnaire Sir Spencer uses when interviewing new submissives.

You need to go over the submissive's medical history. Important facts are:

- Old injuries, particularly broken bones and tendons (for example, a person whose Achilles tendon has been surgically reattached is not a good candidate for many kinds of inverted suspension)

- Diabetes (a diabetic can pass out unexpectedly and is much more prone to long-lasting bruises)

- Contact lenses (these can dislodge during blindfolding; in any case, the dominant should have a supply of artificial tears in case something gets in the submissive's eye)

- Asthma (gags are definitely a no-no and you should keep the medication handy)
- High blood-pressure or heart problems (obvious)
- Allergies (for example, some people get severe skin reactions to alcohol; this would eliminate both Fire on Skin and basic sterilization techniques or latex which would call for gloves and condoms of another material)
- Glaucoma (this does not go well with inverted suspension)
- Orgasmic syncope (people with this condition pass out during orgasm; it is frightening but not dangerous)
- Skin sensitivity (some people have skin that is exceptionally sensitive to cutting and bruising)
- Tendency to muscle cramps or old sprains or strains (for example, a person with a history of charley-horses shouldn't be forced to stand on tiptoe or put in extreme positions)
- Back problems (this would call for care in requiring high heels and the elimination of any hog-ties or arched-back positions)
- Tendency to bladder infections (women with this problem have to be very careful about cleanliness in the area of the urethra)
- Hemorrhoids (this obviously would put a limit on playing with the ass)
- Any psychological problems (a person with claustrophobia is not going to react well to hooding or mummification)

You should also ask the submissive about what his or her turn-ons and turn-offs are, as well as what he or she sees as frightening. However, something that a submissive admits to being scared of is not automatically banished from your repertoire; actually, it may turn out to be a major turn-on for that submissive. The sensation of fear is one of the major driving forces of the scene. Helping a submissive ride that crest of fear is one of the strongest highs for a dominant.

If you wish, you can ask about the submissive's pain tolerance, but, except with highly experienced submissives, I have found such responses to be unreliable. One woman who described herself as a "big sissy" gloried in fifteen to twenty strokes of the cane, something well beyond the tolerance of most submissives. A muscular man who told a female dominant, "I can take anything a woman can dish out," was screaming his safeword before she ran out of her first baggie of clothespins.

This initial conversation is a good place to assign a safeword or words or allow the submissive to choose them. For a detailed discussion of the types and levels of safewords, check the consent chapter. Here, I will only say again that it is absolutely necessary to have at least one safeword so the submissive can stop the scene before it gets too intense. The submissive using a safeword is not an insult to your abilities. It is simply a recognition that Murphy's Law exists in BDSM as well as everywhere else. Things can go wrong.

At this point, you should also discuss any limits on activities, including sexual. It does not have to be detailed. It can be as simple as, "I will not have sex with you, and you may not come without my permission," or, "I feel free to use you sexually in any way that strikes my fancy as long as I use safe sex techniques," or if you wish, you can go deeply into precisely what can and cannot be done.

Some novice submissives tend to go in one of two diametrically opposed directions. Some declare, usually with a dreamy look in their eyes, "I have no limits." Others have a long and complex list of "Things I'll never do."

For the ones with a long list, I recommend a gentle smile. Usually, I suggest writing down the list, sealing it in an envelope and leaving it with me. A year or so down the line, we can get together, open the envelope and have a good laugh. This does not mean that limits are meaningless or you can feel assured that any specific limit will pass away, but just that people tend to grow and change in a new environment. Usually, such lists change beyond recognition as a person becomes more aware of the sensual opportunities and also learns about new things that cause him or her to shudder.

If one or more of the items on the list are things that the dominant really wants to do, you need to talk a bit more. Because the scene has yet to produce a Webster and his dictionary, what you mean by a word may be quite different than what your potential partner means. For example, "whipping" to you may mean a sensually writhing submissive and a deer-hide flogger, but to her it may mean white-hot agony and blood splattered walls. However, sometimes it's a case of you both meaning the same thing, but one with zeal and the other with antipathy. If the other aspects of the potential relationship are not enough for you to put this particular activity on the back burner, then it may be a sign this partner is not the right fit.

There is no shame in this. The scene is a complex maze of pathways and few people walk exactly the same one. Sometimes, it's just a case of both sets of needs and desires being so far apart that a link is not possible. One major reason for careful communication is that it's better to find this out sooner rather than later.

As for the "no limits" submissive, this really isn't all that bad a situation as long as you keep a sense of reality and a sense of humor. What he or she is really saying is "I want my dominant to have the same set of limits as I have." Now, this is a laudable goal, but for that to happen, he or she is really going to have to think about what the shared limits really are.

Usually, I find a gleeful expression and an exclamation of, "Great, I've been looking for someone who would let me cut off some fingers," goes a long way to injecting reality into the conversation.

While you are gathering information about limits and desires, keep in mind that this is an opportunity for the submissive to look over an unfamiliar dominant. For the submissive's peace of mind, you should be careful to maintain a dignified and professional demeanor.

You can either ask about the submissive's fantasies or try a more sensual, voluptuous approach I enjoy. The basic idea of it is taken from Sigmund Freud. He recognized that people can be extremely sensitive to body language and other subliminal clues when they are talking about highly personal matters. Freud suggested that the doctor sit out of sight of the patient during the session to minimize the cues that might make it difficult for the patient to be open. My method modifies Freud's technique for my own, erotic purposes.

If your submissive is comfortable with being nude, have him or her undress and sit in a comfortable chair. If not, have him or her change into loose, comfortable garments before sitting down. Comfort is important because you don't want any distractions. Stand behind the submissive or put your chair behind theirs. The important thing is to be outside of the line of sight. Reach around the chair and gently run your hands over her breasts and neck or his chest and balls. Do not play hard enough to give more than a slight turn on. The imagination, not your hands, should be the primary stimulant.

An alternative is to have him or her put on a blindfold and lie on a bed. You can, if you wish, use light bondage techniques from the other chapters. Since there should not be any struggling, there is little need to worry about binding or nerve damage. The ropes, scarves or whatever should be tied loosely and used primarily for psychological effect. The idea is to stimulate fantasy, not do a full-fledged scene.

If possible, put on some soft, relaxing music. Everything should be designed to promote relaxation and flights of fancy without giving any clues as to what "appropriate" responses should be.

In a low, gentle voice say something like, "Just relax, my darling. Close your eyes. Feel sexy. Be aware of being turned on. Let your imagination run wild. Don't try to guide it or keep from thinking about anything no matter how erotic. Nothing you say now is real. It is all fantasy. Just let me ride through your subconscious with you. There are no rules, no taboos. Tell me what you are thinking and dreaming about."

For the first ten minutes to a half hour, you will usually get conventional sex fantasies. As these begin to wane, there may be a bit of resistance. After all, you are getting into a very, very personal space. Don't be insistent, but just continue as you have been. "You are so exciting, my dear. Tell me more. Let's continue to explore. You are turning me on so much. Share your fire with me."

Never, under any circumstances, show the slightest sign of shock or disapproval. Even a gasp or an "oh my!" can destroy the entire atmosphere. Listen and learn.

Whatever technique you use, you need to explore the submissive's fantasies. While you are not bound to follow any script, this information will allow you to create scenes that can excite and please both of you.

Making a Scene Sing

Defining a scene is about as easy as defining a love affair. Some people like scenes that are very casual, while others prefer formality and a specific set of signals to determine the beginning and the end of a scene which is played in a specific time and place. The majority do both as the spirit strikes them.

However, for the purposes of this section, I'm going to explore the possibilities of formal, pre-arranged, relatively lengthy scenes. It is the most complex kind of scene, so you can feel free to pick and choose from my suggestions when planning your activities. Feel free to add your own twists and kinks.

Whether a scene is to be with an unfamiliar submissive or an old and treasured one, it begins for the dominant long before the submissive arrives. I generally run a scene much like a jazz dance. I know where I am and where I want to go, but the spirit of the moment, my sense of the rightness and the influence of my partner all come together in a complex set of dynamics that changes minute by minute, even second by second.

On a higher plane, there is a strong link between the spontaneity, intensity and passion inherent in the creation of any work of art and in a scene. William Wordsworth defined poetry as "the spontaneous overflow of powerful feelings." He might well have been referring to the joyful exaltation of the whip and the rope. However, even a poet must prepare the pen, the artist the brush.

Preparation

Is the equipment you plan to use available and in good working order? The actual maintenance can be left to a submissive or submissives. It is sheer bliss to some to be allowed to maintain the instruments of their joy. One mistress sets her submissives to chewing the tails of her whips to make them soft and supple.

Still, you are the one responsible for the scene and the safety of everyone in it. You must check the equipment personally.

If the scene will last more than an hour or so, make sure an adequate supply of food and drink will be available. Both you and the submissive are going to be expending incredible amounts of energy. Hunger and thirst can be a distraction from the exciting sensations you want to feel. At a very minimum, I bring a supply of some small, easy-to-swallow treats. Hershey's Kisses or M&Ms are favorites. They are perfect for popping in a submissive's mouth when he or she least expects it. The candy provides a quick burst of energy, and the sweet sensuality of it is a marvelous contrast to the dynamic sensuality of what you are doing.

There is some small risk in doing this because of the level of excitement the submissive is feeling, but I'm sure you know the Heimlich maneuver. If not, read the poster that seems to violate the decor of every restaurant in the country.

Some people plan their scenes with the precision of a German railroad timetable. I've seem some that went: 8:00 to 8:20 spanking, five minute rest, 8:25 to 8:50 whipping with a deerskin cat, and so on. If this is your turn on, so be it. I, personally, feel this kind of scheduling takes much of the spontaneity out of the scene.

This kind of teutonic scheduling is often desired by male submissives and seems to have two sources. With an inexperienced submissive, it is most often an attempt to work out a fantasy which he has had for a number of years. This should be strongly discouraged. Such a person generally has very unrealistic expectations regarding his personal limits and endurance. Also, it is an attempt to seize control of the scene from you. Either situation is a potential disaster.

Less often, such a program may be presented by an experienced submissive who is attempting to recreate a previous experience. While this is much less likely to fail, you should still discourage such attempts. First, you are not the other dominant or top. It is unlikely you could recreate what actually happened, and worse it is almost impossible for you to be able to recreate what his mind now "remembers" of the experience after he has had time to embellish it in fantasy.

Second, and more importantly, repeating such scenes has no potential for a submissive to grow. Part of the dominant's role is to expand their submissive's awareness and experience. We cannot do that by simply repeating the past.

However, even without a detailed design, you should have some plans for transitions between various activities. For example, in an initial scene with a new submissive, I set aside some time between each, increasingly intense activity to talk about her reactions to what was done and how she is feeling.

With more familiar submissives I still try to alternate intense stimulation with gentler activities. For example, although I may use touches of the vibrator during a whipping, I will set aside a few minutes of vibrator play after the whipping is complete and before, perhaps, I go on to waxing. Having such hiatuses gives both of you a rest. The contrast, also, gives a greater intensity to each, individual feeling.

Limits and surprises

If you're unfamiliar with the submissive, spend a bit of time thinking about his or her limits. Of course, no dominant or top would ever ignore a safeword, but one of the more enjoyable games is finding ways to slide around a submissive's limits. Frontal assault is rarely effective in these cases, but a flank attack can occasionally succeed.

For example, my submissive Gale was very sensitive about her anus. If I so much as looked at it too long, she was ready to call an end to the session, but she had never put it down as a hard, never, never, never limit. However, I suspected that the sensitivity that she felt could be converted to sensuality with the right input. Before her arrival, I put a bouncing-ball vibrator in a condom, thoroughly lubricated the condom and put the whole thing in a plastic bag so it wouldn't dry out. The condom served two purposes. This type of vibrator is attached to its battery pack by a single fragile wire. If that wire broke, there would be no way to extract the vibrator without the condom. Second, it kept the vibrator clean.

She loved over-the-knee spanking. I began lightly along the top of her buttocks and slowly worked my way back, toward the "sweet spot" where the buttocks join the legs, while increasing the severity of the stimulation. As the spanking was reaching a peak, I gave the area near her anus a few extra hard smacks with my left hand and continued to spank the lower slopes with my right. Then, with my left hand, I extracted the vibrator from the bag and slid it carefully into her anus.

She was so distracted by the spanking that she felt nothing. Then, I paused to let her get her breath back. After a few seconds, I turned the vibrator speed control to half speed. I could feel her puzzlement and then she shouted, "What did you do to my ass?" Before I could respond, the orgasms hit her. Later, when she could talk again, she admitted that she had always been afraid of letting anyone touch her anus precisely because it was so sensitive.

Music and scent

For many people, music is an important part of the scene. It stimulates the primitive areas of the brain while bypassing the consciousness. Of course, the music must fit with the scene you have planned. For example, during an Inquisition role-play, I play Gregorian chants. The religious overtones and the monotone nature of the music fits right in.

Most often, I simply fit the music to my mood. Because I often want to mix both fast and slow passages, I may use Pachelbel's *Canon*, the theme from *Chariots of Fire*, *The Firebird* by Igor Stravinsky, *Close Encounters Suite* by John Williams or *Rhapsody in Blue* by George Gershwin.

For music that builds toward a peak, there is nothing better than "Music of the Night" from Weber's *Phantom of the Opera*. However, it is a bit short. For a slower, longer build-up, I use albums by Mike Oldfield like his older *Hergest Ridge* and recently released *Tubular Bells II*. I also like Ravel's *Bolero*. Other pieces of this type are Simpson's *Ninth Symphony* or the symphonies of Arvo Part.

Isao Tomita, who works with the Moog synthesizer, has an album, *The Planet*, that supplies a variety of music ranges. His "Mars" piece, in particular, is full of thunder, others are joyous, while others are soft and delicate.

If the lyrics are important and the bottom is calling , one cannot do much better than Madonna's "Hanky Panky (Spank Me)."

The important thing is that the music works for you and your partner.

Don't neglect odor. Incense, like music, creates a mood by bypassing the conscious. Depending on the scene, I use light florals or a heavy musk. The trick is that the odors should tickle the nose, not anesthetize it. You want to accent, not overpower.

You can use incense to provide the odor or a bit of perfume. One effect that I find quite powerful is to take some of the natural lubrication from my submissive's pussy and just touch it to her upper lip.

Beginning the scene

While the kind of detailed discussion I outlined in the previous chapter may need to take place only once before every scene, at least in the early stages of a BDSM relationship, a few minutes of review is a valuable safeguard. During this review, you should go over the safeword or words. If there is going to be role playing, you should inform the submissive about his or her role and the role you will be playing. This does not have to be in detail. It is enough to say something like, "You are a young noblewoman brought before the Inquisition, and I will be your confessor."

Some people use a symbol to begin the scene. For example, I often have a submissive lock her neck chain in place and give me the key. She is mine until I unlock the chain and give her back the key. A dear friend on the west coast uses a blindfold. Others simply begin. Generally, it is just a matter of taste. However, in role-play, there should be a distinct beginning and end to the scene to minimize role confusion.

Clothing is another matter of personal choice, as is its removal. I usually demand that the submissive strip herself as a reminder of her status in the scene. Music can transform this simple act into a seductive dance. Segments of the scene can be marked by a progressive disrobing, or the submissive can be disrobe entirely at the outset.

Depending on your desires, you may or may not undress. If you do, do so in such a way as to add to the scene. Men should never, take their pants off before their shirt. A glance at the covers of romance novels clearly show the female fascination with males naked to the waist. However the reverse, with a shirt tail flapping about bare legs, is a spectacle that no amount of inborn dignity can survive. Female dominants may wish to put their submissives into precisely this undignified situation, but male dominants should carefully avoid it.

The scene itself

The combinations and permutations of activities in a scene are almost infinite, and I'm not about to lay down a "right" schedule of activities. However, for maximum effect, both psychological and physical stimulation should begin relatively gently and then steadily increase. For example, most submissives are not ready for caning at the beginning of a session, but they may welcome that kind of intense stimulation toward the end. Do not forget that the physical activities – bondage, whipping, spanking – are merely the keys that unlock the journey of the mind.

Just which act is more intense than another is a suitable subject for discussion with specific submissives. For example, some see waxing as extremely intense while others find it a gentle stimulation. The perception of the submissive should be the final guide. However, a progression of increasing intensity for most people might be, spanking, whipping, waxing, caning, pricking, cutting. This is only a general guide to intensity and, most assuredly, does not mean that every activity must be present in every scene or even in the repertoire. Some very respected and experienced dominants limit their activities to spanking and whipping. The most valuable characteristic of a good dominant is common sense.

Psychological stimulation like humiliation should also proceed along a continuum. As your submissive becomes more involved emotionally, demands that might trigger a revolt just after the scene's onset will be welcomed with enthusiasm.

With experience, your subconscious will learn to read the subliminal cues that a submissive sends out. Without really knowing why you are doing it, you will feel that it is time to increase or decrease the stimulation, begin another phase or ease up and rest a bit. Much like two dancers working each other's bodies, the two of you will become caught up in a communication with a bandwidth so much wider than that provided by voice or sight alone.

A scene is not simply an extremely erotic activity. In a very real sense, it is a work of performance art.

Ending the scene

The scene can end in a number of ways. You can complete the scenario or end it for another reason. The submissive uses his or her safeword, or it can be ended because of outside guides.

The ideal way for the scene to end, of course, is for it to run to its natural conclusion. However, you should terminate it if you are getting tired or sense that the submissive has passed his or her endurance limits. If you are tired, you aren't going to enjoy yourself as much, but more importantly, you will become sloppy and careless.

A perfect way to end a scene is shown in the video *Geisha Slave*. In it, Sarana says to her slave Mariko, "When I remove your collar and call you 'Lover' the scene will be over." She follows her words with action and then the two make passionate love. Many BDSM films are filled with harmful misinformation. This one is a pleasant exception.

As part of your preparation, you should have provided a place for both of you to rest after the scene. In my scenes, a bit of gentle cuddling is mandatory, both to reassure the submissive and to give me a chance to get my mind out of the scene. One, or both, of you may want to sleep after the scene. Remember, a scene should be intense, but it can also be shattering to a submissive, particularly one who is new to the world of BDSM. If he or she seems to be shaken or have doubts, be supportive. Submissives often need to be reassured about their inherent worth.

Talking it over afterwards

There is some disagreement about when a debriefing should take place, but most people in the scene seem to feel that having one is a good idea. An obvious time is right after the scene ends, while cuddling. Memories are freshest at this time. However, many people in BDSM feel that waiting up to a day is a good idea because it gives both of you time to develop a psychic distance from the scene itself.

With experienced couples, it can be as little as, "Was it OK, dear?" or, "How did it go?" With couples just getting to know each other, the questioning should be deeper and more detailed. You cannot read a near stranger with complete accuracy. However, as you combine what you have observed during scenes with what you learn during the post-scene talks, you can begin to approach the ideal one-soul two-body amalgam. Each person brings a different set of needs and a different set of sensitivities to the scene. A very concrete example would be that Libby loves the paddle more than any other toy while Line prefers much more severe toys and finds a paddle's impact too diffuse for maximum pleasure. Of course, you don't want to beat the experience to death with analysis; it was a BDSM scene, not a presidential speech.

The essence of a good dominant is strength and control, and during these post-scene talks, you must turn those characteristics inward. This is not a time for flowery compliments. These are serious questions. To treat them as perfunctory time-wasters is to miss a chance to expand and grow for both of you. You must press and probe to find ways to improve both your skills and empathic abilities.

The submissive will always be reluctant to say anything that could be taken as criticism. However, by eliciting negative comments and by welcoming them in an open and adult manner, you can do much to build both the submissive's self worth and his or her opinion of you. Besides, wouldn't you rather hear it from the submissive and have a chance to discuss any problems, than hear how bad the scene went from Judy, who heard it from Karl, who was told by Lisa, who had talked to your submissive?

A look at a few specialized types of scenes

Guided fantasy

A guided fantasy is a wonderful way of exploring scenes too dangerous or too complex for realization in the real world. It works by establishing a fantasy in the submissive's mind and then guiding it to an explosive conclusion. However, this technique is not for everyone. It takes quick wits, careful preparation and a flexible imagination.

We've all experienced guided fantasies as children when we read stories of wonderful worlds and great adventures. We would sit back and let our imaginations fill in the spaces between the words. Now that we are adult dominants, it's time to start telling our kind of tales.

It's as simple as telling a fantasy to the submissive. The description alone is a powerful, sensual device that can bring hours of gratification. However, a guided fantasy goes a step further and makes the submissive an active participant in his or her own erotic tale.

To make the guided fantasy work, you must cut off or control as much sensory input as possible. A blindfold is indispensable. I prefer the fur-lined ones because they completely block out all light. I've also used headphones with a low hum to cut off all background noises when I am not talking, although this isn't necessary if the scene is in a relatively quiet room.

Most of the time, during the fantasy, the submissive should be bound in a comfortable position. Any discomfort that is not part of the fantasy can be distracting. You may want to use snap fastenings so that he or she can be moved about if the plot requires it.

Begin your story in a low, sensual voice. Set the scene and then ask your submissive to describe people and things in it. Keep track of these descriptions and weave them into the story. For example, if he or she describes a dark-haired man with a leather vest, refer to the character in those terms and work in references to his stroking of his dark hair or adjusting his leather vest.

By doing this, you are reinforcing the submissive's fantasy by making your story match what is going on in his or her imagination. The two build on each other in the sensory vacuum you've created.

Sound effects can be very valuable. The crack of a whip or the sound of a knife sliding out of a scabbard reinforce the illusion until it becomes almost indistinguishable from reality.

Don't forget the submissive's sense of touch. If you have a vest, you can remind her of her description of one of the characters by saying "As the dark haired man takes off his clothing, he drops his vest on you" and follow your words with the action. To feel the whip at the same time as imagining a whipping is unimaginably intense. One mistress regularly puts her submissives through a degrading male-on-male rape fantasy during which she employs three dildoes simultaneously.

Smell, being one of the most subtle senses, has an intense impact directly on the most primitive portions of the brain. It is a good idea to keep a few small vials of scent and other liquids about. For example, in a cycle-gang rape fantasy, I use the odors of oil, gasoline and rubber to emphasize aspects of the fantasy.

In another fantasy, my submissive surprised me by mentioning that she visualized the floor of the dungeon covered with rose petals. I was nonplussed for a moment because I lacked a rose scent. Then, I remembered a package of assorted incense I had purchased that day. In less than a minute, the room was redolent with the scent of roses.

Because of the relatively relaxed pace and the comfortable position the submissive is in, guided fantasies can go on for a long time. I did one that lasted for more than six hours and there is nothing that prevents one from going on for days.

The six-hour fantasy is a good example of the heights of fantasy that can be reached. The submissive, Marty, had a deep interest in the darker side of the supernatural. She had confided to me that she fantasized that she was the reincarnation of a witch, who had been burned at the stake.

The fantasy began with her tied horizontally in a modified crucifix position with her legs spread. I explained that she was going to be inducted into a witches' coven. In the background, the stereo was playing a long tape of religious chants. We developed the scene with me outlining the entrance of the witches and her filling in details, which I used in my descriptions.

The induction was frankly sexual and during it she had to satisfy each witch orally. To simulate the witches' vaginal areas, I used my own hand flavored with Marty's own secretions. The touch of her tongue on my hand was erotic in the extreme because I could almost see what she was imagining. All the time, candles above her breasts and cupped hands contributed a bit of stimulation as they melted.

Then, the witches summoned Satan to take his newest bride. A pistol shot and a bit of burning sulfur provided the background. For Satan's voice, I used a deep rough tone and spoke with my lips close to her ear. When Satan entered her, Marty let out an incredible scream. Ancient books always spoke of the devil's cock being cold. This one certainly was because I had left the dildo in the refrigerator overnight.

After a bit more erotic play, I changed the pace. I told her that soldiers had broken in, and the entire coven was arrested. I stood her up and tied her hands and arms to her body with a number of coils of rough rope. Another part of the room where I had broken open a bale of hay because the rough cell into which she was thrown.

Naturally, the jailers had to take full advantage of her helpless position. She was repeatedly "raped," a part of the fantasy that both of us enjoyed immensely.

After allowing her to recover, still bound, from the "rapes," I continued the story with her being taken before the inquisition where she was tortured to induce a confession. I had not told her details of the scenario beforehand but I had told her that her safeword for this scene was "I am a witch."

I used the traditional tortures for a witch were flogging, scalding water and being searched for the mark of the devil. The flogging was simple, and I simulated the scalding water by putting her hands repeatedly in very cold water and then shifting them to a container of very hot, but not scalding, water. The contrast made the hot water seem hotter.

The theory behind the witch's mark is that each witch has a place where she has been kissed by the devil. The place is numb. The investigators keep putting needles into the unfortunate's body until they find a point where pricking her does not make scream. I imagine that most suspects confessed while the search was still going on. The investigators may not have used sterile needles or sterilized the area before beginning. However, when fantasy collides with safety concerns, fantasy must give way.

Eventually, Marty "confessed."

I told her that she was going to be burned at the stake and guided her roughly across the floor. Lacking a proper stake, I tied her hands to a hook above her head and turned on a quartz heater directly in front of her. After a few minutes, when her skin was getting a bit red from the heat, I came up behind her, holding a taper of smoldering sulfur and whispered in the devil's deep rough tone, "I've come again for you, my bride," and drove home in her pussy the re-chilled dildo.

The resultant orgasms left her incoherent for more than a half hour.

Anything is possible in guided fantasy. You can travel the length and breadth of the universe and do things that, in real life, would leave the submissive a broken twisted shell. Since much of the action is only in the imagination, the only limits are those of your imagination.

Suggested Reading
Fantasy Made Flesh: The Essential Guide to Erotic Roleplay, Deborah Addington, Greenery Press

Interrogation scenes

One of the classic ways that vanilla film makers slip a BDSM touch into their products is in an interrogation scene where usually the innocent hero or heroine is helpless in the clutches of the evil doers. Therefore, it is not surprising that a common psychodrama in the scene is an interrogation.

There are several common themes in an interrogation scene. We have already covered one, a witch being forced to confess, in the guided fantasy section. Another is a military interrogation. The theme here is that the submissive is an innocent, a brave solder or rebel maid, and you, the Nazi, Viet Cong, English (you may have an IRA submissive) officer, are doing the questioning. In this kind of a scene, there is often a threat of extreme force, even death, made explicitly.

An interesting facet of this stage setting is the use of symbols that would normally be offensive, in particular, Nazi regalia. Because of this, there is considerable debate within the scene about the appropriateness of this kind of play. My personal feeling is that there is an ironic justice using these symbols in the service of a sexual fetish. Imagine the ire of a Himmler or a Hitler upon discovering that a "bunch of happy perverts" were playing with their revered emblems. Rather than honoring them, we are reducing them to a kind of kinky toy.

Of course, for some, these symbols are just too powerful to consider using. Because of this, no responsible dominant would ever spring such a scene on an unsuspecting submissive without probing his or her sensitivities in this area beforehand. Also, if you chose to talk about and do such scenes, be prepared for criticism from some members of the community.

The police interrogation is another standard form of the interrogation scene. Here, the submissive may adopt the role of the bad guy or innocent victim of circumstances. You can be a good cop or a corrupt cop. Force and threats of force are more moderate here than in the military scenario although the actual activities may be very similar.

Like the fantasy rapes covered in the next section, the interrogation requires the dominant to take on a role that may be quite different from his or her personality. For this reason, I recommend a clear starting and stopping point for such scenes. One of my favorite couples goes a step further. Near the end of the scene, he blindfolds her, explaining that he is going out to get some nefarious device. Then, shifting roles, he reappears as her rescuer, lifting her and carrying her out of the dungeon to safety.

You don't have to do anything this complex – although it can be fun. A simple prearranged phrase, such as, "You are free," or an action, like removing the Nazi officer's cap, can signal the transition from scene to reality.

In this kind of scene, the polarity between dominant and submissive is more marked than in most BDSM play. You are the bad guy or gal. All cooperative endeavor is carefully concealed under a camouflage of brutality or coldness. The mood of this kind of scene is clearly adversarial despite the underlying mutual consent.

Scene setting is particularly important during this kind of psychodrama. You want the submissive to be caught up in the excitement of it all and this means providing enough visual, auditory and even olfactory clues so that he or she can achieve what authors call suspension of disbelief.

I like to make the transition between not-scene and scene with the submissive blindfolded. The blindfold is put in place outside of where the interrogation is going to take place and then removed after she has been bound.

Usually, I begin with chair bondage. Not only is this position familiar through hundreds of late night movies, but it also puts the submissive's head at a lower level than mine, an important aspect of psychological dominance.

While, for most scenes, you want your dungeon/black room/ scene room a bit warmer than ordinary room temperature, an interrogation scene calls for a bit of a chill in the air. We want the submissive to shiver a bit. While I rarely use chains for bondage, during an interrogation scene, the cold metal just seems so appropriate. Often, I prepare it ahead of time by leaving it in the refrigerator for a few hours to give it the proper dungeon chill.

It is a special treat for your submissive if you can find somewhere other than your regular scene room to perform the interrogation. For example, all along the East Coast, there are abandoned World War II fortifications. Several times, I took a favorite submissive out to Dutch Island in Narragansett Bay where I had decorated an isolated pillbox. It made a perfect place for a Nazi interrogation scene. These trips were abruptly suspended when an inquisitive soul discovered my hideaway and precipitated a search for what local police believed to be an underground group of American fascists.

However, even in your own house or apartment, you can create the appropriate atmosphere. A bright light shining in the submissive's eyes creates both the appropriate harsh ambience and distracts from any incongruous items in the background that cannot be removed or altered. I would recommend that you light the rest of the dungeon with red lights. Psychologists say that red lighting intensifies hostility and tension. This may not be appropriate for all scenes, but for an interrogation scene it is perfect.

The old saying is "Clothes make the man (or in this case, perhaps, the woman)." Just a few bits of costume can make the scene come alive. A Nazi armband, a black leather trenchcoat, a Chinese communist cap, all add to the verisimilitude of the experience. Posters, wall hangings, even a field telephone on the table can add to the reality.

I have a collection of Nazi marching songs (they were rotten people but they had great marching songs) to play in the background of my scenes, but almost any appropriately military music will do.

In this kind of scene, more than almost any other, you need to keep your submissive off balance and confused, just like a real prisoner. One trick I use is to tie her to an office chair and occasionally spin it around. This effect can be made even more powerful if some of the lights are strobe lights. Even when a person is standing still these lights can be exceptionally disorienting; when a person is spinning out of control, the effect is mindblowing. Of course, when using strobe lights one has to be careful of their effect both on the dominant and on the submissive. A blinding headache could come under the heading of unintended harm, but strobes can also induce seizures in those prone to them. It is also dangerous to use many impact toys under strobe light. You'll find that your accuracy suffers greatly because your eyes are telling you the whip's location when it's actually moved a significant distance from that point.

Another approach is to tip a conventional chair backwards with the submissive firmly tied in it. The suspense and anxiety, I have been told, are overwhelming.

Prisoners are, of course, threatened. I have a dramatic knife (no edges or point) I got from a theater-supply store. It is useless for cutting clothing or anything else, but it looks terrifying. If you are using a real gun as an intimidation tool check again to see there are no bullets in it, obvious, but you want to be completely secure. Do not count on a safety. Some individuals, with less faith in security precautions than I, suggest that only guns with blocked barrels or no firing pin or mock guns be used in such a scene. My feeling is that you should be aware of the risks and make whatever appropriate actions you need to make sure that the risk is zero.

Some people have suggested using blanks in such a scene. I'm strongly against this. Not only do blanks pose a significant risk of injury or even death simply from the wad and the blast, but having any kind of cartridge around runs the risk of getting confused and allowing live ammo to be used.

The section on "Guided Fantasy" covers some of the stimulants available in a witch interrogation scene. I've also used branding irons for intimidation. No branding actually took place, but the woman involved had a great deal of difficulty tearing her eyes off the branding iron slowly heating over a charcoal heater. (Safety note: do not use a charcoal heater in a room. Carbon monoxide poisoning is insidious.)

Electrical devices are often used in interrogation scenes. A typical telephone being used can have more uses than just as a visual prop. Be sure to read the Electricity section of the "Fun and Games" chapter for appropriate hints.

As I noted before, you can end the scene by having the "victim" rescued or by simply giving a prearranged signal. However, in any case, I strongly recommend that you spend a bit of time cuddling and reestablishing the intimacy that this sort of scene pushes into the background.

Fantasy rape

Anyone who has read *Forbidden Flowers* or any of the other books about women's fantasies knows that rape as a fantasy ranks high on many women's lists.

Hold up, ladies. Don't go skipping by this section because you have a male submissive. Being raped by his dominant is one of the fondest dreams of many a male sub. Don't let the female pronouns throw you. If your submissive knew you were leafing through this section, he'd be so hard he could fuck a rock.

Unfortunately, because of the way many men were brought up, actually doing the first rape fantasy can be incredibly difficult. Consensual whipping seems positively easy compared to the playacting a dominant must do in a consensual rape. As in the interrogation scene, you are acting out a role that is much different from your true self image. This can be disconcerting and, if you discover that you are enjoying it (very likely), deeply troubling.

A large portion of this discomfort, I believe, is fear of ourselves. Any man who has come to terms with his dominant tendencies has learned what monsters roam around in the basement of the mind. We have found ways to take them out and parade them for our submissives and even make them do tricks. But, we want them in control, and rape is the biggest and hairiest of monsters. However, we are descended from men who raped. In the history of humanity, consensual sex is a relatively new invention. There is always a bit of nervousness that, once we let this shambling horror out of its cage, we will never get it back in again.

Take heart from knowing that the very existence of this fear indicates that recaging the monster will not be as difficult as you expect. The fear grows from a basic rule of civilized behavior that is part of the bedrock within you. The people I fear are those who are willing and anxious to try this the moment it is suggested. They are the ones who should spend a bit more time on the maintenance of their psychic locks.

Besides, this is a fantasy. The best analogy I can give is to ask if you've ever had a fantasy about flying. Of course, you have. With some people, it is Superman-like flight; with others it is more like a bird hanging on the wind. Well, why haven't you walked to the edge of building and stepped off?

Because it is a fantasy! You had no difficulty telling the difference between a fantasy of flight and a reality of a broken and twisted body on the street. Give your submissive the same credit. She recognizes the difference and can enjoy the fantasy while having no desire to participate in the same events in the reality.

Once both of you are comfortable with this kind of playacting, you can do it on an impromptu basis. In a way, this is easier than the interrogation scene, which I strongly recommend should have a specific beginning and end.

For example, I know one man who "kidnaps" and "rapes" his wife about once a month on her way home from work. She never knows when this will happen, but she looks forward eagerly to each incident.

However, for the first time, a bit of discussion and planning is in order. Sit down, in or out of scene, whatever makes both of you more comfortable, and talk about rape fantasies, how they work and what she thinks would be exciting. As with all scenes, you are not limited by her desires, but they provide a good jumping off place and excellent guidance for what orientation the scene should take.

Explore a bit of history. Has she been raped or molested? Ask, don't assume you know. This is not something that comes up in casual conversation or even in the intense dialogue that precedes an initial scene. The fact that she is interested in playacting a rape does not mean that she has never experienced one in real life. As I noted in a previous chapter, some women look forward to the chance to desensitize a raw psychic scar by reenacting it in a situation of support and love.

Stress that she should not hesitate to use her safeword if things proceed further physically or emotionally than she is able to go. Carefully warn her that she should stop the scene if she experiences even moderate emotional distress. While physical discomfort builds slowly and relatively evenly, emotional distress tends to appear in a rush. Waiting until it becomes overwhelming can be dangerous to her emotional well-being.

One rather exciting variation on the rape theme is to have the submissive go through her closet and choose some clothing that is too worn or doesn't really fit any more. Insist that she wear nothing that is not dispensable. After all, a rape can be a relatively messy business.

Have her put it on and then tie her hands behind her back and slowly cut and rip everything off.

The position I prefer to place the submissive in is with her hands up by her neck. It is described in detail in the Bondage section of the "Fun and Games" chapter. It opens the body almost completely to the knife and does not have to be changed if you want to put her on her back later.

I use the word "knife" in an metaphorical sense. Using a knife next to a woman who may be struggling goes strongly against common sense. What I will often do is show my submissive the knife, and then, walking behind her, discard it and use my EMT scissors for the actual cutting. Make no mistake, you will need to cut. Modern fabrics are tough, and even if you can tear them, grunting and swearing when you get to the seams won't create the image of unstoppable male power you are after.

Amusingly, the hardest part of this scenario is often convincing her to wear old underwear. Women either want to keep them until they fall apart, or they are ashamed of letting you see them with anything but perfection on. In either case, you will get the request, "Can't we just take off the underwear?" Don't give in. One of the hottest parts is the final unveiling. The panties have to be cut off. You can cut them off with only two strokes: waistband and crotch. Or you can slowly and sensually cut holes in them until they resemble indecent Swiss cheese.

One alternative is for you to buy her a set of inexpensive underwear specifically for the scene. I gave one to a young lady with a card that said, "A woman's underwear is intended to make a man want to tear them off. That is just what I am going to do with these." Indecent haste is a good way to describe her reaction to this message.

If she has a bra with a front closure, you can put the knife between her breasts and then snap the bra closure open with your fingers. That allows the illusion that it has been cut without damaging the bra.

Naturally, neither tying nor cutting is necessary. You are probably bigger and stronger than she is. Just make sure she does not get too caught up in the playacting. There is more than one male soprano who underestimated the power of a fighting woman.

If you are planning on a struggle, make sure that you will be doing it in a safe area. Struggles can be very uncontrolled and doing them in places having furniture with sharp corners, extension cords on the floor or movable throw-rugs is asking for an accident. Take care, also, to handle her carefully. Caught up in the spirit of the scuffle, she may forget the availability of her safeword. Bruises are all right, but a broken arm or a wrenched joint will spoil the fun for both of you, to say the least.

Of course as in the interrogation scene, you can threaten her with a gun or knife. Naturally, you should take the same precautions using a weapon in this kind of scene as you would in the interrogation scene.

Language in a rape scene can also be difficult for some dominants who have a deep block against using crude language. However, again, remember you are playing the part of a crude, rough character. It is he, not you, who is telling her to, "spread your legs, bitch, and let me see your pussy." The shift from your normal tone and language can be a terrific turn on for some submissives.

Gentlemen, at ease. I'm going to direct the rest this section to the ladies who have been so patient.

The rape of a male submissive can be done in two ways, forced genital or oral intercourse and anal rape with a dildo. The first is merely seizing control of the situation. It usually consists of pushing the man on his back and using him for your pleasure. You can also combine this with various discipline techniques which may strike your fancy. I know one female dominant who likes to ride a tongue while waxing the owner's cock. I, personally, feel that it must distract from his precision, but the lady does not complain.

A dominant lady of my acquaintance, Lady Pam, has a lovely lavender dildo harness which is designed to accept two didoes, one extending from her pubis, the other entering her cunt. So while she performs the psychologically pleasing act of fucking another, she is also treated to a real fucking for herself.

Dildos can also be held in the hand, but then they seem, somehow, less complete. The best positions for penetration of submissive by a dildo are the same as those described in the section on enemas. While the male submissive should generally be forced to suck the object of his defilement before to being penetrated, you should use large quantities of lubricant for the actual penetration. Saliva is really not effective enough.

For an added bit of excitement, a bit of forced crossdressing fits well with the general theme of the entertainment. Crossdressing is covered in more detail in the Humiliation section of the "Fun and Games" chapter.

The mindfuck

Earlier in this book, I wrote with much disdain about "mindfuckers," who draw out potential partners before dropping them. This is a whole different kettle of mackerel. The mindfuck scene is a scene tailored by the dominant with the intent of making it look a lot more dangerous or edgy than it really is. Naturally, this kind of scene shouldn't be used indiscriminately. While many submissives get off on fear and the feeling that things are out of control, many others will be turned off and may even use a safeword, leading to embarrassment on the party of both parties. Be absolutely sure that fear is one of your partner's major turnons before venturing into these murky waters.

While lying about what is going on is done by some mindfuck players, I won't directly lie since I feel that any lie under any circumstance may damage the delicate trust between players. I will, however, (at this point, imagine me with a feral grin) allow a submissive to draw the wrong conclusion from what is going on. It may be a Clintonesque point, but it is one with which I'm comfortable.

There isn't really any way to teach someone how to do a mindfuck scene. Each is a separate work of art. One disadvantage of being a scene figure is that people tend to talk about my mindfuck scenes so I'm continually having to invent new ones. To be completely honest, I also write about a lot of them, which hoists me from my own petard, or rather flapping tongue.

The best way to learn to mindfuck is to study the scenes that others have done and modify them to fit your own play. The overriding rule is that safety is paramount. The scene may seem to be risky or even insane, but you must have tried to predict any reasonable risks and have taken steps to minimize them.

The first mindfuck scene I did was back in 1969 or thereabout. In those days my relationships would start out vanilla, and I'd inject as much kink as I could find acceptance for. Most of the time it was far short of what I wanted, but with Marty, I found myself challenged almost immediately. In one evening, we went from spanking to whips to needles. In other words, on the outer edges of my skills at that time. As the evening progressed, it became clear that Marty wasn't getting off on the pain or the bondage, but I was most turned on when she was most terrified. This was a big switch for me since, at that time, most of my energy in the early stages of relationships was to keep the young lady from running off in terror.

Frankly, I was in over my head.

Inspiration strikes best through a vacuum of ideas, and I was in the midst of just such a vacuum. Then, it came to me. I got a kitchen knife and began to run it over her body that I'd spreadeagled on the bed, telling her that I really was a murderer (back in those days, serial killers hadn't been invented by the FBI yet, but the concept was there), and she was going to be my victim. This got a rise out of her, but the damned trust reasserted itself, and she regained her composure and lost some of her turn on. As she writhed under the caress of the knife, I talked about the other women I'd killed, but she snapped right out of it, and said rather coldly, "This is bullshit. I don't believe you."

The inspiration hadn't been limited to the story. When these things come, they are like Athena leaping full grown from Apollo's brow. I grinned as evilly as I could manage and told her that I'd kept nipples from each woman. That got her attention. Before those damned critical faculties could reassert themselves, I got up, walked to the kitchen refrigerator and returned with a bottle I slammed down on the bedside table. She looked and gasped. I mounted her and began to fuck her while holding the tip of the knife against her nipple. I said, "When I come, I'm adding your nipple to the collection." The heat built up, and as I pretended to cum, I pressed the knife hard against her skin. She screamed and had a tremendous orgasm.

Have you ever noticed how much dried mushrooms look like nipples?

This is the essence of what I call the "wow mindfuck." Its basis is creating a situation where something seems to be one thing but is actually another.

Here are two more examples.

The first was a scene I did later in my relationship with Marty. One night I brought her down to some railroad tracks and told her we were going to do a Dick Dastard scene with her getting fucked while chained to railroad tracks. Several lengths of chain and locks held her helpless with her neck across one track and her knees over the other. I cut away parts of her black outfit so I had easy access to her breasts and pussy. We were fucking away when about half a mile away, a light came around a bend. The rumble was unmistakable. I fumbled with the keys, dropped them, picked them up, dropped them again and, finally, yelled, "My God" and ran as the train approached at about sixty miles per hour.

Her scream was lovely as the train shot past four feet to her side. I had chained her to a siding.

This scene was considerably more complex than the earlier one. Of course, it helped that the scene was carefully planned rather than being presented extemporaneously. First, I had chosen black outfits for us so the train crew wouldn't see anything. Not that they could have done much, but it was common courtesy. I had her consent. I had rechecked the locked manual switch at the head of the siding when I had taken a "piss break" during the scene. I had been pretty sure that it was OK since earlier I had replaced the padlock on the chain holding the switch open with one of my own, but as I wrote earlier, all risks should be minimized.

I can't take credit for the last example of a "wow mindfuck." It took place in a gay playspace/bar between two very experienced players, who were in an established relationship. The dominant pretended to be a bit tipsy and took an arranged "bet" with a co-conspirator that his submissive had "balls of steel." The submissive found himself naked in a cargo net hoisted about three feet in the air. This may have been fun, but then the dominant brought out a rack of beer bottles, placed them under the net and proceeded to break each with a hammer, leaving what amounted to a rug of glass knives under his disconcerted submissive. The dominant then reached through the mesh and put a blindfold on the submissive. The net shook and got a bit looser. The dominant was cutting one cord after another. The club's dungeon master came over and protested that the scene was too risky only to be told by the dominant that he knew what he was doing. One cord after another was cut, and the submissive was trying desperately to hang on with his fingers and toes. Finally, he fell… onto one of the pads the bar kept handy for "other activities." As soon as the blindfold had gone on, the rack of broken bottles had been removed, and the confrontation with the dungeon master had been play acted.

Another form of this is what I called the "Which Mindfuck." Here, rather than a situation not being what is seems, something essential to the scene has been switched. The mock branding I talk about in the branding section is a classic example of this. Of course, the switch doesn't have to be as complexly as play acted. I once terrified a submissive by playing with her for a bit with some cinnamon oil. Tiny drops brushed on her nipples and her pussy created a burning sensation she both loved and hated. After a bit of that, I rested the familiar bottle of red liquid on her mons, while I casually tickled her. The result was inevitable… she moved, and spilled the contents right on her pussy. The screams were deafening as she begged me, "Get it off! I'm burning up!." I waited a bit before explaining I had switched bottles and what she had just spilled her herself was water with a bit of red dye. The agony was all in her mind.

One day I was idly watching a large house fly bashing itself against the inside of my office window. Inspiration struck.

The next time one of my "terror victims" came over to she noticed a Mason jar with several irate yellow jackets inside. I casually picked it up, gave it a shake to send them wildly buzzing about the bottle and put it down again without comment. A while later, she found herself blindfolded, naked and tightly bound to a frame. It may have taken a moment to realize what the cold, hard circle pressing down on her breast was, but when the first of the flying bodies ricocheted off her skin, the light and absolute terror dawned. She was too tightly bound to move much, but within those confines she was a whirling dervish. When the little darlings got tired and began to walk about on her taut skin, she begged most engagingly. Only when I removed the blindfold did she realize that the jar pressed against her skin contained only a few houseflies.

Another "which mindfuck" that has pleased a number of audiences uses a pair of knives with very distinctive handles. One has an extremely sharp black blade. I use it to slowly cut away the clothing of my victim so she can both see and feel how sharp it is. Then, I slowly and sensually run the knife over her body. When she is flying, I switch the sharp one for one which has an identical handle, but I have carefully dulled the blade and dipped it in black Liquid Latex. Carefully, I draw the blade over her body and then let it slide gently into her pussy. The expression when she looks down and sees that handle protruding from her body is precious. Then, I lean forward and whisper, "Don't move or you'll cut yourself."

The final kind of mindfuck is the "what mindfuck." In this, the mindfuck is the toy itself. There are so many lovely toys that look positively agonizing. Some of them are, but you don't actually have to use the damn things; all you have to do is show them. For example, I have what I jokingly call "my five-inch butt plug." Doesn't sound all that bad, does it? Of course, I haven't told you that the five-inch part is across. This monster is five inches in diameter and almost a foot tall. Imagine the reaction of a submissive tied across a spanking bench, arse high and vulnerable. Then, you bring out this monster and begin to coat it with a nice layer of Crisco.

For those who haven't experienced them, violet wands fall in this category. The glow, the inch-long sparks, the crackling sound is quite enough to terrify someone who hasn't felt the touch of this delightful toy.

While it isn't a toy, but a technique, fireplay also fits in this category. The wonderful part of it is even during the scene watching her breasts burn with a blue flame, most submissives are completely mindfucked, even though they know they aren't feeling any pain. It just looks so damn dangerous.

Mindfucking doesn't work for everyone. Some submissives find that fear shuts off their erotic sense. But for those who need risk as part of their turn on, mindfucking is the responsible dominant's best approach to satisfying that need without subjecting the submissive to unreasonable risks.

Suggested Reading
Toybag Guide to Erotic Knifeplay, Miranda Austin & Sam Atwood, Greenery Press

Opening the Toybox

Toys add so much fun to the scene. Not only do they have a physical effect, their psychological impact is impossible to overestimate. Toys like whips, ropes and suspension cuffs are covered in their appropriate section of the "Fun and Games" chapter. Here, we are going to look at more free-style toys.

Blindfolds and hoods

The best kinds of blindfolds completely block out the submissive's vision without putting any pressure on the eyeballs. While the sleeping-aid-type blindfold is useful, it usually doesn't fit tightly enough to keep the submissive from peeking out next to the nose.

My favorite is a set with separate eye patches on a leather headband. Each eye patch is lined with rabbit fur. When these are on, nothing can be seen. Instructions on how to make these are in the chapter on leatherwork.

Because contact lenses can come detached under a blindfold, you should have the submissive remove the lenses before putting on the blindfold. Of course, with some submissives, removing the contact lenses is the equivalent of putting on a blindfold.

Another approach to blindfolding is hooding. This can be as simple as a bag over the submissive's head or as complex as a custom leather arrangement with removable eyepads, earpads and a gag. However, because a hood conceals more of the submissive's face than a blindfold and hides familiar facial clues indicating distress, you must carefully monitor his or her condition. Hoods can also trigger claustrophobia and restrict breathing.

A trick for covert public scenes is to get the eye pads sold in drug stores. Put them over the submissive's eyes with flesh colored bandages and cover the lot with a pair of large, dark sunglasses. The feeling of helplessness can be overwhelming for the submissive, but bystanders see only a kind person assisting a blind one.

Clips and clamps

Nipple clips are almost a cliché in bondage films and photography, but clips and clamps are popular tools. These can be used on almost any portion of the body, but breasts, labia, cocks and balls are natural and obvious targets. You should always remember that when these are taken off the process is more painful for the submissive than was the initial application.

You should test every clip on the skin between your thumb and forefinger. This does not tell you how it feels on a nipple, but it does give you a gauge for comparison. If one clip felt much stronger than another on your hand, it is reasonable to assume that it would also be more painful on a nipple or elsewhere. Although it would be unusual to do any kind of permanent damage with a clip, one should not be left on longer than fifteen minutes because it does cut off blood circulation to the skin underneath. The triangular paper clips available at stationery stores should be treated with considerable respect.

Complex-looking adjustable clips are available at leather stores. However, many dominants swear by the simple wooden clothespin. Not only are they cheap and easy to obtain, but you can vary their severity in several ways. The simplest is to buy several brands. Different companies have varying degrees of clamp in their pins. Test them on yourself, and color-code each pin with a drop of model airplane paint. I use red for the strongest down to blue for the weakest.

You can also weaken individual pins by putting elastic bands around the part where your finger grips the pin. This is particularly useful when the pins are going to be used on sensitive sections of the body.

Some people even disassemble the clothespins and readjust the spring tension. This is done by heating the spring with a blow torch, altering its alignment with a pair of pliers while it is still red hot, and then quenching it in a container of oil.

Before using clothespins on submissives, you should cut or sand off the tips so the pins end in a flat surface. This will allow them to get a firmer grip on the skin and prevent unintentional pain.

Initially, you should place a substantial fold of skin between the tips. The larger the amount of skin which is gripped, the weaker is the stimulation felt by the submissive. As you become familiar with both the strength of the pins and the tolerance of the submissive, you learn just how large the fold should be to produce a given amount of stimulation. Avoid putting the clip where pieces of bone or cartilage would be caught inside. These bruise more easily than soft tissue.

Alligator clips are not generally used in stimulation because their serrated teeth can easily break the skin. However, you can cover the teeth by taking a piece of shrink-wrap tubing, putting it over the jaw of the clip and then heating the tubing. It may take several layers of tubing before you have a thick enough covering on the teeth.

Mouse and rat traps are fun to play with. They look infinitely more painful than they are because the spring's clamping action is distributed along a relatively wide striking wire. However, before you use them, I recommend that you take off the release arm and the trigger. Not only are these unaesthetic, but the gripper for the cheese can tear the submissive's skin.

To use them to maximum effect, hold the trap about a foot in front of the submissive's shocked eyes and let the striking wire snap on to the wood then take it and insert the breast or cock and lower the striking wire on to the skin.

There are many different types of adjustable clips and clamps. The simplest one is the basic bodkin that was created to pull elastics through waistbands and consists of two narrow fingers with rubberized ends and a ring that can be slid back and forth to open or close the fingers. Because there is quite a bit of friction when sliding the ring while the fingers are held apart by a bit of flesh, I recommend holding the ends of the fingers in one hand, squeezing them until you've got the pressure you want and then, with the other hand, sliding the ring into place.

One of the most expensive and precise clamps I've encountered is The Rolls Royce Clamp. While I haven't mucked about myself in the engine compartment of a Rolls, I am told it's the battery clip from that venerable marque. It consists of a pair of hinged grippers between which base is a cone with a screw through it. The grippers are opened and closed by turning the cone either up between the bases (tightening the gripping end) or down, allowing the bases to come together and loosen the grippers. Because of the gradual movement very precise adjustments can be made.

Simpler adjustable clamps are padded alligator clamps with a screw through the upper jaw. Turning the screw either pushes the jaws apart or allows them to come together.

Tit or ball presses are larger items with two boards or bars that are attached by threaded connections at each end. The appropriate "organ" is inserted between the two elements and the threaded sections are turned to bring them together.

The degree of stimulation from a clip can be increased by several orders of magnitude by attaching weights to the clip. To hang things from clothespins, run a cord through the spring coil. Alligator clips come with a handy screw that is convenient for attaching cords or small chains. Some versions of adjustable clips in leather stores are designed to clamp harder when weights are suspended from them. Always add weight slowly.

Another approach is to pull on the string or, an even more erotic approach, put the string in your submissive's mouth and have him or her pull on it for you. This can also be done when you have two clips attached by a string or chain, a common technique when clamping nipples.

A variation of these dangling weights can be obtained by attaching the weights to heavy elastics or light springs. Any movement will set the weights bobbling, and it will take a while even when the submissive is standing stock still for the weights to stop bobbing.

Japanese or Clover Clamps were originally created to stretch silk without tearing it. They have a lever arrangement built in so as the pull at the base increases the jaws clamp tighter. This means, as you add weights, not only does the clamp pull down harder, the squeeze increases.

One particularly evil trick is "the zipper." To make one, you can tie several clips (clothespins are most often used in this) to a single line so they look like beads along a cord. You may attach them to the submissive at various points and, when the time is right, pull hard on the line so they pop off one at a time like shots from a machine gun. For an even more intense variation of "the zipper," drape the submissive with a light fishing net and attach the clothespins so they grip both the skin and the cord of the net. This allows them also to be pulled off with a single tug. Think of it as a two-dimensional zipper.

If a clamp causes a minor cut, you should treat it with antiseptic. However, torn skin requires a doctor's care to prevent permanent disfigurement.

Suggested Reading
Toybag Guide to Clips and Clamps, Jack Rinella, Greenery Press

Collars

A symbol of submission is the collar. It can be as simple as a dog collar or as complex as the kind of collar worn by O in *The Story of O,* which was made of many layers of thin leather with an attached ring. Rings provide convenient attachment points for leashes or wrist cuffs.

The most common error in buying a collar is to buy one that is too wide. Unless it is only for short-term wear, one inch is the best width. Anything wider will have a tendency to abrade the neck over a period of hours.

Neither collars nor other around-the-neck devices should be used to attach a standing submissive to anything solid. Think what might happen if he or she stumbled or fell. If a person is attached in this manner, use cotton thread. This will provide the feeling of capture, but in the event of an accident, it will break without causing further harm.

Another common error is to attach the collar too tightly. If you cannot slip two fingers under the collar, it is too tight.

In recent years, there has been a lot of talk about "official collars." People have held forth about "training collars," "consideration collars," "ownership collars" and god knows what else. If it resonates with your needs and fantasies go with it, but don't feel there is any way you must do it or any symbol or collar you must adopt. Your scene is yours.

Gags

I don't use gags much. They cut down on the complex verbal interaction between the submissive and the dominant, i.e. I like screaming and begging. They also can be risky.

However, in a semi-public environment, like an apartment with thin walls or motel rooms, gags can avoid premature termination of the scene through external influence, such as someone calling the cops. Some submissives also enjoy gags. The mild ache from the stretched jaw muscles is a reminder of their status. The ball gives them something to bite down on while you are stimulating them, and for those who enjoy humiliation, the uncontrollable drooling provides the dominant endless opportunities for comment.

Before you use a gag, establish a safe signal that will work when the gag is in place. Like a safeword, it should be something that would not take place as part of a scene. This eliminates random grunting, but using a rhythm is acceptable. Don't get too complex. It may be easy for your submissive to hum *The Stars and Stripes Forever* when the only thing you are doing is watching. It is entirely a different matter to do it when you are playing connect the dots on his or her skin with a needle.

Simple physical signals are effective too. Some submissives use opening and closing both hands to signal unacceptable discomfort when gagged. Others use slow and purposeful eye blinks.

Before playing with any submissive, you should ask about breathing problems, asthma and allergies. If you are going to use a gag, ask again and listen carefully. A blocked up nose can kill someone who has a gag in his or her mouth.

There are a multitude of commercially available gags and an even greater variety that you can improvise. At one point during a session in an expensive hotel, the phone rang. I just grabbed my companion's panties and put them in her mouth. She later told me that the mere casualness of this action made it extremely arousing.

Most important, the gag must be comfortable. If it isn't, that is a signal that it doesn't fit and can cause harm. With an inflatable gag, have the submissive inflate it. Dominants invariably overestimate how big it has to be. I have seen some face masks that cover both the face and the nose. I neither like them nor do I trust them. If either the nose or the mouth is blocked, the other should be completely free.

Ball gags that do not go completely into the mouth are particularly good if a person has a bit of trouble breathing. If the ball is attached with a single elastic, it can be easily pushed out of the mouth in an emergency by the submissive's tongue.

A submissive friend lists three benefits that go with gags. It is fun to bite down on a gag during intense stimulation. It gives the submissive a feeling of being controlled, and finally, it causes drooling which, in turn, gives the dominant an opportunity for a bit of verbal humiliation if both enjoy this type of activity.

Dildos

For whatever reason you are using a dildo, it is always a good idea to cover it with a condom before use. At the very least, it makes cleanup quick and easy and assures that you and/or your submissive will have a sterile surface in contact with all that sensitive flesh. If you will be doing a scene where the dildo will be moving back and forth between people (yourself and the submissive or between two submissives) or will be used in both the anus and vagina, one or more condoms are mandatory.

If I am planning a complex scene, I may put four or five condoms on a single dildo. As soon as I am ready to shift from one area to another, I just take off the top condom and the next is already on. A neat trick I borrowed from my motorcycle racing days when I would wear five or six face shields, one under the other. When one got muddy, I'd just pull it off. This also has the added advantage that, if one condom tears, the others are intact.

In my opinion, the best dildos are made of silicone rubber. They have a more lifelike texture, are exceptionally smooth and retain body heat or cold, see the section on guided fantasies in the making the scene sing chapter, best. However, they are expensive.

Latex dildos are less aesthetic but are also less expensive. Dildos made of harder material must be used with care, but they are often useful in the scene to make a psychological point. One mistress has a custom-machined, eight-inch, stainless-steel dildo with brass balls which is enough to drain the color from the cheeks (both sets) of the hardiest submissive.

Obviously, when using a dildo in the anus, copious lubrication and care are the order of the day. You must always keep a good grip on the dildo and allow no more than two-thirds of it to enter the anus if there is nothing at the base to prevent it from going all the way in. For safe anal play, butt plugs are more sensible, or you should use a dildo with a flange or set of balls at the base.

Some dildoes are made with a clitoral stimulator at the base. While some find this fun, my opinion is that it limits the range for movement of the dildo if you want to use the stimulator at the same time. A well-lubricated thumb is infinitely more versatile.

Squirting dildoes which simulate ejaculation should be cleaned very carefully. The artificial urethra provides an ideal environment for bacterial growth. However, squirting a bit of bleach-water mixture or alcohol through it should be enough to clean it out.

Male chastity belts

Male chastity belts are popular items in leather stores. Some are made of leather, some of metal, and I've seen a few that were made of clear plastic.

Evidently, these toys predate the current interest in BDSM. In doing research for this book, I encountered the McCormick Male Chastity Belt, patent number 587,994, patented in 1896 – yes, 1896. According to the application, the purpose was to protect a man from himself. However, it seems ideal for any lady seeking to make sure her submissive remains pure and sweet when he is not under her supervision.

The appliance had a plate, "having an aperture through which the proper member is passed." The plate was attached to the body by a belt and had a series of what the inventor termed "pricking points." (Could this be the source of the slang word for the member in question?) "When, from any cause, expansion in the organ begins, it will come in contact with the pricking points." This, in turn, was considered enough to turn the wearer's mind to purer thoughts.

Although the inventor wrote that he intended this device to be worn voluntarily, he did note that arrangements could be made to be permanently attached to certain "irresponsible wearers."

While I've never encountered Mr. McCormick's gadget in any store, a similar device can be made using leather through which the prongs of snaps have been forced. Normally, these prongs are bent over to hold the snaps in place. However, if they are left extended, they can provided a "pointed reminder" for the wearer. Another product is a non-skid run mat designed to protect carpets from rolling chairs. The bottom of these is covered with sharp plastic prongs. A small piece snipped off and placed in a jock strap provides most interesting sensations.

Sportsheets™

Sportsheets are an interesting little product that uses a Velcro loop sheet to provide points of attachment for a set of Velcro hook wrist and ankle cuffs. Because the sheet fits tightly over a conventional mattress, you can convert any bed into a versatile bondage surface. It takes a bit of practice to attach the cuffs so that a strong person cannot break the attachment to the sheets, but it can be done. An added bonus is that the sheets are comfortable enough to sleep on.

Of course, with enough strength, enthusiasm and incentive, one can get loose from Sportsheets. Libby and I were introduced to Sportsheets early in the '90s at a party given by Mistress Sia, a dear friend and a delightfully creative sadistic dominant. Both Sia and I were playing with Libby when we were amazed to see her rip apart the chain connecting one of the leg cuffs to a pad. Libby at that time was an enthusiastic swimmer and walker so she had really strong leg muscles, and what we were doing was just plain "mean," but when I mentioned the incident to Tom Stewart, the president of Sportsheets, he let me in on a business decision they'd made in designing the product.

"When we were developing the Sportsheet we experimented with a lot of different hardware that connected the cuff with the anchor pad. As a result of our customer feedback, we used a metal key ring and snap link for the connection. The reason for this choice of hardware was for a last ditch, fail safe means of getting free from the Sportsheet. The question many people asked us was, 'What if I can't grip the anchor pad and I panic?' or, 'What if the bed catches fire and I'm tied up, how do I get out?' If we had used stronger hardware, say, a welded D-ring versus a key-chain key ring, and a stronger snap link, our answer to these types of 'what if' questions would have been something like, 'Well, then I guess you're screwed.' The key ring was selected because it will fail under circumstances where a person pulls very hard and the key ring will open up and the person gets out. If we had made it escape proof that would have defeated the 'you can get out anytime' feature of the Sportsheet. For some heavier players we have suggested adding an additional key ring and/or another snap link to make the connection stronger."

Spreader bars

Spreader bars are simple wooden or metal bars with loops at the ends or at points along their length which attach to wrist and ankle cuffs. When properly in place, they prevent the submissive from bringing together the limbs to which they are attached. Some of the commercially produced models are adjustable, but many dominants simply make their own from lengths of one-inch dowel.

While there is rarely a problem using a spreader bar between wrist cuffs, care should be taken not to use one that is too long between either ankle or knee cuffs. If a submissive is forced to spread his or her legs too widely, the hips could be injured. This is particularly likely if weight is placed on the hip region while the legs are spread. As the appropriate angle varies among individuals, you should demand feedback from the submissive the first few times you use a leg spreader.

For an interesting effect, a second bar can be attached at right angles to a leg spreader. This bar can hold either a vibrator or a dildo, which the submissive can move in his or her anus or cunt by straightening or bending knees.

However, because submissives have been known to desire too much of a good thing when they become excited, I recommend attaching the two bars together with a rubber band rather than cord or tape. This way, if the submissive tries to agitate the device too violently or tries to drive it home too firmly, the elastic will stretch and moderate the action or break entirely, hopefully, before injury is done.

Vibrators

Just hearing the hum of a vibrator is enough to bring joy to most submissives' hearts. I like to use a vibrator for teasing and contrast during the scene, pushing the submissive over the pleasure-pain-pleasure edge and during cool down after the scene ends.

There are basically two ways to produce vibrations. The first type to appear was the coil-driven vibrator. These usually have a vibrating head. They usually have only two speeds, low (sixty beats per second) and high (thirty beats per second). (That isn't a misprint. The body interprets the slower speed as faster than the faster speed, and the manufacturers went with perception rather than reality.)

Motor-driven vibrators, on the other hand, use a rotating, off-center weight. This allows them a broad range of vibrating speeds. There are two types of these. The wand vibrators that look like an old-fashioned hand-held microphone, and Swedish vibrators which strap on the back of the hand and turn the entire hand into a living vibrator. Most wand vibrators are exceptionally large, but this spreads out the vibrations and makes it a more effective massage tool. I tend to like the heft of a large vibrator.

Swedish vibrators are sensual and versatile tools. Their drawbacks are that the softness of the hand mutes the impact of the vibration a bit, the constant vibration can make your hand go numb fairly quickly, and the straps that hold the vibrator on your hand can catch pubic and body hair.

Vibrators are also classified by their power source. In the early days, I shunned vibrators powered by replaceable batteries. They were generally shaped like dildos, but produced the worst of two possible worlds as they were ineffective dildos and underpowered as vibrators. Generally, if I wanted to use vibration inside a vagina or anus, I didn't use a plastic vibrator, but instead, inserted a dildo or butt plug and then held an AC-powered vibrator against it.

Because of these drawbacks, the only setting where I found the battery-powered plastic dildoes useful were in wet scenes in baths, showers and hot tubs. Because they were battery powered, there was no chance of a dangerous shock, and their size let me waterproof them by slipping them in a condom and knotting the end. However, improved design and more powerful batteries have changed my mind. Many battery-powered vibrators are wonderfully effective these days.

Many battery-powered vibrators have the speed-controller/battery-pack connected to the vibrating unit by a cord. These offer an opportunity for the dominant because these can be worn under the clothing, they allow you to take your submissive for a walk or to a restaurant while covertly stimulating him or her. The speed control/battery box can be draped over the waist band, and you can discreetly play with the controls throughout the public session. If you use an vibrator in the anus, you should put it in an unrolled condom first. This will allow you to withdraw it safely if the cord breaks.

Even better for this are the radio-controlled vibrators. Sadly, at the time I'm writing this, the RC vibrators I've used have a range measured in tens of feet, but I have high hopes for the future. Even with the limited range, these offer interesting opportunities for the control and simulation of your submissive.

Several years ago, Libby broke her arm in a fall. At that time, she had, Rio, a personal slave. It was her idea to insert an RC vibrator in Rio's pussy so Libby could summon Rio with just a touch of a button. Normally attentive, Rio became a paragon of vigilance while she awaited Libby's summons.

As cell phones have decreased in size, their kinky potential has expanded. No great sewing skill is required to create a small pocket near the crotch of a pair of panties where a cell phone can be secreted. I leave the potential applications to your imagination.

For those with a bit of skill with a soldering iron, it is possible to build a do-it-yourself version of an RC vibrator. Sartan of Treve, a kinky entrepreneur, has the plans of this on his website (http://www.saroftreve.com/workshop/vibe.shtml).

Thanks to micro-chips, vibrators are no longer limited to slow-fast. For example, The Pulsetron by Lady Calston has the conventional slow-medium-fast range, but it also has pulses of vibration interspersed with pauses and a buffet of patterns as the vibration becomes stronger and stronger and then softer and softer.

The Lady Calston people have carried this idea over into a wonderful device for those who are trying to make a long-distance BDSM relationship work. The Televibe is a pulsetron that connects to either a telephone or a computer. The unit is plugged in, and the recipient inserts the vibrating probe into the appropriate bodily aperture. Then, even thousands of miles away, the dominant can take control of his or her pleasure while listening and talking on the telephone or in a chat room screen.

AC-powered vibrators are more powerful and have a greater range than those powered by replaceable batteries. Their only major drawback is the need for an electrical outlet. However, when you are playing in an unfamiliar area, that can be a major inconvenience. For example, in many public dungeons, major play areas are in the center of the rooms. Using a vibrator, generally means running an extension cord through the shifting, milling crowd. This is hardly a satisfactory state of affairs.

Rechargeable vibrators are usually built along the same lines as a wand vibrator, and their batteries are generally good for 15 to forty minutes of stimulation. This may not seem like a lot, but you should remember that AC-powered vibrators overheat. Most manufacturers recommend sessions of no longer than thirty minutes without a cool-down period. Therefore, you may not get significantly longer sessions with AC- than with replaceable-battery-powered vibrators.

Like dildos, many vibrators can be covered with condoms for safety and ease of cleaning. You will be surprised how big you can stretch those suckers, and it is unnecessary to cover the body of the vibrator. For example, only the foot of a coil vibrator actually touches the skin, and this is relatively easy to cover. However, a few of the wand vibrators are just too big. Use a rubber glove to cover their heads.

Once, what I had expected to be a single-submissive scene became a two-submissive scene, and I didn't have any condoms or gloves. However, I had two riding crops. Rather than stop using what I find is a very effective tool, I mentally designated one crop for each submissive and, holding the shaft of the crop against the head of the vibrator, used the tip of the crop to touch the submissive. Since each crop only touched one submissive, there was no chance of cross infection. An added bonus was that the submissives found the intense, localized stimulation of the vibrating crop so arousing that I made the technique a standard part of my repertoire.

Finding toys in the vanilla world

One thing that consistently amuses me is the recurrent drives by single-minded do-gooders to, as one of them puts it, "close down the places where people buy devices of pain and agony." I won't quibble about the "pain and agony" part, but what is so amusing is that there is more kinky stuff in the average K-Mart than in any leather store.

This last section isn't about specific toys or how they are used. I want it to be more of a consciousness-raising exercise. Let's take a walk through our local discount store and see how many things we can do kinky things with. I'm not going to try for a complete list. I'm just trying to give you some inspiration for your future shopping trips.

You've already read about the wonderful things that can be done with clips and clothespins. The *Secret Dungeon* chapter has other cute ideas, but let's start our stroll and see what we can find.

Gardenware shop

Not even inside the door yet, and there is this lovely display of canes. I suppose they expect us to use them to train tomato vines. Any other ideas as to what to train?

Kitchenwares

We may have discovered the mother lode, with wooden and plastic spoons, mixers and spatulas. What wonderful spanking devices. Cheese boards come with the convenient handgrip. Wouldn't it make a nice splat on some rear end? Hanging on the wall, we have clips and clamps galore. How about an egg opener? It looks like a pair of scissors with a loop on one end. Notice how the loop is just big enough for a man's cock.

Toys

What interesting stuff. The makers call it Slime™, and it really looks sickening. Might it have potential for a humiliation scene? This Nerf™ paddle may not do any harm, but it certainly stings. What about jacks? Wouldn't it be interesting to see how someone would walk while she was holding them between her legs? My goodness, a treasure trove of little girls' play makeup. Wouldn't this be handy for a reluctant TV? It has an added bonus in that it comes off easily.

I think I'll take a pass on these toy handcuffs though. The plastic has hard edges and they could hurt someone who struggles.

Hardware

What a treasure trove with all the hooks, pulleys, rope and clamps. Anyone who can't imagine uses for vise-grips should be sent back to BDSM 101. The trick is to close the handle before putting it on and use the little screw to adjust the tension. In a given aisle there are five locks that open with the same key. That is a handy safety precaution.

Automotive

Ratcheting tie-downs are designed for pickup trucks, but they would be handy for firmly attaching a submissive to a frame. Key rings come with a nice feature. It has two rings attached by a mechanism that needs to be pushed together to separate them. Wouldn't it make a handy emergency release for light bondage?

Sporting goods

Sir Spencer was once going to a birthday party for some scene people. He knew the crowd would include a sprinkling of vanilla people, who knew nothing of the birthday girl's interests. His lovely and brilliant wife recommended that he buy a game that featured a pair of charming Lucite paddles. As she pointed out, the vanilla guests would take the gift at face value, and the scene people would realize that the real value of the gift was somewhat lower than the face and on the other side.

Weightlifter's kidney belts can be useful. The same kind of belt, to protect a submissive's kidneys during a whipping, cost five times as much in a leather shop. Sinkers are heavy, and I bet they would be a lot of fun hanging from nipple clamps.

Hobby supplies

This place is full of perfect materials for making cuffs and bondage toys, maybe even paddles and floggers.

Jewelry

Nylon replacement watch-straps with Velcro fasteners can be backed up with a felt pad (to keep them from cutting into the skin) from the hobby department to make a fine cuff. One warning: jewelry for pierced ears shouldn't be used in body piercings. It can cut and cause damage.

Pet supplies

The pet store is just full of leashes, collars and humiliating squeaky toys that you can run a cord through and make into a great gag. Giant corkscrews, that screw into the ground, might be intended to hold Fido's chain, but when used in pairs or fours, they are wonderful for spreadeagle outdoor bondage. Nylon leashes can be tied to bed legs and then clipped to cuffs.

Miscellaneous

A mysterious scissor-shaped wooden clamp is, in the vanilla world, a glove stretcher. We have other uses for it. A baby's pacifier makes a nice symbolic gag.

Tack shop

The places where the "horsy set" goes to shop is packed solid with riding crops and whips as well as all kinds of leather straps and such. Even better, they are less than half the price you'd pay in a leather shop. What could an imaginative person do with a bridle? Stirrups are useful for supported suspension. One gentleman at The Vault modified a standard saddle and delighted in giving ladies rides about the place.

Look around. If you keep a kinky thought in your head, the world becomes a kinky place. You may never look at a cucumber the same way again.

Fun and Games

Spanking

It is so classic. The stern schoolmistress, strict nun or angry father orders the miscreant to bend over, and the pleasure begins. Hey, Wait. Isn't that "punishment?"

Well, to each his or her own. To some people, being in one role or the other of this little scenario would be but one step away from heaven. Spanking is perhaps the most common BDSM activity. Drop by your vanilla video store's classics collection, and you can spend hours watching mainstream stars warming each other's celebrity fanny.

It also has served for the entry point to BDSM by more than one couple. Spanking seems like so much fun. It seems so wholesome, so American. Besides, could anything that John Wayne did be so awful? In a very practical sense, it is probably one of the safest of the BDSM activities. The buttocks, while abundantly supplied with nerve endings, are well padded, and the physics of the event guarantee that the hand partakes of much of what it gives.

Only when straps, paddles and strapples make their appearance is it necessary to consider a modicum of safety, and that is only to avoid the portion of the upper buttocks where the bone is close to the skin. There are nerve junctions in that area which do not take kindly to being pounded. However, the rest of that delightful protrusion is fair game. The area between the top of the leg and the point where the arse begins to turn in again should be a particular target; as one masochistic lady put it, "It is the sweet spot with a direct line to the pussy."

Comments from two submissive gentlemen indicate that the same effect is present in their anatomy with a slightly different destination.

Suggested Reading
The Compleat Spanker, Lady Green, Greenery Press

Bondage

Who can look at the bound and helpless submissive and not feel a stirring of excitement and pride? In a very substantial way, this is the scene made real. While not all submissives long for rope, leather and chain, all long for the spiritual essence of these things, confinement, restriction, being controlled and held.

A man in a French maid's costume kneeling quietly at his mistress's feet can be more tightly restrained than one in a cocoon of rope and leather. Freedom through constraint is the quintessential nature of BDSM.

Sadly, however, few things are done more poorly than bondage. Like Olympic-level gymnastics, to do it well is to make it look easy. It is far more than simply grabbing a length of old clothesline, wrapping it around your partner and tying a granny knot at the end.

Before we go any further, remember bondage, unlike diamonds, is not forever. You should always have the means to quickly and efficiently release your submissive. No one should ever do any bondage without a set of EMT scissors, also called paramedic scissors. They have extremely sharp, serrated blades that can cut rope or even heavy leather. Also the bottom blade has a spoon-shaped end so that they can be used next to a struggling person's skin without doing any damage. Of course, they won't cut heavy chain. If you are doing chain bondage, keep a bolt cutter handy.

What should not be used for bondage

Let's look at the actual tools for bondage. First, what should *not* be used? If a submissive is going to lie quietly, without any movement, almost any long, flexible material, including barbed wire, could be used. However, short of posing for a cover shot for *Hogtied Quarterly*, submissives do not lie there quietly. Many enjoy struggling for the confirmation of constraint it gives them. Others are stimulated to movement by the dominant's activities.

Therefore, it is best to assume a certain degree of struggle. This eliminates many of the favorites of the bondage artist or photographer. Handcuffs, for example, are notorious for causing abrasions and can even cause nerve damage and broken bones. While this quality may be considered a plus by policemen seeking a docile prisoner, it is definitely not a plus in the scene. This is particularly true when we recognize that "struggle" is not always intentional, not only do people trip and fall, but orgasms can bring on a more spectacular "struggle" than most whippings.

If you insist on using them for anything more than an attractive ornament on your belt, you should be aware of two schools of thought concerning handcuffs for bondage. The first recommends you buy good-quality handcuffs. These are available to the general public in many states through police supply stores. This school of thought mandates that you avoid the cheap handcuffs sold in novelty and leather shops. The differences are twofold. First, the quality of the professional handcuffs is much better, and there is less likelihood of burrs or rough edges which can tear the skin.

The second reason is even more important. Professional handcuffs have a lock that prevents them from continuing to tighten after they have been applied. This lock is either missing or ineffective in the cheaper models.

The other school holds that in spending a substantial sum of money for the handcuffs will tempt the buyers to use them more often than they would have otherwise. This group, with whom I'm finding myself in more and more agreement, holds that since handcuffs should be limited to psychological or light play scenes where there is no possibility of struggle, cheap handcuffs are preferred so there will be no temptation to use them for inappropriate scenes. Regardless of the quality of the handcuffs, they should never be used for suspension or, even for holding the hands above the head for a substantial period.

There are also some precautions which can reduce the risk of injury. Since nerve injury most often happens when the submissive tries to pull his or her hands out of the cuffs, either intentionally or unintentionally, causing pressure against the base of the thumb. This can be minimized by tying the elbows so the submissive cannot spread them. They need not be tied so they are touching. Indeed, this position can injure some people's shoulders. Just a few loops of rope should be enough to keep from getting too far apart and putting pressure on the cuffs.

I occasionally take someone for a walk in cuffs, with the handcuffs hidden under a long jacket. Since if she were to fall, she might injure herself, one of the links of the handcuffs is replaced with thread. The feeling of being "handcuffed" is perfect, but if needs to she can get her hands free. I needn't even tell her of the substitution since the brace-me movement is instinctive should she find herself falling.

Police have begun to use long plastic strips with self-locking tabs as disposable handcuffs or plasticuffs. Because they were developed by electronics companies for bundling cables, these are available through places like Radio Shack. While they should not be used when the submissive may struggle, they are nice props for psychological scenes. Once the tab has been inserted through the lock, the plasticuffs are sealed permanently and must be cut off.

Another bondage item that should not be used in connection with any potential struggle is the hose clamp. These are long strips of metal with a screw-locking mechanism designed to tighten over hoses until they are sealed to a nipple. They come in sizes big enough to hold a pair of legs. However, they have several important drawbacks. They are metal and can do damage if they are overtightened or if the submissive struggles. They take a while to take off because the tab must be slowly unscrewed. Because paramedic scissors may not be able to cut them, if you are going to use these, you should have a pair of bolt cutters handy in case something goes wrong.

Articles of clothing, like scarves and pantyhose, figure commonly in bondage fantasy. However, in the real scene, they should be used with care. Both can clump until they are very narrow and cut deeply into the skin. A silk scarf is soft, but if you pull it tightly between your hands, it forms sharply defined folds. Imagine those folds cutting into your submissive's wrists, and you can see what I am warning about.

Knots in scarves and panty hose are also notorious for jamming. Eventually, you are going to untie your submissive. It is definitely anti-erotic to break fingernails while struggling unsuccessfully with a balky knot. You are the dominant; you are supposed to be in control. Being bettered by an inanimate hunk of silk is not the image you are trying to project. Even more importantly, it interrupts the flow of the scene and destroys the mood for both of you.

Plastic, clothesline rope is a definite no-no. Not only can its wire core cut deeply into the submissive's flesh, but it has an uncanny ability to jam almost any knot put in it.

Leather laces are definitely another no-no for immobilization. First, they are so narrow it is almost certain to cut into the skin and stop circulation. Second, leather shrinks when it gets wet. Even if you're not into water sports and don't plan to dunk your submissive into a bathtub, he or she is going to sweat. Just a bit of sweat is enough to turn a tight, but safe, tie into a tourniquet. Worse, this same contraction will turn a relatively safe knot into a solid mass of dense leather.

Thin cord or line can be used for a decorative binding to produce interesting patterns on the submissive's body or for controlled compression of body parts, like the breasts or cock, but it should never be used for immobilization. For example, these should never be used for securing the wrists to each other or to a solid object. Keep thin cord for decoration or for secondary tying where a lot of strain will not be brought against the binding.

What can be used for bondage

What to use, then? The best bondage tools are well-made leather restraints. Although they are expensive, and may be daunting to the novice, they are actually the safest way to render a submissive helpless. Their width and the nature of the material make it harder, although not impossible, to do something wrong, like cutting off the blood supply.

Of course, leather binders do cut into the dominant's creative flexibility. Wrist cuffs go on wrists. They won't go around waists or upper legs. When using them, at least part of the choreography is already laid out.

Rope is cheaper and inherently more versatile. Sisal or manila rope is rough and stiff. Some submissives like the harsh touch of these materials, and some dominants enjoy manila's ability to hold knots without jamming. Both, however, have to be handled carefully because they can cause severe rope burns. Polyethylene rope, the yellow stuff that floats, is stiff and hard to handle, as is mountain-climbing rope which consists of a core of nylon lines inside a jacket of woven nylon.

Before the ghost of my father, a Merchant Marine Officer, descends to crack me alongside the head and yell, "You're talking about *line,* son!" I'll admit that what seafarers call "rope" is more suitable for fastening the QE2 to a dock than a submissive to a table. However, rope is what most people call it. Sorry, Dad.

Perhaps the best all-around material for bondage is plaited cotton rope. Cotton rope used to be used primarily to hold sash weights in windows and for clothes lines. With the passing of sash weights and the use of non-rotting nylon for clothes line, cotton rope largely disappeared. The modern version has a plastic stiffener inside which renders it inappropriate for use in bondage. However, some pure cotton rope is still available, and those who have been able to obtain it swear by the material and guard their supply with care. A number of these lucky individuals report buying theirs at a magicians' supply store.

If you are lucky enough to find some without the plastic stiffener, wash it first to get rid of the starch that manufacturers use to make it look pretty in the store. Follow the directions in scrubbing up in the appendixes for washing unless you want to spend the next few hours untangling a Gordian knot.

The best generally available material, in my opinion, is nylon rope. It is smooth and flexible and takes knots well without jamming. I prefer 5/16- and 3/8-inch rope for immobilization bindings, while 1/4-inch and the so-called parachute cord are best for decorative bindings. Ropes of a half-inch diameter or larger are relatively difficult to work with, but can be worked into the scene as psychological props.

Nylon rope usually comes in two surfaces, three strand twisted and plaited. Plaited rope slides more evenly over skin while the three strand can leave "interesting" patterns when it is removed and lends itself to splices. Three strand twisted should be cut by wrapping it with electrician's tape and cutting through the tape. This also provides a nice temporary whipping.

The ends of both kinds should be sealed with a flame so that they will not unravel. When you are melting the ends, keep away from the smoke, it is not healthy to breathe it. Work outdoors or in a well-ventilated room. The melted ends are also very hot. Use a stick or pencil end to tamp them down. Don't even consider using your finger. If you are cutting a lot of nylon rope, you might consider getting an attachment that goes on a soldering gun and turns it into an electrically heated knife.

For a really kinky look, dye the rope black or red. Cotton rope dyes easily with any commercial dye. However, nylon rope requires something more "enthusiastic." I use a dye manufactured in Germany called Deka L. A ten-gram package is enough to easily dye fifty feet or so of 5/16 inch nylon rope.

Another interesting bondage medium is mountain climbing webbing. Available in a number of colors, this nylon webbing is fairly thick and comes in widths from one to three inches. Because it is so broad, there is less chance of cutting off circulation, and it can be tied as easily as rope and does not jam. You can cut and seal it in the same way as nylon rope.

The most common mistakes beginners make with rope is, first, to buy too little of it and, second, to cut it into lengths that are too short. The shortest useful length is generally five to six feet. Anything shorter tempts the dominant to tie the submissive incompletely and too tightly.

You should have several lengths available. My kit usually contains five five-foot lengths, five ten-foot lengths and a twenty-footer. If I am planning a webbing (see further along in this chapter), I bring two fifty-foot lengths. Of course, specific plans may call for a different mix, but this combination is good for, say, a visit to Paddles or to a private party.

It is a good idea to code your ropes according to their lengths so you can quickly and easily select the proper one for the job. I use plastic tapes on each end of the rope. As a mnemonic aid, they are coded by the spectrum. Blue (blue has the shortest wavelength of the visible colors) is for the six-foot length, yellow is for tens, green is for twentys and red for the fiftys.

Colored tapes are also useful for establishing ownership at the ends of group scenes. All of my ropes have a black piece of tape at one end in addition to the color code.

Of course, rope isn't the only material to use for bondage. Fiberglass-reinforced packing tape is impossible to break. I like to run a few turns of gauze bandage over the area before putting the tape in place so that the adhesive does not bond to the submissive's skin. That isn't necessary, but if you are going to use the tape against the submissive's skin, experiment by putting a small piece on his or her skin in an earlier session and checking later for any redness or other signs of an allergic reaction. In later scenes, keep checking because a single exposure may not be enough to trigger a reaction. Also, pulling fine hairs out as the tape is being removed may not be what your submissive would call positive pain.

I've seen photographs of submissives bound in 12- or 14-gauge heavy-duty electrical extension cords. It looked attractive, and the thick plastic coating would provide more than adequate protection against cutting into the skin.

Velcro provides impressive opportunities for creative bondage. One couple I know has glued strips of hook and loop Velcro together to make a versatile tool. To tie it, all she does is give the strip a half turn and presses it against the opposite side. I've seen Velcro replacement wrist-watch bands that look like they would be quite effective as cuffs if they were attached to wide pads so they wouldn't cut into the skin.

Hook Velcro will also stick to nylon rope although the bonding is not as strong as against the proper loop material. Velcro does have the tremendous advantage in that the dominant can free the submissive quickly and easily from most bonds using this material. SportSheets, mentioned in the toybox chapter, use Velcro in an interesting fashion to turn any bed into a bondage device.

As you have read, I'm a fan of nylon rope. However, to be fair, there are a large number of bondage enthusiasts who prefer natural fiber rope. Because I'm not an expert in this area, I asked Tatu, a nationally recognized Japanese or Asian styled bondage expert to write the following section. You can read more of his work on his website (http://www.Ds-Arts.com) or write him at Tatu@Ds-Arts.com.

Natural Fiber Rope for Bondage By Tatu

Terminology

There is confusion in terminology in the retail marketplace concerning natural or vegetable fibers. The word "hemp" in the retail bondage marketplace erroneously refers to rope made from cannabis sativa as "hemp." However, the word "hemp" in the industrial marketplace refers to any natural fiber rope that is made from the bast fiber of a plant, which would include jute, sisal and manila.

Bast fiber is material from the skin, or bast, surrounding the stem of a plant. These fibers are selected because they have a much higher tensile strength than other portions of the plant. Tensile strength is the breaking point of any fiber or rope. They are used in the industrial marketplace to make rope, as well as paper, burlap and yarn.

So the term hemp can be applied to any natural fiber rope, and it is used in that way by those who make natural fiber ropes.

Sisal is a hard, vegetable fiber used in gardening, shipping, petroleum, mining, fishing, lumbering, architecture, and communications industries. There is also a large market for sisal in the pet industry in making scratching posts as well as in the arts & crafts market. It is what you buy at the U-Haul store for moving purposes, and it is not well suited for bondage.

Manila is a hard, vegetable fiber used a lot in the public utilities, as it will not burn easily when in contact with electricity.

Both sisal and manila are both very scratchy and can cause some nasty abrasions for bondage, which actually might be a plus for some. These ropes can also contain some very nasty chemicals that can cause other problems when in contact with roughed up skin. Be sure and read the packaging, before you use in contact with human skin. In general, sisal and manila are not the best choices for bondage and probably should be avoided.

Jute is a soft, natural fiber rope in the hemp family, and, contrary to popular belief in the west, it is the rope of choice by traditional rope artists known as "Kinbakushi" or "Nawashi" in Japan. It is however harder to find in the west on the retail market. If you can get it, it is a lovely rope to use. Jute is mainly used commercially for wrapping bales of cotton, sacks, and a course cloth. In North America we generally refer to it as burlap. Its strength is similar to hemp.

Hemp is a hard, fiber rope, which comes from the cannabis plant, specifically the cannabis sativa variety, which is the non-psychoactive variety in contrast to the cannabis indica variety, which has poor fiber quality and is used for recreational drug use. Cannabis indica has high levels of tetrahydrocannabinol (THC). Hemp (sativa) is what our bondage ropes are made from, so you won't get a chemically induced high from your bondage rope. You may however get a natural high caused by the energy of your scene.

It has historically been used mainly on sailing ships. Its fibers in an unfinished state are somewhat softer than sisal and manila.

Finishing or conditioning hemp rope

You can buy finished hemp from several retailers on the Internet. If you choose to buy unfinished hemp, which comes in a scratchy and rough state, you will need to know how to end up with very nice finished form with a wonderful feel for bondage. I highly recommend a seven-step process pioneered by Angelene Black from the now closed "Helios Rope," a process which is now used by Erotic Hemp of Chicago (www.erotichemp.com).

- Washing
- Drying
- Scorching the irritants off the outside of the rope
- Oiling the rope
- Hand rubbing the oil into the rope
- Pressure cooking the rope for softness
- Drying

This process is completed a total of 3 times.

After Helios Rope went out of business, I was able to obtain special permission to post at my website their process for finishing hemp. See *http://ds-arts.com/RopeArt/hempropefinishing_angelene.pdf*.

Why hemp?

The choice of bondage rope for many is often based simply on feel and cost so many will automatically gravitate to synthetic fiber ropes. Hemp and other natural fiber ropes, however, challenge the senses in other ways. Natural fibers have a feel to the skin which is desired by many. Some say they can feel the rope becoming one with their skin as opposed to the slippery feel of synthetics. The natural hemp color, which will vary from a light to dark brown, can look very natural and visually pleasing against the skin. Its look is appealing in an artistic sense to many, especially photographers. The earthy natural smell appeals to many rope bottoms and tops as well, as it challenges their senses in a very erotic way that synthetics do not. Many report that these natural fiber ropes gives a special energy to the rope scene.

Hemp ropes also are superior at holding knots and stretch minmally, which makes it more appealing for those "get out" scenes centering on escape.

Hemp rope care

Rope inspections should be done regularly. Get into the habit each time you bring out a rope of pulling it through your fingers to feel for abnormal broken or twisted fibers, excessive wear, cuts, nicks, signs of abrasions, reduction in diameter, or anything unnatural to the feel.

Hemp rope can be washed. You should wash it in cold water with an unscented natural laundry detergent. Do not use any kind of fabric softener. Be sure and use a hosiery bag or you will end up with a tangled mess. Stretch your ropes out under some weight to dry.

Natural fiber ropes will tend to dry out over time and will need to be re-oiled. Mink oil is my choice. Simply place light amounts in a heavy cloth and pull along the rope.

Allergies are another factor in all rope choices, but especially in natural fiber ropes. Some people will have sensitivity to hemp and can have experience a breakout on the skin or cause excessive itch and dryness in the eyes. Hemp can be dyed in various color choices. It is the choice of many in the west who do Japanese styled bondage.

Whipping the ends of your natural fiber rope

If you choose natural fiber rope, you normally will be able to buy it with the ends of the rope already whipped or perhaps it will come with a wall or crown knot in the ends.

To whip the ends:

1. Select a thin piece of a strong twine about ten inches long
2. Begin by making a loop in the twine and laying it lengthwise near the end of the rope
3. Hold the loop in place as you wind the twine around the rope ten-15 times starting about ½ inch from the end of the loop
4. Once you reach the loop end, pull the twine through the loop
5. Tighten by pulling both ends
6. Trim off the ends and do the same at the other end of the rope

Size and strength

Natural fiber ropes will come labeled in global measurements (millimeters) rather than western inches. So when you buy hemp you should know that 6mm is about to 1/4 inch and 8mm about 3/8 of an inch. These will be the ideal choices for bondage use.

One final consideration of natural fiber ropes is strength. Natural fiber ropes are not as strong as synthetic ropes. The recommended load is ten times the actual weight of your subject. So a 200-pound person should be held by a minimum 2,000 pounds of rope strength. Generally their breaking point for natural fiber rope is about 800 pounds so, if you use them for any sort of load bearing with a human, you need to use three or four strands to meet acceptable safety standards for safe support of your rope bottom.

Knots: knot so mysterious

There is nothing mysterious about knots, and a dominant need not become an apprentice to a pipe-smoking old tar to learn how to join two ropes together or how to fasten a submissive down securely. However, a thorough knowledge of a few knots should be part of your repertoire.

Square or reef knot – This is one of the most common knots. It works best with two ends of the same rope or with ropes of the same size and material. It is simply two overhand knots, one in each direction. Millions of ex-Boy Scouts tie it every day, muttering under their breaths, "Right over left; left over right."

square knot

Slipped reef or safety knot – This is a modification of the square knot in which one end has been doubled back like a half bow under the other rope. In an emergency, the dominant can give a good yank on the doubled back end and the knot will just come apart.

Two half hitches – Because this can tighten, you should never use this knot directly on a submissive's body. However, it is an effective knot to attach a rope to a ring or other inanimate object. Run the rope completely around the object and then back along the rope. Loop it around the rope with the end coming out under itself. Go down the rope a bit and then repeat this.

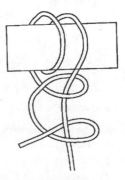

two half hitches

Bowline – The bowline lets you make a loop in a way that is less likely to slip than two half hitches. However, particularly with nylon rope, you have to be careful to tighten the knot after you tie it. The classic description of a bowline is, "The rabbit (the end of the rope) comes out of the hole (the loop you have made) goes around the tree (the part of the rope above the loop) and then goes back in the hole." It sounds cutesy, but it is an effective memory aid.

bowline

Fisherman's bend – This is a knot that allows you to use rope as a less effective substitute for bondage cuffs. First wrap three or four loops of rope loosely around the submissive's wrist or ankle leaving at least two feet of free end. Then wrap the end around the rope, loop it through the loose loops and then tie it off with a bowline. This makes the loops less likely to tighten independently and cut off circulation.

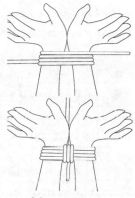

fisherman's bend

Sheet bend – This knot is used to connect two ropes of different size or to connect a rope to an eye. Make a loop in the larger rope. Then run the smaller rope through the loop, around both portions of the loop and then under itself.

sheet bend

That's it. There are many other useful knots, but these are the basics. If you want to learn about bottle knots, Spanish bowlines or rolling hitches, I direct you to any book on knots.

When tying and untying a submissive, you should always be aware of the rope ends. More than once, I have seen enthusiastic novices inadvertently smacking the subject of their attentions with the end of the rope while attempting to tie or untie a complex knot. When being pulled through a loop, a rope can move at substantial speed. As the end of the rope approaches the loop, it can easily be slingshotted to one side or the other. Three-eighth inch rope with a fused end can have a substantial impact under such conditions.

Trying to work too fast can also lead to rope burns. While such burns are less common with the recommended cotton and nylon ropes, they can happen. Work slowly and carefully. When you must drag a rope across the submissive's body, put your hand under the rope so you are aware of the potential for burning and are partially shielding the submissive from it. If your submissive is rope burned, clean the area with warm water and a mild soap. Then, disinfect the affected skin with alcohol or Betadine (povidone-iodine).

A precise, careful dominant is a lot more impressive and gives far more pleasure than one who works fast but seems to be on the edge of losing control or, worse, actually injures the submissive because of ill advised speed.

Bondage positions

Of course, the tying is only part of a gestalt, the whole of which goes together to excite both of you. While a wonderful feeling of helplessness can be created by simply tying a submissive's hands behind his or her back, there are positions that amplify that feeling by magnitudes.

They can be as simple as adding an additional tie at the elbows to bring the arms closer together. This is particularly exciting with a woman because the position forces the breasts into greater prominence. However, there are two dangers with this position. The elbows should never be forced to touch. While some people can bring their elbows together behind their body, doing that with others can result in permanent shoulder injury. Also, a person should never be placed so that the body is resting on the tied wrists for more than a very short time.

Another position that puts the submissive in a very erotic helpless position is with his or her hands up behind the neck. First, run a length of rope (climbing webbing is even better) behind the neck, bring it around in front of both shoulders and then back across the upper part of the back. With a female submissive, moderate tension on this rope will also make her bring her breasts into greater prominence. Then, with another length of rope, tie the hands together in front with about a foot of rope between them. Leave another foot of each end of the rope loose. Bring the hands up and over the neck and tie them to the rope across the back and neck.

This position leaves the submissive completely helpless, exposes the entire body line, back and front, and can be used either standing or lying down. This is the position I use when I am doing a knife-stripping as described in the fantasy rape section of the *Making a Scene Sing* chapter.

A very versatile position is to have the submissive sit on the floor, knees bent and leaning forward slightly. Tie the wrists to the ankles and the elbows to the knees. A spreader bar can be attached between the ankles, but in most cases, only the most flexible submissive will be able to bring the legs together in this position. Because the genitals are in forced exposure in this position, one of my submissives named it naked-making.

Another position that many submissives find naked-making is to be placed horizontal on the ground or on a bed with their legs vertical and spread widely. I used to have ring bolts in my ceiling beam for just such a situation. A spreader bar attached to a single line also works, but I've found the feeling of helplessness is greater when each ankle is attached to a separate point. You may want him or her to wear boots (and nothing else) during this both for erotic contrast and to protect the tendons. If the tendons are protected, the legs can be left up and spread for quite a long time.

A very secure position is "the fold." In this position, the submissive's hands are behind his or her back. The forearms should be horizontal and each wrist should be tied to the opposite elbow. This folds the arms behind the back. Next, have him or her sit cross legged in what the yoga people call the lotus position and tie each ankle to the opposite calf. Then you can take a ten-foot rope, fold it in half, loop the middle under the already-bound forearms and tie if off. This will leave you with two four-foot-long or so lengths of rope tied to the submissive's forearms by bringing one length over the shoulders on either side of the neck. Next you can lean the submissive forward until there is a bit of stretch, but no discomfort, then tie each length of rope to a calf or to the ropes connecting the wrists and the calves. He or she can be left in that position to "mediate upon sins" or tipped backward, an action that exposes the genitals for casual play. Because the arms are bound in the small of the back, there is less pressure on them than in the conventional wrist-wrist tie.

Hog-tying is a classic position, but it should be used with care. It can put a lot of strain on the back and knees. To start you can position the submissive on his or her stomach and tie the hands behind the back, wrists together, with enough rope so that you have a three-foot tail on either end after you have finished. Next, the dominant ties the elbows together with a number of coils of rope. You must take care not to put pressure on the shoulders doing this. As I wrote before, some people cannot touch elbows without severe injury. You want the submissive secure, not injured.

Then the dominant ties the ankles together, folding them up against the thighs. Run the rope tails from the wrists and tie them around the ankle rope. This positioning of the final knot makes it much harder for a SAM to reach it.

Hogtied submissives should not be placed on their backs nor should any portion of the tie go around the throat. This is a popular photographic subject, but is much, much too dangerous for real play.

There is no hard and fast rule for how long a person can be left in bondage. Some positions are extremely stressful and should be used only for a few minutes. Others are so comfortable that sleeping in them is possible. Submissives' tolerances also vary. It should go without saying that you should carefully watch anyone in bondage, and he or she should never be left alone.

Aside from asking them how they are, you should check that extremities do not become cold and that they can wiggle their fingers and toes on command. Blue skin is a good indication that circulation is not all that it could be, as is a complete loss of sensation.

This does not mean that a bit of circulation restriction can't be part of the bondage scene. Some submissives love the helpless feeling a numb limb gives them and glory in the pins-and-needles effect of

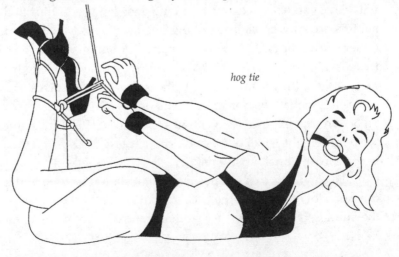

hog tie

returning circulation. However, this sort of scene must be monitored even more closely than conventional bondage.

For submissives who enjoy these feelings, I prefer to let gravity rather than ropes restrict the circulation. Anyone who has his or her hands held above the head can attest to how fast they go numb. After roughly a half an hour, most people begin to lose sensation in their elevated hands. Releasing them produces the sought-after tingling.

Decorative bondage

Many women enjoy having their breasts singled out for special bondage attention. Some report that the reduction of the circulation by the bondage increases the sensitivity, while others just like the way it looks. There are several ways to do this.

An approach that is often the choice of bondage photographers is to encase each breast in a coil of rope. A thin rope, like parachute cord (1/4"), is easier to use for this than the thicker rope we have been using for immobilizing ties.

You should have her lean forward, and begin with an anchoring loop over the shoulder and down under the arm. The rope then passes under the breast, up between the breasts and down the outside. Each successive coil should go outside the previous one. The rope should be tight enough to that it gets a good grip on the skin, but it shouldn't be so tight that it will cut off all blood circulation.

Repeat this for the other breast. Finally, tie the ends of each rope behind her neck for a very effective rope bra. As this will reduce blood circulation, it should not be left on for too long. Many women report that the breasts lose the extra sensitivity created by the rope bondage after about ten minutes.

Some breasts are simply too small and firm to offer the rope a good grip. As this can be a very hurtful point for some women, your failure to achieve a solid decorative bondage with rope can have more impact than you realize. You can avoid this problem by doing a full chest binding.

One way is to wrap several layers of plastic wrap around the chest. When the chest has been wrapped, take a pair of EMT or bandage scissors (do not use anything with a sharp point) and cut holes through which the breasts or just the nipples can protrude.

You can also use coils of rope around the upper chest to provide a similar experience, except that you can't simply cut holes in the coils.

While you are wrapping, leave room between strands for the nipples to protrude.

Naturally, since both of these techniques have the potential to interfere with chest expansion and, therefore, breathing, you must monitor the submissive very carefully while the bondage is in place and be ready to cut it off if she becomes disoriented or dizzy. Also, when a woman is menstruating or is about to begin her period, her breasts may be extra sensitive and what would be pleasant at another time becomes very painful.

Men, of course, have cocks. For the female dominant, these can provide hours of delightful fun. In the scene, this is often known as cock and ball torture or CBT, and bondage is an important part of this specialty.

Since this is a binding rather than an immobilization, parachute cord or other relatively narrow twine can be used. One scenario that parallels the previously described breast binding is to anchor the cord around the base of the genitals and then circle the scrotum with successive coils. The balls are forced further and further into the sack. The same approach can be used on the cock. However, its more uniform shape provides a surface for more artistic endeavors. At least one mistress performs macramé with a thick yarn over the cock and balls until they resemble a teapot in its cozy. Of course, eventually the cock will lose its erection and escape the bondage, providing an excuse for the mistress to punish her slave for this infraction.

Another approach is, after making the loop around the base of the genitals, you can bring the cord around and between the balls, separating them and pulling them upward. This process is repeated until the series of X's are in place.

If the submissive has a tight little sack that makes getting a good grip difficult (fear often makes the balls retract), let them rest in a pan of moderately hot water. The reproductive system's temperature control scheme will lower them right into your waiting hands.

Some leather shops and bondage magazine advertisements have clever little toys for binding, restricting and clamping cocks and balls. The best of these lace rather than snap so as to provide a snug fit, regardless of the size of the endowment.

As with any bondage that has the potential to interfere with circulation, you should undo or reposition cock and balls bondage every ten to 15 minutes.

Suggested Reading

Family Jewels: A Guide to Male Genital Play and Torment, Hardy Haberman, Greenery Press

Whole-body bondage and mummification

A subspecialization of bondage is whole-body bondage. The goal is to extend the experience of binding over much of the body surface.

Japanese bondage is one technique that combines the whole-body experience with an aesthetic exercise. Because it is, essentially, a binding, you can use almost any smooth, flexible material including twine, parachute cord or yarn. I tend to prefer my favorite 3/8 inch rope, and I will admit that sufficient rope to do a proper Japanese bondage can be rather bulky.

Because this is a lengthy tie, you must have a pair of sharp bandage or EMT scissors handy. In the event of an emergency, this type of bondage cannot be untied quickly and must be cut. Also, because it is usually done with the submissive standing up, you should make sure that at no time the little rascal locks his or her knees. Locking the knees makes it easier to stand still, but it also makes it likely that he or she will pass out on you.

One easy approach to Japanese bondage requires a minimum of fifty feet of rope or cord. Double up the rope. About a foot from the bend which marks the center, hold them together and tie a simple overhand knot (half a square knot). One end of the rope over should be placed over each of the submissive's shoulders. The knot should rest, not press, against the back of the submissive's neck.

Then you should tie another overhand knot just below the ribcage and above the navel. The third knot goes about eight inches below the clitoris or the cock. The fourth knot goes three to four inches below that.

Next the dominant passes both ends of the rope through the submissive's legs and brings them up along the submissive's back and tie another knot about half way up the back. Finally, the rope is passed through the loop made by the first knot (just behind his or her neck) All the rope is drawn all through this loop but don't pull it tight. It will get tight soon enough.

Passing each end of the rope around one side of the submissive's body, you can "trap" the arms at this time or pass the ends under the arms and secure the arms later. Both ends of the rope go through the loop between the first (behind the neck) and the second (below the ribcage) knot, and then each end goes back around the submissive on the same side that it came forward. Thus, the rope that came around the submissive's left side would go through the loop and then back around the left side toward the back. The whole point is that the rope is free to slide over itself.

Pulling the rope moderately tight, the third knot should move above until it is just forward of the arse. Above the knot in the middle of the back, the dominant passes both ends of the rope through the two ropes and brings the two ends back around the same side. This time, the rope goes through below the second knot and, then, go back around the submissive's body. This will bring the third knot on a woman right over her clitoris or on a man just under his cock. The other knot should be pressing on the arse.

By now, you see the pattern, an interlocking series of diamonds progressively tightening the entire pattern of ropes. At this point, you should have plenty of rope remaining, and from this basic design, you can extemporize, looping and tying, until the submissive is a lovely piece of macramé.

Because there is not enough constriction to impede blood flow, a submissive can remain in Japanese bondage for an extended period and can, with some designs, actually don street clothes and venture out in public while remaining in this exotic bondage. When the entire pattern is completed, any strain should be evenly distributed across the entire body so the submissive can be lifted off his or her feet by attaching a hoisting rope to the web.

If the submissive's hands are tied to the web, this should be treated as an immobilization tie, and appropriate precautions taken. For example, it is acceptable to web the entire arm to the body web with twine or narrow cord because the pressure will be distributed across several loops. However, if you are doing a wrist tie with a single strand, you should use a wider rope and knot the rope with a fisherman's bend or use cuffs to protect the wrist from damage.

Another whole-body bondage technique is mummification. Again, you should not try this unless you have a pair of sharp bandage or EMT scissors handy in the event the submissive needs to be released quickly. Because there can be a gradual build-up of heat during a mummification, you should regularly monitor the submissive's alertness. Any faintness or disorientation is a danger sign, and if it occurs you should give him or her a cool drink and consider moving on to another activity.

The simplest approach to mummification is to slightly dampen an ordinary sheet and roll the submissive in it. The moist sheet will adhere to itself and to the submissive. The submissive's head should always be outside the roll.

Another, similar technique is to use plastic wrap. The kind you get from the grocery store is acceptable, but many dominants like to buy industrial shrink wrap in 36- to forty-inch rolls. Simply wrap your submissive like a large leftover. You can then have the wrapped arms lowered and enclose them as you make turn after turn around the upper body. A hair dryer can speed up the shrinking action, but the submissive's own body temperature will activate the process in any case.

This material conducts heat, cold and impact very well. So you can whip or wax right over it with the well-wrapped submissive getting the full stimulation. However, you may enjoy using your EMT scissors to create openings through which all sorts of nice things can pop and be played with.

Many dominants keep a supply of regular or elastic bandages available for whole-body bondage. The usual procedure is to start with a few turns around the upper body and apply the wrappings in overlapping turns. As each bandage is put in place, it is secured with butterfly clips, usually supplied with elastic bandages, or with adhesive tape. A figure-eight pattern is used over the nipples to leave them exposed as you don't want to cut elastic bandages, and if regular bandages are cut, they tend to unravel at the most inopportune times.

There is some debate about whether it is better to wrap the arms at the same time as the body, either crossed over the chest in Egyptian style or along the sides, or bind them separately. Those who prefer the same-time wrapping argue that it is more aesthetic to have a single package. The arms-separate school holds that keeping them separate allows more options in the continuing bondage process.

The most important thing to remember with whole-body bondage is that it usually cannot be undone quickly. You must have some means by which you can cut the submissive free if something untoward happens.

Self-bondage

First, and foremost, self-bondage is dangerous. If you've read the sections on bondage carefully, you'll notice I stress how important it is for a dominant to be able to free a submissive on a moment's notice. In self bondage, this is generally difficult, if not impossible.

The best thing is to find a dominant and have him or her tie you up. I accept that it isn't all that easy, but please consider doing this.

The next best thing is to limit yourself to partial immobilization. Many submissives secure only their feet and one hand. The main incentive for this is that the free hand is used for masturbation, but it is also available for getting them out of bondage in the event of a fire, break in or other emergency. Others secure only their hands and, in an emergency, could escape from their homes or apartments.

However, I recognize that, for some, nothing but complete immobilization will do. In most cases, they use some locking device with a system to withhold the key for a certain interval. Many of these systems are extremely dangerous. One, which has appeared in more than one bondage film, is a burning candle that cuts a cord, dropping the key within reach. Unless you enjoy being helpless in a burning building, I do not recommend this approach.

Another, less dangerous approach uses keys suspended from a string which runs through a pulley and down to the minute hand on an old CrayLab timer. When the hand approaches the zero position, the cord slips off and the keys drop from where they have been hoisted.

A common technique is to freeze the keys into a block of ice. The keys are unavailable until the ice melts. The size of the block determines the length of the bondage, and submissives have used gallon milk containers as molds for their "bondage cubes.'

It is possible to arrange a weak equivalent of the safeword in self bondage. Put an extra set of keys into a valued vase on a high table. The logic is that in a real emergency you won't hesitate to knock over the table, smashing the vase and making the keys available. If you lack a Ming antique, put the spare keys in a regular jar in the middle of the living room rug and then fill it with vegetable oil. Again, knocking this over isn't something you will do casually, but it will provide you with a set of keys when you need them.

However, remember that you won't be able to get your extra keys with anything like the speed with which an attentive partner can free you. Self bondage is only a choice if a trustworthy partner is not available and you feel you must be in bondage. It is not something that should be tried casually.

Suggested Reading
Jay Wiseman's Erotic Bondage Handbook, Jay Wiseman, Greenery Press

The Seductive Art of Japanese Bondage, Midori, Greenery Press

Whipping

A whip is almost the icon of the scene. Hanging from a dominant's belt or flying through the air to land with a resounding crack on a submissive's back, the whip, to many people, *is* the scene.

Selecting a whip
Contrary to popular impressions, it is the multi-tailed cat rather than the bullwhip that is the whip of choice for most dominants. Although the bullwhip is spectacular and makes an impressive crack in the air when used properly, even a short one requires an inordinate amount of room and is very difficult to employ in such a way that does not reduce the expectant submissive (and occasionally, the novice dominant) to bloody shreds. After all, the loud, snapping sound characteristic of the bullwhip is caused when the tips travels faster than sound. It is very difficult to caress anyone with a hypersonic piece of material.

Bullwhips are used in the scene, but their role is often restricted to that of a noisemaker and intimidation device. Using one directly on a submissive is either the mark of a highly skilled whipper or a complete fool, and the distinction is rarely in doubt for long.

Generally, when a singletail is used in direct contact with skin, no attempt is made to crack it. Instead, the fall is drawn across the back often with a wide swinging horizontal arc or flicked against a muscled area with a flick rather than the explosive movement that creates the cracking sound.

On the other hand, the cat whip is a tremendously versatile tool. It can deliver as stimulating a whipping as most submissives can tolerate, or it can be as soft and gentle as a baby's touch.

The most common material cat whips are made of is steerhide. It is relatively inexpensive and easily available. However, it can be a bit rigid and inflexible, particularly if it has not been prepared well. I and many other dominants I know prefer deerskin or moosehide. These are softer and more flexible than steerhide and have a very pleasing feel.

Suede is an interesting material. It has a lovely texture and is very soft, but anyone using it should be aware that it has a tendency to abrade rather than cut. Only a few strokes with a suede whip will redden skin. Too much may draw blood despite a complete lack of visible cuts. Whips of this material are a good adjunct to a dominant's kit, but I don't think they should be used as a primary whip for extended whipping.

Another popular material that can be deceptively harsh is horse hair. Horse hair flicks are sold in both tack and leather shops. Used lightly, horse hair are an unmatched erotic tease while with forceful blows they can be quite stimulating. However, this is another material you should watch with care because the hair's surface is so rough that abrasion will take place during an intense whipping. This effect can be reduced somewhat by using soaking the hair in a solution made from a capful of hair conditioner to a gallon of water and allowing it to air dry. For those desiring a fashion statement, commercial hair dye can be used to make the flick match your own hair color or the color of your outfit.

Midnight, a Boston dominant, who is an artist of the horse hair flick, says, "I use it as a warm up. it tends to redden the bottom a little faster for me. It also leaves very, very small welts so that the stings seem to last much longer. I also use it to caress."

Cat whips with beads or knots at the end of the tail should be avoided early on. Later, you may want one or two for special effects or as scene-enders when you want a burst of high intensity stimulation. However, they have to be watched carefully, and you can't use them for too long. To me, that cuts into the fun.

Although they are not technically whips, canes belong more logically in this section than in the spanking section. The canes used from a scene aren't the sturdy supports elderly people use to get to the corner store but are, instead, light, whippy pieces of birch, rattan and bamboo so beloved by the English schoolmaster. In recent years, fiberglass and even graphite canes have made their appearance for those more interested in durability than tradition.

Canes call for considerable care in their use and should not be used unless you are very familiar with both the specific cane and the submissive's limits. More than one budding affair almost came a cropper over too enthusiastic application of a cane too early in a relationship. The feeling from a cane is much more intense than that from a paddle or, even, most whips, and a cane stroke, particularly where it passes over an existing welt, can draw blood.

Returning to the traditional whip. In my opinion, the best whip for a novice is a cat whip with five to ten broad, moderately heavy tails between 12 and 18 inches long. It is a fallacy that thinner tails are less injurious. Actually, they cut and abrade the skin very easily. One of the most feared whips in my collection is a simple ring with four leather shoelaces attached to it with hitches at their midpoints, making an eight-tailed whip.

On the other hand, a weighty, wide strip will make a satisfying splat when it hits and sting a bit but won't cut the skin. Lighter whips also have the disadvantage of making the dominant work harder.

Suggested Reading

Toybag Guide to Canes and Caning, Janet W. Hardy, Greenery Press
Flogging, Joseph Bean, Greenery Press

Using a whip

There are several standard techniques for using a whip. The standard stroke comes largely from the muscles in the back and arm. The motion is much like a child would use spreading on paint with a paintbrush. Because several of the body's major muscles are involved, it can be quite a powerful stroke. It is generally delivered diagonally, but it can be delivered at anything from zero to ninety degrees from the vertical.

The sling-shot stroke is more precise. The handle of the whip is held away from the body in one hand and the ends of the tails are held close to the face in the other. The handle is moved farther away until a degree of tension is built up in the tails. When the tension feels right, the tails are released and the handle is moved toward the submissive with a snap. Just before the tails strike, the handle is jerked back. With a little practice, a whipper can become quite accurate with this motion. However, the impact is deceptive. It is considerably harder than it seems, so careful monitoring is advisable.

While the sling shot stroke is best for accuracy, the spin provides the most continuous stimulation. The whip is held by the end of its handle or by its handle lanyard, if it has one, and is spun like a biblical sling. If this is used on the breasts, you should place your hand under the submissive's chin and lift the head up and back. This not only moves the vulnerable face out of primary danger but if the strokes are hitting too high you will feel them on your hand before any damage is done.

It should be obvious, but I think I should point out that the whipping area should be well lighted. To have the kind of control you need, you have to be able to see what you are doing. If you want darkness for dramatic effect, use a spotlight to illuminate the submissive and leave the rest of the room dark.

The secret to a satisfactory and safe whipping is to hit only fleshy muscled meat. You don't want to hit skin that is tightly pulled over a bone nor do you want to hit any place where internal organs are close to the surface. The primary safe zones are from below the shoulders to above the lower middle of the back (not including the spine), below the upper curve of the buttock to above the knees. These are places where a moderate whipping is unlikely to do any permanent damage. The biceps and the back muscle of the lower legs are also acceptable targets. Extreme danger zones are kidneys, spine, joints, hands and feet. When whipping the upper back, avoid letting the whip hit inside the arm pit. There is a nerve junction there that is quite vulnerable. Naturally, these danger area apply when something other than a whip, like a strap or cane, are being used. In these areas, you have to be very careful that the ends of a whip don't wrap around the body and hit there.

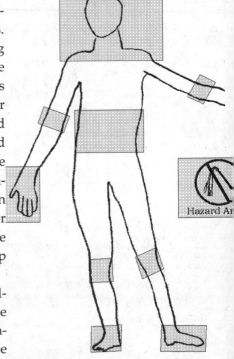

Hazard Ar

Other portions of the body, including cocks, balls, breasts and pussies, can be whipped. However, even more intense monitoring of the submissive's reactions must be maintained when you are stimulating these areas. For best results, a whip with six- to twelve-inch tails should be used for these areas. The shorter tail gives better control and allows you to concentrate the stimulation on the intended area rather than having it spread about.

As a personal idiosyncrasy, I tend to prefer to stimulate the genitals with a short strap or a riding crop. However, that is something that is completely personal. There is nothing wrong with a carefully and lovingly applied whip here.

Whipping should always begin slowly so that you can increase the intensity as the excitement builds. Even submissives who insist, "I'm not into whipping," can get quite turned on by a gentle introduction followed by a slow escalation. That is where the soft, heavy whips come into their own.

For example, one technique would be to first require the submissive to kiss the whip you are going to use. Then, tie his or her hands to an overhead hook, stand behind the submissive and just drape the whip over his or her shoulder and then slowly pull it back. The sensation of the soft leather mixed with the knowledge of what is coming next is almost impossible to stand. Next, very leisurely, lightly whip the back with a standard diagonal stroke and, slowly walking around the vertical body, whip the sides and front. Don't work at it, just flick the tails on to the skin. If you are hitting hard enough to tear a sheet of newsprint, you are hitting too hard. At this stage, don't worry about safe zones because you can't do any damage in any case. Obviously, the head and face are never legitimate targets, but the entire rest of the body is fair game.

Now, you can step up both the timing and the intensity of the strokes. One per second would be about right. At this point you are at a place where the spot you are whipping is becoming important. For the rest of the session, do not allow your whip to strike in any of the danger zones.

Watch the marks left by the whip. Do only the amount of damage you are comfortable with. As you judge it appropriate, increase both the tempo and the force of the strokes. Stop every once in a while to stroke the submissive with the whip, a hand or a piece of fur. Genital stimulation short of orgasm is appropriate here. However, the recess should not be longer than a minute or there is a danger you could lose the plateau that you have built.

Canes should only be used full force on the thickly muscled buttocks and thighs. However, they can be used lightly on the chest and upper back. In any case, you should remember that the cane is flexible, and for best results, you should use the flex instead of fighting it as some novices do.

All caning should be done with the end of the cane beyond the submissive. Allowing the tip to hit skin is both bad form and likely to cause cuts and deep bruises.

Genital shaving

While shaving of and by itself isn't limited to BDSM, it often figures into scenes, and shaven genitalia have a special attraction to some people. Dominants often view them as symbols of possession, and submissives remark on how the "special, intimate" nakedness reminds them of their status.

As with so many other activities, success is often more a matter of preparation and follow-through than the actual execution. Many people who have tried genital shaving have been put off by the appearance of ugly red spots and itching and burning after the initial shave. While even intense stimulation during the scene can be an erotic turn on, stimulation that appears hours later and continues for days is just annoying.

However, this unfortunate side effect of shaving can be minimized by a few simple procedures. Trim the hair as short as possible with scissors or a clipper. The less tangle the razor has to deal with the more smoothly it will cut. Steam the remaining hair with a towel soaked in hot water. This will both soften the hair and partially clean the skin.

Use shaving cream or shaving gel and a slightly used razor. This is very tender skin, and I have found that a razor which has been used once before is less likely to scrape than a brand new one. An electric razor, particularly one of those battery-driven units that is designed for use on a wet surface, can also be used.

Once the hair has been removed, wash the area with a mild soap and apply an antiseptic lotion. Although it has an unattractive color, betadine is an excellent choice for this. The red marks are often caused by minor infections in nicks in the skin. By killing the bacteria on the skin's surface, you are reducing the chances of such an infection. For this reason, the area should be cleaned regularly with a mild antiseptic. Four or five times a day during the first three days would not be excessive.

Regardless of the appearance of red marks, you should plan on shaving the submissive daily for at least four days or he or she should be instructed to shave each day during that period. Eventually, the red marks should disappear.

Naturally, the shaving can be made part of the ritual of a scene. Bind the submissive for maximum exposure and work slowly and carefully. An alternative approach is to have him or her kneel before you and do the shaving without assistance.

A straight razor makes an interesting prop, but requires a high degree of skill to use. Novice barbers train by scraping shaving cream off inflated balloons. Once you are capable of doing this without bursting the balloon, you should practice on your own body before exposing your submissive to your nascent skills. Also keep in mind that, regardless of your skills, if the submissive is incapable of remaining absolutely still, the razor can inflict serious injuries from the slightest twitch.

A safer and easier approach might be to conspicuously sharpen the straight razor while the submissive watches, and then blindfold ing him or her, after which, you put aside the straight razor and use a conventional safety razor for the actual shaving.

Pony play

Pony play combines elements of bondage, display, control and service to create a unique kink that is enjoyed by a very active subgroup within the BDSM community. Basically, in pony play, and other kinds of animal play, the submissive takes the role of a pony and is used and presented as such. Pony play can include sophisticated, lovely and expensive rigs, including harnesses, saddles, bridles and even carts. The pony can carry or pull the dominant or can be put through elaborate movements guided by the signals of either a mounted rider or dismounted trainer, or the submissive can take part in races modeled after the various forms of horse racing in the vanilla world.

Pony play can be an exclusively private-play activity, but because of the strong exhibitionistic component, it usually leads to public play either at parties or at events organized by aficionados of this lovely kink.

Like much of BDSM, the attraction to this activity is in the soul. However, it would be hard for the most insensible individual to look at the sheer joy radiating from a pony girl going through her paces and not recognize the unmitigated hedonism, the release and the joy that is coursing through her.

Many people have been drawn to pony play after reading the *Beauty* series, a trilogy written by Anne Rice, under the pseudonym of A.N. Roquelaure. In these books, the sexual slaves are set to pulling riding carts for the enjoyment of the masters and mistresses of the castle.

Many submissive men and some women prefer to be mounted rather than using pull carts. The feel of a rider on his or her back lends an intimacy that is lacking when the dominant is some feet behind in a sulky-type cart. Many of these people use specially designed saddles that allow them to stand upright with the rider's hips level and behind their shoulders. In this position, they can carry a surprising amount of weight. Except in the pornographic videos, one rarely sees a human pony carrying anyone while on all fours. The spine simply is not designed for this activity. When it happens, the rider either sits on the shoulders with his or her legs on either side of the pony's neck or on the arse with the legs near the waist. In any case, this kind of prone-carry should not be done for very long.

Suggested Reading
The Human Pony, Rebecca Wilcox, Greenery Press

Suspension

Suspension is a touchstone of bondage films and fiction. Unfortunately, this has given many the perception that it is both indispensable to enjoyable bondage and is safe. Both are wrong.

Many people enjoy years of intense bondage activity without anyone's feet leaving the ground. There is nothing that makes suspension the *sine qua non* of bondage. On the contrary, suspension is an activity fraught with hazards, one that needs to be approached, if at all, with care, thought and preparation.

Some of the physical conditions that would make suspension unwise are if the submissive has had his or her shoulders dislocated previously or if he or she has diabetes or any other condition that would restrict the flow of blood to the extremities. Suspension usually causes a shortness of breath because the rib cage is compressed by the body's weight, so you should think twice about suspending someone who has difficulty in breathing.

If you are intent on going ahead with suspension, I recommend you have at least one additional person to assist you. While a two-person suspension scene is possible, a third person provides the extra margin for error needed in the event of an emergency.

Where to suspend

Your preeminent need is to locate a place from which to suspend. Ask any mountain climber; finding a place to safely support a person's weight is harder than you might realize.

After they have succeeded in pulling down the shower curtain rod, the towel racks and a closet hook or two, the next thing most people think of is sinking a screw eye through their ceiling and into a support. This has three basic problems.

First, if the supports are there (a significant number of modern buildings have surprisingly little support holding up the ceiling), how are you going to find them?

Knocking on the ceiling or using a stud detector usually gives you a good enough idea of a support's location to hang a picture, but consider what would happen if your screw eye did not hit the center of the support. As weight was applied, the screw would work its way sideways, and splitting the wood, it would come out unexpectedly, through the side of the support. You must be able to see the support you are using.

Second, the supports between a ceiling and a floor are designed to accept pressure from above. There is no guarantee that they can stand a very concentrated pull on their underside, particularly after you have weakened them with a hole that is an appreciable fraction of their total width.

Third, a vertical screw eye is one of the worst things you can use for suspension. Never use anything that can unscrew. What makes this specific situation so much worse is – if you use a screw eye vertically, weight on the eye makes it easier, not harder, for the screw to come out.

The safest support is something strong enough to support three times the weight you intend to put on it when that weight is bouncing up and down with enthusiasm. The safest way to attach something to that support is to use a length of chain looped up and over it and then bolted or snapped together.

That piece of information usually leads people to the cellar, where there are often a lot of pipes running along the ceiling. It is very easy to throw a length of chain over a pipe, and isn't a steel pipe strong enough to support almost anything?

True, but not having energetic perverts in mind, most plumbers don't attach the pipe to the ceiling with clamps strong enough to support much more than the weight of the pipe. So, therefore, while steel pipes can be fashioned into an outstanding bondage and suspension frame, putting unexpected strains on the pipes that are in your house for other purposes isn't advisable.

Also, the pipe is also likely to break if you pull it loose from its supports. If it is water pipe, you will be very wet. If it is a sewer line, you will be very sorry. If it is a gas pipe, you will be very...

However, while you are in your basement, look at the floor supports. These are usually 2"x6" or 2"x12" boards on edge. These are relatively safe to use. Take an eye bolt (an eye bolt is like a screw eye except instead of ending in a point the grooved part has a nut on it), drill a hole through the support about two-thirds of the way up, put the bolt through and tighten it in place, using washers to prevent either the eye or the nut from sinking into the wood. The part of the eye that is open, although bent back against the shaft, should be at the top in the unlikely eventuality that it works its way open under stress. Some dominants use hooks instead of eyes. I avoid anything that can let the rope or chain go unexpectedly. It may be easier to lift a rope or chain out of a hook than to pull one through an eye, but I see it as a safety factor, not an inconvenience.

Consider the load you are going to be putting on the bolt and get one more than large enough to handle it. Because you are able to put things horizontally in to this support as opposed to one hidden behind a ceiling where the only approach is straight up, screw eyes can be used here. Vertical weight on a horizontal screw tends to hold it in place rather than allowing it to work out. Again, drill the pilot hole about two-thirds of the way up, and make sure that the screw eye is big enough for the load.

This technique can also be used with exposed ceiling beams and with room supports in the attic. Some exposed beams in cathedral ceilings are some distance down from the ceiling itself, making it possible to run a rope or chain over and around them, eliminating the need for an eye bolt.

Suspension gear

Suspension can be done with rope, chain or a combination of both.

Chain should be the kind with welded links. The light-duty chain with unwelded links, or plastic decorative chain intended for supporting plants and lamps, is completely unsuitable. Twisted-link chain is capable of supporting the strains on it, but it lacks aesthetics and is uncomfortable to work with or even to brush against when it is under strain. If you are using locks and snap links (mountain climbers call them carabiners), you should make sure that the individual links in the chain are large enough to accept them.

Snap links and locks can also be used when chain is attached to eye bolts either by directly linking the chain to the eye bolt or by having the end of the chain pulled through and then attached to itself with the snap link. Permanent connections between two chains or between the end of a chain and part of itself can be made with split links rather than the S-shaped pieces of chain material sold in some stores. However, these S-links can open under pressure.

Keep in mind, when using a snap link as a temporary connector, you should note that it is difficult or impossible to open them under strain. At some point in your chain arrangement, you should have one or more panic snaps. These are snaps that are designed to open safely despite strain on the chains they are holding. Panic snaps allow you to release the submissive quickly and safely in the event something goes wrong. Obviously, panic snaps should never be located where suspended SAMs can get their hands on them.

Although it has never happened to me, I have heard about panic snaps breaking under stress. Because of this possibility, I recommend that you have a separate, safety chain bypassing the panic snap. Because this safety chain would not be under stress while the panic snap was intact, you can use an ordinary snap link to attach it to the chain above the panic snap.

In the event of an emergency, you would first disconnect the safety chain's snap line. Then, you would release the submissive using the panic snap. However, if the panic snap broke during the scene, the safety chain would take up the strain and prevent what could be a serious fall.

Locks can act as a kind of inferior panic snap, as most can be opened under pressure. However, chains have a tendency to get caught in the clasp's notch at the worst possible times. Also, only the best quality locks should be used; inexpensive locks may open under strain. For a psychological effect, inexpensive locks can be used to fasten chains that already have snap or panic locks taking up the strain.

Keys should be clearly marked and kept on a hook near the suspension or on your person at all times, and spare keys should be kept in the first aid kit.

The kind of care that is involved in tying knots for bondage is all the more important in suspension. This is not the place to have a poorly tied knot come undone or unexpectedly tighten.

Neither chain nor rope should be used against bare skin during suspension. I prefer heavily padded suspension cuffs designed just for that purpose. They have an extended brace so that submissives can grip the cuff itself and ease the pressure on their wrists. If you use conventional cuffs, make certain that the inside of the submissive's wrists, where the veins are, are toward the outside. This way, the weight is borne by the outside of the wrists and the danger of cutting off circulation is reduced. In any case, you must monitor circulation regularly and terminate suspension at any time you notice symptoms of circulation being cut off or your submissive reports numbness or chill in the supporting extremities.

Once you have everything, and everyone, rigged, you still must suspend them. After all, that is what it is called, suspension. Even with rope through a simple pulley is difficult to lift a full-grown human; trying to pull links of chain through a eye bolt with more than 100 pounds of flesh on the other end is something that would challenge Conan.

With chain, the best approach is for the submissive to step off of a box or other movable object, like in an old-time hanging. However, unlike in the hanging, the drop, the distance between where the person is standing on the box and where she or he will be while hanging, should be not more than four inches. This is to make it possible to get back on the box after being exhausted by the session.

Most dominants, however, prefer to hoist their submissive into position. Auto supply stores sell chain falls that are ideal for this purpose, and hoists are available from boating and hardware stores. The safest kind is a screw hoist, which uses a crank attached to a screw drive to turn the drum. Unfortunately, it lacks the wonderfully erotic click-click-click of the cam hoist. Surprisingly, the safety of the screw hoist is a disadvantage in an emergency. Because the cam hoist uses a cam riding on a notched wheel to prevent the cable from unwinding, it is possible to quickly lower someone by moving the crank to remove tension from the cam, lifting the cam off the notched wheel and then letting the drum freely rotate as someone else supports the suspended person. A screw hoist, because of its design, cannot allow the drum to run free.

Do not expect to run the rope all the way to the hoist, which should be attached firmly to a wall or another such immovable object. Rope, particularly nylon rope, has an amazing ability to stretch. A 15-foot length of nylon rope can be expected to stretch to 25 to thirty feet under strain. Not only does that mean a lot of cranking before anyone leaves the ground, it also makes the suspended individual bounce in an annoying manner that is more laughable than erotic.

You can use wire-cored plastic or wire cable to run most of the way from the hoist to the lifting rope or chain. The cable will not stretch, and the submissive will stay about where you want him or her. Where the cable has to change direction to convert the downward pull of the winch to a lift, you should use a pulley, both to cut down on the friction and because cable is more vulnerable to abrasion and more likely to abrade that it rubs against than rope.

When lowering and releasing a suspended submissive, you will welcome an extra set of hands. The submissive is likely to be confused and disoriented, both by the suspension and by the activities that went with them. Expect a sort of collapse and be ready to support him or her when the strain is removed.

Inverted suspension

Cuffs for inverted suspension are also available, but, if care is taken to protect the Achilles tendon, tight-fitting boots can also be used. The ideal device, however, are the '70s fad, gravity boots, which can occasionally be found at yard sales, eBay and flea markets. A more recent sport, bungee jumping, also provides suitable equipment for inverted suspension. The feeling of partial inverted suspension can also be obtained with tables, intended for meditation or relaxation therapy, which someone can be strapped to, while the entire table-top tilts.

Some submissives report that the feeling of being suspended in an inverted position mimics, in a somewhat safer way, erotic asphyxia, an extremely dangerous activity, but one that a number of people find stimulating. Unfortunately, this position also tends to cause sinus blockage. Because of this, the dominant should monitor the submissive's condition during inverted suspension even more carefully than during conventional suspension.

Because the valve system in the veins and arteries is designed to keep an even pressure when people are upright but not inverted, you should not suspend anyone in an inverted position who is extremely near-sighted, has glaucoma, high blood pressure, heart conditions, diabetes or other circulatory problems in the extremities.

Great care should be taken while raising and lowering the submissive as a moment's carelessness can result in a fall directly on the skull and back of the neck. A compression fracture can mean a lifetime as a quadriplegic.

A common-sense safety precaution is leaving the submissive's hands and arms free during hoisting and releasing prior to lowering. I also like to have a third party present to steady and support the submissive's body, while I tend to the winching.

Supported suspension

Supported suspension eliminates many of the problems inherent in conventional, by-the-wrist suspension while providing the off-the-ground out-of-control feeling valued by submissives. In supported suspension, the primary stress is either distributed at several points, or it is placed so that it mimics the normal stresses of standing or sitting.

Obviously, regardless of how the submissive is suspended, there is no reduction in weight, so you shouldn't scrimp on the supporting ropes and chains or on how you attach them to the supports. None of the hardware requirements I've stated earlier are in any way relaxed.

The simplest and most popular form of supported suspension is the swing. This can be as simple as a child's swing with the submissive's arms tied above the head along each of the risers. This way the submissive's entire weight is resting on the horizontal board, and there is no pressure on the wrist ties.

More complex swingers' swings or bondage swings allow the submissive to lie back and have both his or her feet and hands firmly attached to the four supporting lines. These swings are often sheets of leather or canvas or meshes made from broad nylon strapping. The support is more broadly spread, and because of this, these swings are more comfortable than the simple board.

Of course, with swings, there is limited access to the parts of the body, the ass or the back, that is doing the supporting. However, a creative dominant can lower the conventional swing until it is just above floor height and have the submissive stand on the seat. Extra ropes can hold the ankles and wrists against the rope. In fact, the entire length of the arms and legs as well as the waist can be attached to the swing's risers. This leaves both the front and the back of the body available for stimulation.

A homemade swing with an extra-wide seat is useful here. In this way, the seat substitutes for a spreader bar and keeps the legs well apart. As with any spreader, you can include a place for a dildo or vibrator support.

A more complex solution to the problem of supported suspension is to use a harness. These range from a simple climbing harness like those used by rock climbers, to something similar to a parachute harness. In fact, enthusiasts often haunt flea markets and surplus stores and snap up surplus parachutes. The shroud fabric is useful for many applications. The chute cord can be used for decorative bondage where there is no tension on nerves or blood vessels, and the harness itself is a joy forever.

For those who are unable to obtain the conventional parachute harness, or who find it unaesthetic, a leather harness can be acquired from a number of leather craft shops around the country at a considerable cost.

To create one style of climbing harness, you need about ten feet of nylon webbing, sold in mountain sports shops, and a device called a carabineer from the same source. A carabineer is a kind of D-ring with a spring-loaded gate that snaps shut whenever you put something into the ring.

I prefer the two-inch-wide nylon straps. The three-inch-wide straps provide better support but are harder to tie. This fabric feels soft but there is a chance that it can abrade the submissive's skin.

Dominants should be aware of this, and monitor it closely. Some dominants prefer to put lambswool or other padding under stress points.

You can put the middle of the strap across the submissive's back and tie it over the belly button with an overhand knot (first tie). The two free ends go between the legs. Each free end should cross one of the buttocks diagonally and then go under the horizontal strap at the point where the outside pants seam would be if you were nice enough to allow your submissive to wear pants. Then you need to bring both ends forward and knot them over the belly button with a square knot. Finally, you must take a carabiner and put both the first and second tie inside of it.

That completes the climbing harness. The carabiner provides a point of attachment for your hoisting rope or chain. You may wish to tie the submissive's wrists to the hoisting rope or have him or her hold on while you lift. There is a certain tendency for people to hang upside down in this harness so, naturally, a behind-the-back wrist tie is a very dangerous idea unless you somehow secure the upper torso to the rope so this does not take place.

Suspension is a lot more difficult to do well and safely than most people realize. Many of the desired effects can be obtained by other, safer approaches, such as standing bondage or tight spread-eagled bondage. However, if you and your submissive feel that suspension is what you want, do it carefully and sensibly.

Waxing

Candles cast such a lovely glow across the bedroom or dungeon. Their gentle light hides and reveals. Their flickering flames draw the eye like little magnets. In the scene, candles can also perform another function: waxing. At first, it may sound horrifying, dripping hot candle wax on bare skin. I assure you it will sound horrifying to a novice submissive.

However, properly applied candle wax can be no more stimulating than a brisk spanking and considerably less so than whipping. The secrets are choosing the right candles and letting the wax cool by letting it fall a distance before it hits the skin.

Most novices attempting their first waxing are likely to go out and buy expensive candles. After all, they think, this is a special occasion so it calls for special candles. Unfortunately, these are may well be the wrong candles to use. Expensive candles are often made from beeswax. This is because it is easier to mold into exotic shapes and burns for a long time.

Unfortunately, the reason a beeswax candle lasts for a long time is that it has a melting point considerably higher than the cheaper paraffin. The stimulation caused by melted beeswax striking the skin is very likely to exceed a submissive's ability to transmute it into pleasure. This, in turn, can lead to a truncated session and general unhappiness all around.

Scene people consider the best candles to begin with are generally the cheapest: the ugly white votive candles sold for chafing dishes and such, or standard Jewish Sabbath candles.

However, Professor Spectrum, a kinky chemist, has done extensive research on waxing using scientific apparatus rather than simply relying on anecdotal evidence, and he found that the many of the "facts" we had believed were not necessarily true.

Modern candles are made up of such a complex mixture of waxes, dyes and plasticizers that it's almost impossible just to judge the melting point from the label.

This is why I recommend that you test the temperature of any candle before using it on a submissive by letting it drip onto the skin on the underside of your forearm.

Another of Professor Spectrum's discoveries is that, in reality, the height from which the wax is dripped has little impact on how hot it is when it arrives.

In my first waxing session with a submissive, I prefer to have her firmly tied down. This is because the stimulation provided by the hot wax can inspire considerable thrashing around. However, once she is familiar with it, I can generally forgo bonds unless they are needed for psychological reasons.

Generally, I begin dripping the wax on a less sensitive part of the body like the shoulders, slowly working southward as I feel her going into that transcendental state. I, also, keep a bowl of ice cubes handy. They come in handy for chilling down a bit of wax that was too hot, and they are handy for some erotic techniques I'll describe later.

Dripping can be done in several ways. The candle can be held horizontal and rotated by the fingers so that the top is melted evenly and the drips are fairly regular. To speed up the dripping, you can lower the lit end so the flame is flowing over the wax. This delivers the hottest wax because it is coming directly from the flame area. To get better control of the timing of the drips, you can tip the candle, drop a bit of wax and then return it to an upright position until you want to drop a bit more wax. This also delivers cooler wax because it has spent some time in the bowl at the top of the candle away from direct contact with the flame.

Splashing is more shocking. You allow a pool of wax to build up in the candle and then dash it on the submissive's body. Because of the unexpectedness of the action and because the larger quantity of wax holds heat better, this is much more stimulating. Another way to splash is to use a brandy warmer, one of those little gadgets that holds a brandy glass above a small alcohol lamp. (Personally, I cannot imagine a better way to ruin the bouquet of a fine brandy by overheating, but it does lend itself to waxing.)

Simply take some wax; the flakes you remove from your submissive at the end of a session are fine. (Recycling can be fun.) Put the wax in a brandy glass and let it sit over the flame until the wax is melted. You can then slowly dribble the melted wax or dash the contents all at once. You should test the temperature of the wax with a finger before using it; the alcohol flame can raise the temperature of the wax considerably above the melting point. Also, a pool of wax will not cool anywhere near as fast as single drops. If it does not run off as a thin sheet, spread it around with your fingers or use an ice cube (more on that soon) to cool it down.

If one candle is good, aren't more better? I wonder how many antique candelabra are sold for purposes that the dealer couldn't even guess? This is particularly effective with different colored candles in each cup. Some dominants like to spin the candelabrum so the wax literally flies off the candles. Of course, this makes a major-league mess and often results in the dominant getting as completely waxed as the submissive. But it is spectacular.

With a little common sense, the entire body is an appropriate target. Obviously, open sores, eyes and vulnerable places like that are off limits, but more than one man has watched in pleasurable horror as his mistress has converted his cock to create a surreal wax sculpture.

Colored candles can burn hotter and can contain dyes that can irritate a submissive's skin. For this reason, I do not use them during an initiation to waxing. Normally, I'll add a few drips of each color in my "paint box" to the next session. Later, I carefully examine where each of the drops landed. All by itself, this examination can be fun. If there is any redness or irritation, the color which caused it is off limits in future sessions.

Colored candles also allow the artist in the dominant to come forth. It is possible to produce very attractive designs using your submissive as a canvas. One of M's greatest pleasures was to parade around The Vault or Fetish Factor clad primarily in different colors of wax.

Avoid dripless candles. They contain chemicals that are very likely to irritate skin and the outer layer that makes the candle "dripless" has a much higher melting point than the wax that makes up the rest of the candle, so you can't really be sure of how hot each droplet is.

BDSM is a study in contrasts. This is nowhere more true than in a waxing scene. There is no reason why you have to limit yourself to hot wax. You can drop by the kitchen for a refreshing drink and pick up a glassful of ice cubes while you are there.

There are a host of ways to combine fire and ice. The simplest is to alternate touches, nipple cold, neck hot, stomach cold, armpit hot. Particularly if the submissive is blindfolded, it is amusing to randomly vary the kinds of stimulation. It keeps the submissive guessing.

Another approach is to use both on the same spot. For example, a section of skin can be chilled for a few seconds with an ice cube, and then the skin can receive a splash of hot wax. After a while, your submissive may be surprised to discover that he or she can no longer distinguish between hot and cold.

Most waxing is done with the submissive horizontal. That affords the maximum of available targets and the easiest application. However, sometimes this may not be possible or aesthetic. A vertical body calls for some variations in technique.

First, and most obviously, you must use or create horizontal surfaces on which to drip the wax. Some are natural, breasts and cocks come immediately to mind, but don't forget feet and shoulders. If a male has allowed himself to become so out of shape as to develop a potbelly, this is an obvious time to make him regret his lack of exercise. The head can be bent forward or back to put the neck in an appropriate position for waxing, and legs and arms can be brought out to the horizontal.

One danger should be noted here. You should keep a close eye on what is above your candle flame. I was present when a careless mistress badly burned a submissive's stomach while she was waxing his cock. True, his protruding stomach was most unattractive, but the injury was unintentional, an indefensible error for a dominant.

Vertical bodies are also appropriate for the splashing technique noted earlier. However, you should exercise care that the forward, toward the submissive, motion is as smooth as possible. Jerking when you begin your toss is likely to splash wax on you or to waste it on the floor. The jerk should come as the candle stops its forward motions to that the liquid wax is projected toward the submissive with skill and accuracy.

There are many ways to remove wax. One way to remove much of the wax is simply to allow the submissive to wear it. M, the first submissive with whom I tried the brandy glass trick, greatly enjoyed being paraded around wearing cooled wax. Of course, this option may mean that flakes of wax will be turning up in the most unlikely places for the next millennium. At home, that's your call. At a party in someone else's house, it can lead to your not being invited back.

Of course, the submissive can be set to removing his or her wax, but I feel this is declining an opportunity for me to get in a bit of additional provocative stimulation. It can, however, be visually amusing, particularly when the submissive is forced to remove significant amounts of body hair along with the wax.

While it is superfluous when the submissive is removing the wax, the wax should be allowed to cool completely before the dominant begins to remove it. This makes removal easier. If you are in a rush to cool the wax, a glassful of ice water works nicely. Ear plugs are recommended against the resulting scream.

You can, of course, pick the wax off with your fingers. This method is particularly alluring when done by a female dominant with long, attractive fingernails. Other dominants attempt to whip off the flakes of wax off the submissive's skin. My preference is for a large, sharp knife. (For personal protection, I generally eschew large knives for serious play where the skin might be broken. After all, vital organs are rarely more than two inches away from an opponent's skin. However, the scene puts image above practicality.) Watching a submissive's widened eyes following the shiny steel sliding over her breast and caressing her nipple, while the flakes of wax are removed, can be a most delightful experience.

There are a three pre-waxing exercises that can make wax removal much easier. The most erotic of the three is to use massage oil on the skin before waxing. It greatly increases the flakiness even when there is noticeable body hair. The existing layer of oil allows the hardened wax to be much more easily lifted off, and spreading the warm oil all over the submissive's body can be a sensual experience for both of you.

Another approach is shaving. Most people have fine hairs over most of the body, not to mention the not-so-fine collection at several of the most logical targets for waxing. When these hairs are trapped by the cooling wax, it becomes quite difficult and time consuming to remove the result.

Another approach that makes wax removal a snap is using plastic wrap. Ordinary kitchen plastic wrap or the industrial strength product conduct heat and cold quite efficiently and provides a surface which the wax will not cling to. Prior to waxing, you can elect to mummify the submissive, or you can simply put the plastic firmly over the sections to be waxed.

In most cases, the plastic wrap goes on quite tightly and sticks very well. Unfortunately, this is not true in the case of the genitalia. Both cocks and balls and pussies are so irregular and, often, so hairy that the plastic wrap is cannot find a smooth surface on which to stick.

This problem can be remedied by taping both ends of the plastic. Some people use masking tape. I have found the clear plastic tape sold in hardware and stationary stores for sealing boxes is better. Because it comes in three-inch wide rolls, there is plenty of adhesive surface to distribute between the plastic wrap and the skin. It also bonds quite effectively to skin.

You can have the submissive lie on his or her back, attach one end of the plastic wrap to the stomach, then have the submissive roll over and pull the plastic tight and attach the other end to the back. Not only will the heat or cold be transmitted directly to the submissive's skin through the tightly drawn plastic wrap. The sight of the "shrink wrapped meat" is an appropriate topic for light banter.

Wax removal consists of simply removing the plastic wrap. The wax comes right off with it.

Suggested Reading

Toybag Guide to Hot Wax and Temperature Play, Spectrum, Greenery Press

Fire on skin (fireplay)

A more spectacular, and a bit more dangerous, activity akin to waxing is putting fire itself directly onto the submissive's body. Both ethyl and isopropyl alcohol will work, but do not use methyl alcohol because it is quite poisonous. I used to prefer ethyl alcohol, but it can be hard to find and expensive. Also, diluting it to the right concentration is time consuming and distracting. Now, I generally use 70% isopropyl, right off the drugstore shelf.

Before doing any fireplay, clear the area of anything flammable. This includes but is not limited to pillows, drapes and your own and your partner's hair. Many female dominants (and some males) who have long hair carefully pull back their hair and secure it with an elastic before beginning any fireplay.

Anytime fireplay is brought up, someone will suggest a fire extinguisher. While this isn't a bad idea, having only a fire extinguisher can be. The reason is that fire extinguishers are inherently messy. Unless the situation is clearly out of control, most people will hesitate to use one, particularly if a naked body is in the immediate vicinity. My intermediate solution is to have a damp towel in reserve. It can handle most small fires without the drama of the conventional fire extinguisher.

To learn how to do apply alcohol to a body, take an applicator (I use a Q-tip with a cardboard, not a plastic, stem for testing) and rub a bit of the alcohol mixture on your arm. After all, we use submissives for play, but we test techniques on ourselves. Dip the Q-tip again and light it; then, touch it to the wet spot on your arm. As it begins to burn, run your other hand along your arm, sweeping the fire away.

The reason you can do this is that alcohol doesn't burn, but alcohol vapor burns. Thus, the flame is a short distance above the skin. Sweeping pushes the flame away from the vapor concentration so it goes out. If you wait until all the alcohol vapor has burned off, the flame may have gotten close enough to the skin to cause a burn.

During a scene, I use a riding crop with a relatively narrow slapper as an applicator. I wet the slapper and place a bit of mixture on the submissive. Then I use the wet slapper as a torch to ignite it. If the fire burns for more than a second or two, I put it out with my own hand. Letting it burn for too long can lead to a first- or second-degree burn. Be careful not to use an applicator that soaks up too much alcohol. At one party, a lovely submissive begged me to do a fire scene with her. I didn't have my equipment, but there was a drugstore near. For the applicator, I got a package of cotton balls and attached them to a bamboo stick. I didn't realize how much of the alcohol the applicator had soaked up until I touched off what I thought was a small smear. Almost her whole chest burst into flame. It took several rapid waves to extinguish. She, and the audience, thought it was a spectacular start to the scene, but I was covered in cold sweat.

This technique works best in a relatively darkened room so the pale flames stand out. Although the intensity of the stimulation from the burning mixture is slightly less than would be received from a close waxing, the psychological effect the submissive feels watching his or her own skin flickering with a bluish flame is quite intense.

When I set up for this scene, I try to avoid areas with strong drafts from fans or air conditioners. These either blow out the flame prematurely or cause it to burn in unexpected directions.

Obviously, you shouldn't put the alcohol on mucus membranes or on the face. Also, some activities can make areas super sensitive. Once, after a spanking, I went to do a little fireplay on Libby's ass. No sooner than I had touched her with the applicator, she safeworded. She thought I had ignited it and let it burn, but it was simply the effect of putting alcohol on skin that had been a bit abraded.

Also, as with candles, you should be careful that the flame does not burn anywhere where there is something above it. For example, do not allow it to run under a breast where the flame will be burning upward against the skin. The vapor barrier works only when it is below the active flame.

As I've noted before, if you get careless about making up the mixture or using the technique, you can cause a first-degree burn. This is where a bowl of ice cubes like those used in waxing scenes comes in handy. First aid for minor burns is covered in the first aid section.

One effect of the flaming-skin technique is that it will effectively burn off body hair because hairs stick up into the active flame area. Because I have a sensitive nose, I avoid areas where much hair will be cremated, but I know some, particularly female dominants, who use this odor as an effective intimidation tool. Of course, this technique can be used to remove body hair before a waxing session.

Suggested Reading
Flames of Passion: Handbook of Erotic Fire Play, David Walker & Robert J. Rubel, Power Exchange Books

Humiliation

Nowhere is the difference between the psychologies of male and female submissives so markedly different as on the subject of humiliation. While any generalization is suspect, and I am scarcely an expert on all submissives, the gender differences I have observed are much too consistent to ignore.

The majority of male submissives seem to crave some degree of humiliation as part of their servitude. Sometimes, this craving is for extremely intense humiliation. The vast majority of female submissives, even those who seek out intense physical stimulation, seem turned off by humiliation. This, of course, does not mean that all women reject humiliation as part of a scene. I have met a few whose cravings are as fully intense as those of any man. However, this is an activity which a male dominant should approach with caution.

A quite handsome English gentleman came to the TES meeting one night. He was middle-aged, with a ramrod straight posture and a neatly trimmed thin moustache. It was quite clear that he was making a most positive impression on the ladies, particularly the unattached submissive ladies.

However, later, during a general discussion among members and visitors about their needs and desires, he said that what he enjoyed most was humiliating a woman. While condemnation and criticism of another's orientation is unthinkable in that environment and no one moved an inch after he had said it, I got the definite impression that a vast gulf had opened up between him and the women who, until he made that comment, had been hanging on his every word. Later, one submissive woman commented, "Damn, up to then, he was turning me on."

Male submissives often have a very different outlook. At another meeting, a submissive man recounted, before a rapt and admiring audience of other male submissives, how his girlfriend had lured him into the woods with the promise of sex. Then she made him strip, rolled him in mud, urinated on him and left him naked and bound.

Part of the answer to this difference may be that an essence of BDSM is contrast. Consider that the only women I have ever found deeply attracted to this role were strong, intelligent and forceful. Many say it is precisely the surrender of control that is so seductive.

Taking it from this point of view, you can see why humiliation is not attractive to most women. It offers little contrast between many women's daily lives and the scene. They find they are served a full daily diet of humiliation by our society. They hardly need to seek more.

Men, on the other hand, are largely shielded from humiliation and, when they experience it, they are permitted by society to strike back in a physical manner. To experience humiliation in a controlled environment is a novel and exotic experience.

Another explanation for the love of many male submissives for humiliation was put forward by Michele, a lovely and intellectually dynamic female submissive. Her suggestion was that because men are dominant and controlling, they are unable to tell whether a women desires them for their power or for themselves. If a woman strips them of their power, their dignity and self-respect and still cares for them they are reassured of their essential worth.

A submissive man explained his love for humiliation by citing the Woody Allenism that sex feels dirty only if you are doing it right. "I guess that I feel a bit of shame at my submissive tendencies," he said. "Humiliation plays on this, magnifying it and making it more intense, more 'forbidden' and, therefore, more desirable."

To further confuse the issue, humiliation is quite different from erotic embarrassment. Quite a large number of submissives of both sexes are turned on by embarrassment. To me, the primary difference between humiliation and embarrassment is how the activity causes the submissive to feel about himself or herself. Humiliation degrades and causes the person to feel that he or she is less valued and treasured, while embarrassment can bring out a greater sense of self-worth.

Here is an illustration quite separate from the scene itself. Imagine you are at a formal dinner and the speaker says several complimentary things about you then asks you to come up and say a few words. You might be embarrassed by the activity, but it would make you feel that you were valued. Then, as you walk to the rostrum, the speaker steps forward and pulls your pants down, and the audience laughs. That is humiliation. There is no gain or advancement there.

Early in the 1990s, there was a Best Submissive contest at Manray, a local BDSM club. I entered Libby, one of my submissives, in it. She was embarrassed as I led her to the stage, but she was also turned on that I thought enough of her to enter. She was also flattered by the attention of the audience. However, one uncouth type called out during the whipping, "Hit her harder." I spun and snapped my whip within inches of his face. He shut up. His cry humiliated her, and I would not stand for it.

In short, embarrassment is what happens when you force submissives to do what they would like to do anyway if society and their own inhibitions would let them. Humiliation originates and is imposed from outside.

As with many psychological aspects of the scene, humiliation can hurt more than any whip. Also, the level of discomfort seems to build at a geometric, rather than an additive rate. For this reason, I strongly suggest to my submissive that, as soon as the humiliation seems to be building to an intolerable point, she should use her safeword. Macho shit on the part of the submissive can do more lasting damage in this kind of scene than in any other.

Another factor to consider is that humiliation often occurs in a public place. I am of mixed feelings about these scenes. They seem to be a terrific turn-on for those who enjoy them, and in a place like The Vault where everyone knows what is going on, there is no problem. However, an axiom of the scene is consent – consent by everyone in the scene. A woman walking her five-year old in a public park did not give her consent to be confronted by a half-naked man being led by a chain.

I'm not excluding the public venue. However, I am asking that you think carefully before forcing members of the public to be part of your scene. Spencer's M greatly enjoys public bondage. I have taken her for walks in Central Park with her hands tied behind her back, but the ropes were hidden by an artfully draped coat. Another time, her master displayed her at The Renaissance Faire in chain bondage.

However, both of them were in period costume, and she was pre-sented as a witch on the way to the stake. In each case, the public was used, not abused.

There are many techniques for humiliation. Because this activity is an almost exclusively male penchant, I will use the masculine pronoun from here on in.

Forced cross-dressing is a potent tool. The incongruity of a male form in female clothing is often enough. However, when the clothes in question are particularly frilly or feminine, the effect is quite marked. Perhaps the height of this approach is to force him to wear negligee or outlandishly erotic garments. The inherent instability of a man in high heels and a French maid costume is a subtle but effective means of bondage.

Other humiliating attire is baby clothing. Several manufactur-ers have lines of oversized diapers and other items intended for the "middle-aged" baby. Forbidding the use of toilets because the baby is too young for them, and requiring him to use the diaper, augments the indignity.

Men have filled the English vocabulary with insulting terms for women. It is completely appropriate to use these terms on the "horny slut" who grovels at your feet. However, don't neglect the animal kingdom in your search for the appropriate term.

As cleaning has largely been the work of women, putting him to work, especially in appropriate clothing, can be an effective humilia-tion. There is no need to make his work easy. Toothbrushes do a better, if slower, job than scrub brushes, and mildew is best removed with a Q-tip and toothpick.

A dominant friend has a toilet brush that has been reshaped to be held in the clenched teeth. As she puts it, "This brush puts him close to his work." She also rewarded a submissive who had been cleaning her bathroom for several hours with a beating. She explained that he had missed something. When he returned to his labors, he discovered that she had shit in the middle of the floor.

Food can be a source for humiliation. Obviously, baby bottles and formula can be used, and as formula often causes diarrhea in adults, this will lead to more productive use of the diaper. However, the consumption of almost any food stuff without use of the hands can be humiliating, particularly if a firm grasp on the hair is used to "assist" the process.

I had one of those rare female submissives who desired humiliation. Her specific scene was to treat her like a dog. To this end, I had her name placed on a dog dish. She thought it was just a bit of scene setting until I emptied a can of dog food into it and commanded her to eat. Later, she admitted that she had come within a hair's breadth of her breaking point.

While real dog food is perfectly safe to eat occasionally, as some elderly people on a fixed income have discovered, I had cleaned out the can without her knowledge and replaced the contents with beef stew. She remained unaware of the substitution throughout the scene.

There is something powerfully evocative about the foot. Foot play can be an important part of a humiliation session. Simply having the submissive remove your shoes and get down on all fours so you can use him as a hassock is a good way to begin. While you are comfortably reclined, you can consider other activities.

If your feet are not perfect, it is the submissive's fault, and he should rectify the situation. Set him to work washing your feet (you may specify tongue or a soft cloth, or both), then clipping, smoothing and painting your nails. Foot massage feels heavenly and any slacking or carelessness should be punished.

A perfect position for all of this is to have him lie on his back with his feet and legs under your chair. His cock and balls should be directly under the front edge of the chair. With him in this position, you can knead his cock with one foot while extending the other for his loving attention.

Many men and a number of women love to be trampled or walked upon with bare feet or shoes. A word of warning here: this can be risky for the dominant as well as the submissive. A human body is hardly the firmest of surfaces, and the trampler faces the risk of a bad fall. Sailors used to have a saying, "One hand for the company and one hand for yourself." For tramplers, it could well be "Two feet for your partner and one hand for yourself." Always have a firm handhold when you go for a flesh-based walk. Be sensible in your choice of footwear. Stilettos are lovely to look at and lick, but when you have both feet on someone's back, you may think you have all your weight on the sole of the toebox – but it only takes a moment's loss of attention to transfer it back onto the heel, with potentially disastrous results.

A one-footed trample is a bit safer than using both feet for both the trampler and the tramplee. It also allows you to have more of the body to play with since most of the human body just isn't meant to support another person standing on it. With one foot, you can trap a wrist or press firmly on the genitals. One female dominant I know loves to order men to stick their tongues out and carefully positions her stiletto heel on the tongue and gently presses down.

Food can be combined with feet for further humiliation. A bit of food on the foot can be offered to the submissive, and he can be required to lick it off. For more intense humiliation, you can grind your feet into the food before offering it to him. If you leave dirty footprints on the floor, so much the better. He can clean them too.

Too often, submissives from whom we demand oral services become overly enamored of what they see as a power to give pleasure. This attitude should be carefully guarded against. Prior to her initial submission, the editor of a well-respected magazine expressed a certain interest in humiliation and, also, said she had a justified pride in her skill at fellatio. Early in the scene that followed, I reclined in a chair and directed her to demonstrate her vaunted oral skills.

Her expression of nonchalant confidence vanished when, after she had made only a few tentative licks, I put my foot on her shoulder and pushed her backwards to the floor. "You are careless and clumsy," I shouted. "You don't deserve my cock. Here, practice on this," I said, extending my foot. After a few minutes, I let her, chastened and contrite, return to her original task. Later, she admitted that it was one of her most exciting experiences, precisely because it was so unexpected.

Suggested Reading
Toybag Guide to Foot and Shoe Worship, Midori, Greenery Press

Golden showers, analingus and coprophagy

Unlike a lot of what we do, urine consumption seems to have been studied extensively. The consensus of both the scholarly and empirical seems to be that drinking it in moderation is a pretty low risk. Absent a bladder infection, urine is generally sterile on departure. So much so, that I was informed by a corpsman in my military days, that fresh urine was considered more acceptable than nonsterile water for a wound dressing. Research done in WWII indicated the dangers of drinking urine to replace water were twofold. First, drinking too much of it could lead to a build up of salts and toxins in the body. Second, urine is corrosive to tooth enamel. It seems that both of these risks could be handled by keeping the amount of urine consumed symbolic and by following it with a rinsing drink of water or some mouthwash.

In the same physical neighborhood, but bacteriologically light-years away, feces are an entirely different kettle of fish. These are far from sterile. Analingus can be performed in relative safety using a dental dam as a barrier between the tongue and the anus. Some people insert their tongue into a condom before licking "that" area. However, coprophagy or "shit eating" is a lot more problematic. Feces have been found to contain all sorts of pathogens from HIV to giardia. Even the ordinary denizen of the lower digestive tract, Escherichia coli or E. coli, is known to cause sickness when ingested. The only really good news is the most dangerous form, strain O157:H7, isn't native to human guts – so unless your partner is a deer or a cow, you probably aren't going to die. But even the strains that reside in us aren't particularly friendly when they leave their regular neighborhood south of the stomach.

This doesn't mean that coprophagy doesn't have a long history, dating back to the Old Testament where Ezekiel was told by God to make his bread with human feces (Ez 4:12). Even later, the Church held that coprophagy was an acceptable practice of self-humiliation.

Enemas

Enemas are occasionally used as a sensual/discipline/stimulation device in BDSM. My observation is that they seem to be most frequently used by gays and by female dominant couples. However, they are far from unknown in male dominant games.

The theory is quite simple. A quantity of water or water-based substance is placed in the lower bowels through the rectum. It is held for a period of time and then released. The practice admits quite a bit more variation.

For one thing, there is a strong psychological element in giving and receiving an enema. First, and most obvious, is the humiliating position and the sense of being invaded in a most intimate area. Moreover, many find it exciting that you are taking away their control of one of the most forbidden bodily functions. People, particularly men, can adapt to urinating in public, but almost everyone retreats into privacy where defecation is involved.

The enema also brings into play an intense contrast. The submissive will want mightily to defecate but can only do so with your permission. You are commanding something that lies close to the innermost being of the submissive.

The mechanics are easily mastered. For example, while water is often used, medical authorities suggest adding one or two teaspoons of salt per quart to minimize negative effects from the enema. A small amount of castile soap or Liquid Ivory creates a cramping effect that some BDSM practitioners seek. Castile soap is available in gourmet and camping stores.

Although some enema players have been known to use diluted alcohol, this is a very bad idea. The lining of the intestine is more permeable to alcohol than the stomach, and it is impossible to judge a safe dilution. Alcohol poisoning can be lethal. In any case, even a slightly drunk submissive cannot properly judge tolerances and limits, and therefore, cannot judge when to use the safeword.

Hot (cooler than you'd use for a hot bath) and cold water can be used to produce different effects. Again, as with all BDSM techniques, this is something the dominant should try on himself or herself before using on a submissive.

For safety reasons, no more than two quarts of liquid should be used in any single "cleansing" operation – a pint is plenty for an inexperienced submissive. The bag containing the solution should not be more than 18 inches above the anus to keep the pressure from becoming too great.

Although enema bags come with their own nozzle, gay and BDSM suppliers have come up with a multitude of specialized types, including some that are actually modified dildoes and butt plugs. One popular commercial type of nozzle is the Bardex, which has one or two balloons. With a single balloon-type it can be expanded after it has been inserted in the anus to prevent the tube from being expelled. The two-balloon Bardex has one balloon inside the anus and another outside to make a more secure seal.

Always use an enema bag or syringe. I have seen arrangements where tubes were connected directly to faucets. However, unless there are complex control systems, you will be unable to reliably control the pressure and temperature this way. Internal scaldings are bad, bad news.

While wearing gloves, you can lubricate the rectum with KY or other water- or silicone-based lube, let a bit of fluid run out the nozzle to make sure that there is no air in the tube, and then insert the nozzle no more than three to four inches into the anal canal. Be careful: the lining of the intestines is much more delicate than skin and a tear or puncture is very dangerous.

Insertion can be made with the submissive in a "bend over and grab your ankles" position, kneeling with his or her head on the floor or lying on his or her side. Insertion while the submissive is in a seated position is possible, but I believe there is too great a chance of ripping the intestinal wall in this position.

After the submissive has been "filled," you can remove the nozzle (If you are using a Bardex, deflate it first) and replace it with a butt plug available in most sexual supply stores. Do not use a dildo unless it has some guard to prevent it from completely entering the anus; as there is nothing to keep dildos from going in all the way, they can be lost in the rectum.

After an enema session, the submissive may complain about diarrhea or gas. This can be dealt with through a diet of yogurt, or through packets of intestinal bacteria that can be purchased from a drugstore.

If cramping continues more than one hour after the session ends or if there is a bloody discharge, go to an emergency room.

The effects of an enema can last for several hours, and you should be prepared for "accidents," particularly when a submissive orgasms. If such an accident happens over a sheet of plastic, it can give you an excuse for a delightfully scathing and humiliating lecture. However, should you be unprepared, it can be a messy and inconvenient end to an up-to-then-enjoyable scene.

Suggested Reading
Intimate Invasions: The Erotic Ins and Outs of Enema Play, M.R. Strict, Greenery Press

Fisting

While neither anal nor vaginal fisting is a BDSM activity *per se*, both are commonly used by members of the scene as part of their play.

Naturally, the first rule is play safely. The human body is a remarkably resilient device, but the linings of the anus and the vagina are much more delicate than the skin. A jagged fingernail can create havoc.

Prior to the AIDS epidemic, in the lesbian community, even more than the red handkerchief in her left pants pocket, the mark of a fister was a right or left hand with short, carefully filed nails. Now, of course, any responsible fister dons latex gloves before beginning, so the length of the nails is of less importance.

The best gloves are individually packaged surgical gloves. They not only fit better but they are a bit longer than the laboratory gloves which come in large packages. If you are going to do anal fisting, which often involves deeper penetration than vaginal, you might like to use a "calving glove," which has a longer sleeve. These are available from farm supply stores. Anal scenes should also be preceded by one or two enemas to clean the area.

There are two requirements for a fisting: Lubrication and patience. There is no such thing as too much lubrication. I tend to favor ForPlay, Probe or Elbow Grease, but any thick sexual lubricant is satisfactory. KY tends to be a bit too thin and dries too quickly for my taste, but others use it.

Crisco, an icon of the fist-fucking scene, is rapidly fading from popularity because it is an effective culture medium for bacteria. Those who still use it are careful to avoid contaminating their supply jar. Before the scene, a quantity of Crisco is placed in a smaller container, or containers if there is to be more than one submissive. If there is any left after the scene, it is discarded.

The secret of a good fisting is to seduce the body into doing something it doesn't expect that it can do. Fiction may show the dominant smashing a dripping fist into someone's arse or cunt, but in real life, it is a much more gradual process.

A single finger at a time, you touch and tantalize. Only when the body is comfortable with the intrusion do you add another finger. The process is not a simple progression. For best results, it is more a series of advances followed by slight withdrawals. Both verbal and tactile communication should continue throughout the process with the intent of soothing the submissive's very real fears and building the sexual tension.

The crux comes with the insertion of the thumb and the advance of the knuckles through the quivering ring of tightly stretched muscle.

The alignment of the hand should be up and down rather than horizontal at this point, and generally entry can be made with a gentle rocking motion rather than a direct push.

Once you feel the muscle closing around your wrist, pause for a moment and reassure the submissive that everything is all right. Then, begin a gentle series of motions with your encased fist. One of my favorites is to slowly and gently open and close my fingers.

The hand's strongest muscles are flexors in the palmar fascia which are responsible for closing the fingers. The extensor muscles on the back of the hand are relatively weak. However, I have found that they can be strengthened somewhat by enclosing the thumb and fingers with a heavy elastic and exercising by repeatedly opening the hand against pressure.

You can also use a push-pull motion or rotate the wrist. The important thing is to do everything slowly and carefully. You want to stretch and stimulate, not tear.

At this time, if you are fisting a vagina, you can also slide a lubricated gloved or cotted finger (a finger cot is a condom for a finger) into her ass. It is best if you plan this ahead of time. Putting on a latex glove with the other hand trapped in a vagina is an exercise in creativity and frustration.

Don't get overenthusiastic. A little goes a long way. One or two fingers is plenty. Once your other hand has touched the ass, do not use it to touch anywhere near the vagina.

When the session is over, removal should be gradual so as not to shock the system or in the case of anal fisting, prolapse the rectum, in effect turning the submissive inside out.

The opinions on a slight amount of blood from an anal fisting vary. Some individuals feel that it can be ignored. Others insist that any blood at all is cause for major concern. My gut feeling (yes, I meant to say that) is that fecal material and blood just don't mix. Peritonitis is a lousy way to die. There is no disagreement about a significant amount of blood. Go to an emergency room, immediately.

The vagina is a bit safer environment so a smear or two of blood is probably nothing to be concerned about. However, again, a significant amount of blood is a sign that something very serious is going on. Go to an emergency room.

Suggested Reading

A Hand in the Bush: The Fine Art of Vaginal Fisting, Deborah Addington, Greenery Press

Trust, the Hand Book: A Guide to the Sensual and Spiritual Art of Handballing, Bert Herrman, Alamo Square Distributors

Cutting, pricking and play piercing

Contrary to what most vanilla people think, ordinary cuttings and temporary piercings ("play piercing," "temporary piercing" and "pricking" are all the same thing – which expression you use depends on what part of the country you live in) are not extremely painful. The primary impact of the scene is in the submissive's head. Having metal penetrate our skin touches something deep into our primal instincts. Of course, some of the more creative approaches also can cause intense stimulation that could easily pass the pleasure/pain threshold.

Cutting and pricking should be done only after the most careful consideration of the risks and ramifications. The skin is the body's first line of defense against disease. While this has always been true, AIDS and hepatitis have made it, literally, a matter of life and death. In fact, anyone who is planning to do this activity should seriously think about getting vaccinated for hepatitis B.

While pricking almost never leaves a scar, cutting, depending on a person's physical makeup, may. This is particularly true of those with an African genetic heritage. People from that part of the world seem to have a marked tendency to develop keloid tissue over cuttings. Therefore, the possibility of a permanent marking from even a small cutting cannot be ignored.

Never penetrate the skin casually. While the preparations for a relatively safe cutting or pricking may interrupt the flow of a scene, aesthetic considerations have to give way to safety. Cleanliness is a primary consideration. Both the area to be played with and the tools you are going to use must be absolutely clean. Despite sterilization procedures, you should never use the same tools on different people.

The submissive must be absolutely immobile. For any initial play of this type, regardless of a submissive's certainty of her ability to remain still or our mutual experience with other forms of stimulation, I insist on using stringent bondage techniques. A futon frame is perfect for this because its slats provide a multitude of tie-down points.

Later, as I become more familiar with the submissive's ability to handle this specific stimulation, I may forgo the bondage. However, I always remain acutely aware that a single, unexpected, involuntary movement on the part of the submissive could have serious repercussions.

Always wear latex gloves (or nitrile if you or your submissive is allergic to latex). Not only are you breaching your submissive's skin, you will also be exposed to his or her blood. In today's world, anyone's blood has to be considered a bio-hazardous material. A tiny hangnail or scratch on your hand might expose you to an unacceptable risk. However, keep in mind that gloves do not provide a protection against needles or blades. Anything that can penetrate skin can go right through latex. A moment's carelessness with a needle or a blade can still be fatal.

The best gloves are surgical gloves that come packaged in separate, sterile containers. Ordinary lab gloves are sufficient, although they do not provide the tactile sensitivity of surgeon's gloves. Also, remember lab gloves are not sterile, and you should wash your hands with Betadine after putting the gloves on.

Be generous with the antiseptic when sterilizing the part of the submissive's body with which you will be playing. Betadine is cheap, and the submissive shivers so delightfully both at its chill and what it promises for the future. Some dominants use the surgical antiseptic Betadine for sterilizing the skin. Betadine does a better job than rubbing alcohol but has a distinctly unappetizing color. However, you can first sterilize with Betadine and, then, after a minute or so, clean it off with alcohol, and have a fairly sterile area.

Whatever you use, spread it around with your gloved hands. This is both sensual and helps makes sure that any airborne bacterial that have landed on the gloves will have a short and unhappy life.

In my opinion, the best toy for a cutting is a surgical scalpel. It is easy to handle because it is designed for exactly what we are setting out to do. Also, it is much sharper than art or utility knives. Sharpness is very important. A sharp blade is less likely to result in an unintentional scar. Also, you want to be able to work as smoothly as possible. One piece scalpels are intended to be discarded after each use. Others are made so that the blade can be replaced with a new, sterile one. In any case, you should never use the same edge on different individuals. Straight razors with disposable blades are also used by some dominants. These can be obtained from beauty-shop supply stores.

I met a west coast dominant who carried a tiny knife in a locket between her breasts. Seeing her extract the knife from the hidden scabbard was a distinct turnon, but I think I'll still stick with my scalpels.

I like to use acupuncture needles in my pricking scenes. They are very thin and easy to use. For more intense stimulation, I like standard hypodermic needles. Other dominants use medical suturing needles or those designed for carotid angiography or arterial catheterization. The popular sizes of hypodermic tips range from quite small to quite large.

Except for those packaged for medical use, the needles must be sterilized. The ideal sterilization tool is an autoclave, a device that disinfects with live steam. However, if you don't work in a hospital or a laboratory, you can use a pressure cooker. Keep the pressure up for at least forty minutes.

Needles should be thrown away after each scene, and in no case, regardless of sterilization, should a needle that has been used on one submissive be used on another.

Naturally, neither cutting or pricking should be done in any area where joints, nerves or blood vessels are close to the surface. Safer, but not absolutely safe, places are the upper arms and legs and buttocks.

When cutting, hold the blade perpendicular to the surface of the body. Begin with light pressure and increase it only to the point that the blade breaks the skin. You are doing a shallow, erotic cut, not dissecting a frog in biology class. Take your time, and allow the first cut to clot before you begin the second.

When you are finished, lightly swab the entire surface again with an Betadine-soaked pad. Some people, to make the cutting permanently visible, put a bit of autoclaved ink on the skin before wiping it. The ink is then trapped under the skin when it heals and makes a tattoo-like mark. Remember that this is permanent. It will not go away, and surgical removal is troublesome and not always effective.

In the pre-AIDS/hepatitis era, it wasn't unusual for a dominant to taste the blood from a cutting. I greatly enjoyed doing this. In the day, it was a powerfully symbolic bit of eroticism. Today, doing such a thing outside a monogamous or fluid-bonded relationship is a form of feeble-minded Russian roulette.

Unlike a cutting blade's vertical position, needles should be put into the skin at a very acute angle. The intent is not to penetrate deeply, there is little sensation below the skin, but to produce the desired stimulation. Grip the needle firmly close to the tip to minimize any wiggle and insert it smoothly. I use a hemostat to get a good grip. If you want to insert it further slide your grip further back and push again. You can have the tip come back out through the skin. When the needle is removed, it is important to re-disinfect the area.

Some people create further excitement by making several prickings and then connecting them with sanitized thread or monofilament. I've observed very erotic scenes wherein several submissives were connected with threads running between their temporary piercings.

Permanent piercings

A friend succinctly summed up the difference between non-pierced people and pierced people. She said, "Pierced people don't wonder what it would be like not to have a piercing."

While some people do permanent piercing as part of a scene, I prefer to leave that to professionals because the puncture will remain open for a significant length of time, and because there are considerations regarding placement and such that requires experienced judgment.

You'll find that most piercing professionals are very obliging if not active members of the scene, and they'll usually go out of their way to accommodate any ritual or such you want to include with the piercing.

Almost any area of the body can be pierced, but I'll list the most common types of piercing. For both men and women, aside from the ear, the nipple is probably the most common kind of piercing. Aside from aesthetic considerations, nipple piercings often make the nipple more sensitive.

In India, nostril piercing is as common as ear piercing, and it is becoming more common here. The most customary type of piercing is through the outside of a nostril, but a ring or bar in the skin at the end of the septum, the piece of cartilage separating the two nostrils, is being seen more and more.

The mouth is not a particularly clean place; therefore, tongue and lip piercings require special care when they are healing. However, they are show stoppers. Also, members of the oral sex cognoscenti have been known to rave about the effect of a tongue piercing.

Less common piercings are seen in the eyebrow, on the bridge of the nose and in the navel. The latter is another piercing that requires special attention when healing. Clothing rubbing against sore skin may be exciting for a few minutes, but even the most dedicated masochist can get very tired of it over a few weeks.

There is something about a cock that has drawn the eye of piercers for centuries. The *Kama Sutra*, India's equivalent to *The Joy of Sex*, mentions the apadravya, a vertical piercing of the glans, or head, of the cock. The ampallang is similar but horizontal. The apadravya can also be made behind the glans in the shaft. According to legend, the women of Borneo refused to have sex with men lacking one of these piercings. The dydoe is a piercing through the ridge of the glans. Dydoe piercings are often done in pairs.

Foreskin piercings were developed in ancient Rome as a means of enforcing chastity. According to some authorities, they retain that function today.

The frenum is a piercing through the skin of the cock just behind the glans and often includes a cockring. The Prince Albert is a piercing that goes through the urethra and exits behind the glans. Legend has it that Prince Albert, Queen Victoria's consort, had it done so he could strap his cock tightly against his leg and avoid spoiling the fit of his tight trousers.

A piercing through the outer skin of the scrotum is called a hafada, and it originated in the near east where the piercing went considerably deeper and was part of a rite of passage. Finally, the guiche is a piercing in the flap of skin that connects the anus and the scrotum. Because of its proximity to the anus, there is a significant danger of infection while this particular piercing is healing.

Although a woman's genitals are less "outstanding" than a man's, they afford a number of interesting sites for piercings. The hood of the clitoris is often pierced. However, authorities and aficionados have mixed opinions about piercing the clitoris itself. One group holds that it is unwise to puncture something with such a concentration of nerve endings. The others argue that this is exactly the reason to do it. In any case, all agree that piercings in this area increase the sensitivity of the clitoris. However, some women have had the piercings removed, reporting that it is possible to have too much of a good thing.

Although both the inner and outer labial lips can be pierced, most people prefer piercing the inner. Paired piercings on both lips provide an opportunity to put a lock or seal across the opening as both a symbolic and practical chastity belt.

A piercing that goes from the end of the vagina toward the anus (much like a guiche) is called a fourchette. This piercing has the same inherent dangers as a guiche.

Earring jewelry should never by used in a body piercing. The wires that hold earrings can tear the skin if the jewelry catches on clothing or, as has happened, part of your lover. Body jewelry is expensive, because it is handmade in small quantities. However, one piece per piercing is quite sufficient. Body jewelry isn't changed regularly like earrings. You don't need different sets for the office, dates and formal affairs.

Generally, jewelry is made from gold, niobium or stainless steel. Other metals can be used after the piercing has completely healed. However, some people show negative reactions even to niobium and stainless steel.

There are several types of common jewelry used with body piercings. The most common is the bead ring, a simple ring that is straightened, inserted in the piercing, and then bent back into a circular shape. The break in the ring is held closed with a bead. Occasionally, the bead is not attached to the ring, but simply held there by tension in the ring. This is called a captive-bead ring.

A barbell is a bar with a screw-off bead at each end. Sometimes the barbell is bent into a partial ring. Another variation substitutes a fine wire for the screw-off beads.

If you choose to have a permanent piercing, remember to carefully follow the piercer's instructions about after-piercing care. This may mean a period of sexual abstinence. However, everything nice has its price, and infections are not fun.

As noted, simply wearing body jewelry can add to sensation. However, body jewelry on a submissive has other uses. As with clips and clamps, they provide handy attachment points for weights of various sizes. You can also run strings through them and attach them to each other. By tightening the thread, you create all sorts of interesting stimulation. As with temporary piercings, two submissives can be attached to each other by strings through their body jewelry.

A word of caution though, be very careful of how much pressure you put on a piece of body jewelry. They are threaded through the piercing by a relatively thin wire which can cut the skin. Light pulls with a lot of checking are the order of the day. Never jerk at pierced jewelry and never bind a person by the jewelry when you might expect him or her to jerk. (For example, do not bind a person in this way and then do a spanking or whipping.) A minor drawback to piercings are that they can get conduct an uncomfortable amount of heat from saunas and hot tubs inside the body.

A common question is, "What happens if I have an car accident and get taken to the hospital?" Relax, even if you are in East Podunk, Idaho, emergency room people have seen lots weirder things than piercings. My friend's stomach ache became full-fledged appendicitis. When she woke up in the hospital after the operation, one of the first things she saw was a bottle on her nightstand, neatly labeled "body jewelry," with all her rings and barbells inside.

Another common question is, "Won't the jewelry set off metal detectors at airports?" It depends on how much you are wearing. However, given the current state of paranoia, the security people have been cranking up the detectors until they would probably detect the iron in a leaf of spinach. You have two alternatives. First, take off the jewelry for the trip. Second, you can behave like one of my friends did on her way to Living in Leather. After the alarm went off, a guard used a hand-held detector to localize the "suspicious metal" to the area of her breasts. When he said, puzzled, "Do you have any metal in there?" she smiled, pulled up her blouse and showed him. His jaw, and about a dozen others, hit the floor. As she walked away, the waggle in her hips indicated that she had enjoyed the entire process.

Electricity

In my first fiction book many years ago, I put in a scene where a young woman was tortured by a mad scientist. While she was bound spreadeagled to a frame, he connected wires to her body and gave her electrical shocks until she confessed. Whenever I meet anyone who has read that piece of trash, the conversation shifts around to that particular segment and I'm complimented on how "hot" the scene was.

In the first edition of *The Loving Dominant*, I warned against using line current (household current). I still stand firmly behind that belief. One hundred and ten volts is simply too dangerous to play around with, and most transformers can short out. This means the "nice tingle" from a phone recharger can become a mind-blowing blast of electricity if a wire frays or a connection comes adrift.

The "no play above the waist" I previously subscribed to is now less draconian. The instructions provided with TENS units (much more on these later) often show pads on the lower back and some accessory manufacturers provide nipple attachments for the units. However, it's still a good axiom. Electricity causes muscles to contract. The heart is a muscle. In fact, it is a very sensitive muscle. According to Underwriter's Laboratory, as little as one microampere (one millionth of an amp) can disrupt the heart rhythm. It seems sensible to keep electricity away from that particular organ, doesn't it?

Add to this, that electricity does not always travel in a straight line. It travels along the lines of least resistance, and no one, as yet, has come out with a fool proof way of charting those in a specific human body.

So, we play the odds, and a good way to do that is to keep the shocking stuff below the belt. Fortunately for us, that's where most of the "fun bits" can be found.

I'm a big supporter of people learning CPR, but I've heard occasional comments, particularly concerning electrical play, that I feel demand a warning. These comments usually go something like, "Oh, I don't have to worry about that, I know CPR." The implied assumption is that if a heart problem occurs it can be fixed with a few chest pumps. The human body is not like a Windows-based computer. It isn't just a matter of rebooting and going on with whatever you were doing before. CPR is valuable in the same way a seat belt in a car is valuable. Both save lives. Neither is a guarantee. You wouldn't ram your car into a wall simply because you have a seat belt on in the same way you shouldn't do dangerous play simply because you know CPR. A chilling statistic is that the survival rate from unaugmented CPR (no defibrillator or such) is less than fifty percent. It's valuable, but it isn't perfect.

Technological progress has added another rule to electrical play. The cardiac pacemaker was invented in 1958, but when *The Loving Dominant* was first being written, it was still relatively rare. That's no longer true, and electricity in any form and pacemakers don't go together. You don't even need to touch the body with an electrical source to drive the gadget out of its silicon mind. They are sensitive to the radio waves produced by many electronic devices. The best rule here is if the submissive has a pacemaker you probably should avoid electrical play of any kind.

One toy gets to break all the rules, except the pacemaker one. The violet wand plugs into the wall and can safely used almost all over the body. It was originally manufactured at the beginning of the previous century as a medical device which claimed to cure everything from gout to impotence. It didn't cure anything, but hurt just enough so people felt it must be good for them. Fortunately, it is still being manufactured. It can often be located in barber supply stores where its overt purpose is to give "stimulating scalp massages."

Because it uses exceptionally high-frequency electricity that doesn't enter the body cavity and presents no danger to the heart, you can use it everywhere on the body except the eyes. Because the output is directed through a gas-filled tube, there is no danger if the unit shorts out because the glass won't transmit the lower frequency electricity of the line current.

The machine consists of a plastic tube, about a foot long and two inches in diameter, containing a Telsa coil. One end has the power cord and an adjustment knob and the other has a cylindrical opening into which attachments can be inserted. As noted above, many of the attachments are hollow glass tube, which glow bluish violet and give the wand its name. When these attachments are brought near anything, a spark will jump to the object. The effect is like that from walking across a nylon rug with rubber shoes during dry weather and touching a door knob.

The spark is relatively harmless. With some people, it can produce a tiny burn, particularly if the electrode is held over one place for a while. Also, because the output can be rich in ultraviolet, the skin can become slightly sunburned. The current easily penetrates clothing, a convenient feature when one is playing in a club where nudity is forbidden. Also, if the cloth contains metallic fibers, the current will run along them, spreading the shock and making the fibers twinkle like tiny lightening bolts. A small warning: twice in all the years I've been playing with wands, I've had the submissive's clothing catch fire. In both cases, she was wearing a fuzzy material like angora, and she had been a heavy user of hair spray which might have gotten on the sweater. Neither incident caused any serious damage, but they've caused me to shy away from using wands near this kind of material.

However, you can use this effect to ignite alcohol on a submissive's body in a fire scene. Generally, I've found that to get a reliable ignition the alcohol has to be warmed a bit. Usually, I do that by lighting the surface of the bowl of alcohol I'm using and letting it burn for a minute or so.

One interesting technique is for the dominant to grab the attachment when the unit is turned on. If it is gripped directly, there will be no spark and no pain, but then by reaching out toward the submissive, he or she can "fire" sparks from a fingertip. Since there is a bit of a sting when the spark leaves as well as when it arrives, I like to control it with a small piece of wire or a coin held between two fingers. You can also use a Wartenburg wheel, which has an entirely different sensation when used with an electrified-dom.

Another interesting toy for the charged-up dominant is a cheerleader's pom-pom. You can get the kind that is made from Mylar-coated plastic. Hold the wand in one hand and the aluminized pom-pom in the other. You can either drop-and-draw the strands or use it like a flogger. If you want a more intense effect, drape the pom-pom over the comb attachment of the wand and let the strands directly conduct the electricity. However, be careful. Used this way, you aren't part of the circuit so if you hit yourself on the backswing you'll get the same shock as your partner.

Because holding the wand this way can be tricky, accessory manufacturers have produced a contact pad that fits under your belt to give you a hands-free link to the wand. When looking for such a pad, I recommend you only consider those that have a segment of ceramic as part of the current flow. This will protect you in the unlikely event that the Telsa coil shorts out in the same way the gas-filled tube protect your partner.

There are lots of things out there that can give a pleasurable zap without resulting in a call to the paramedics. One mistress uses a single nine-volt battery to deliver tiny but noticeable shocks to the tips of her submissive's cocks. She uses no amplifier or wiring. She just pushes the battery onto the dampened skin.

Fortunately for those who enjoy more technological gadgets, back in the early part of this century, quacks were fascinated by electricity. There were a multitude of devices manufactured so that the quacks could give people a tingle of electricity and a lot of lies.

A good friend of mine, Goddess Sia, has such a device. It is called an Electreat, and it looks a bit like a flashlight. It takes two flashlight batteries and can deliver quite a jolt when the sliding control is all the way up. What it was claimed to accomplish, no one seems to know, but her submissives are quite outspoken in their enjoyment of the stimulation it provides.

Another one I've see actually wraps the balls in a metal mesh before delivering some substantial shocks. Again, I don't know what it was supposed to cure, but I'm sure that I'd be yelling, "I'm cured! I'm cured!" shortly after it was turned on.

Up until the 1960s, one company manufactured a passive exercise machine called the Relaxacisor. It worked (or rather didn't work) by stimulating the muscles with tiny electrical impulses. Here the erotic charge is not from conventional electrical shock, but from the disconcerting feeling of having ones muscles performing without having willed it. Some couples have reported combining the Relaxacisor with conventional vaginal or anal sex with considerable success.

TENS units (Transdermal Electrical Neural Stimulator) are battery-powered units that are legitimate medical devices. Doctors use them for pain management.

They put out a controllable series of DC pulses that are intended to interfere with the pain receptors. The sensations can vary from a tingling and twitching as the current takes control of the nearby muscles to a pretty substantial zap. While the original TENS units are prescription items (but can be picked up used at flea markets and online auctions), a mini-industry of kinky types has sprung up supplying both the box and electrical butt plugs, urethra probes, dildos clips and clamps.

The typical TENS unit has two channels. This means that two pairs of positive and negative electrodes can be placed on the body. Each channel has a separate intensity control, usually located on top of the unit next to where the wire for each channel connects. In addition, most units have two other variable controls, one for the pulse width (how long the current is on for each "blip") and the other for the pulse rate (how many "blips" per second). These two work on both channels simultaneously. Generally, the controls allow you to set the unit to give from between two and 150 pulses per second and to have the current stay on from fifty or sixty microseconds (1/20 of a second) to 250 microseconds (a quarter of a second).

The conventional TENS unit comes with stick-on pads. One pad represents each end of a circuit that flows through the body between them. These are excellent starting toys and represent what are called mono-polar units. This means two will be required to complete any circuit. Bi-polar units have both the positive and negative poles on the same toy.

For example, if a mono-polar dildo is inserted in the vagina, no current will flow until another mono-polar toy (let's say a pad on the small of the back) attached to the same circuit on the TENS unit is put on the body. However, a bi-polar dildo will work just fine with the current flowing from one pole on the tip to the other pole on the base.

One troublesome "feature" of TENS units is that different brands often have differently designed plugs. Some use the standard bi-polar jack also used for personal tape players and IPods, but others use proprietary designs that mean you can only use accessories from that company or find a converter that changes the proprietary design into a standard jack.

Fortunately, if you're reasonably handy with a soldering iron you can make an adapter, because the pins that attach the TENS unit to the pads are standardized and the same size as a 3/32" subminiature plug (Radio Shack #274-245). The pins are mono-polar so you need three jacks. Let's call them A, B and C. You can start by running a wire from either pole of A to the top pole on C and another wire from either pole of B to the bottom pole on C. Then, you can connect one pin into A, the other pin into B and plug the bi-polar plug from the accessory into C.

One injury I've seen turn up regularly in TENS play is a small burn because the toy didn't have good contact with the skin, and instead of the current flowing smoothly into the skin, there was a spark every time contact was broken. The best way to deal with this is to use a conductive gel on the toys that is designed to fit against the skin and a sex lube for the insertable ones. Special care needs to be taken with the ones designed for urethral play since this area is particularly sensitive to infection. The recommendation here is for the use of a sterile surgical lube.

A favorite electrical interrogation device around the world is the old hand crank telephone. Turning the crank sends a substantial charge down the line. Interrogators in Cambodia would remark that they "would have to call information" when they were about to use this technique. Pepperpot generators in old-fashioned telephones can be used in the same way.

There are two ways of reducing the stimulation level produced by these devices. The first is simply to turn the crank slowly. The faster the crank is turned, the more electricity is produced. The second is to remove several of the U-shaped magnets. Because of the current being used, burns are common, particularly if the method of contact is thin like a wire. To minimize the chance of burns, TENS-type pads can be used. Electrical burns can be very painful and slow to heal. Not many would find them erotic

Another popular shock device is a cattle prod. In general, these produce too much of a shock for most submissives. However, the shock can be reduced by removing one or more of the batteries and replacing them with dowels wrapped in aluminum foil.

When I wrote the first edition, I was sure the so-called "stun guns" powered by nine-volt batteries had no place in BDSM play. I strongly believed the electrical impact they produce was well beyond the threshold I consider safe. At that time, I hadn't encountered many electrical players, but I did I know of one submissive who was traumatized when her dominant used one on her. Although she had a substantial ability to transmute pain into pleasure, she spent several hours in a state of semi-shock after a single application. However, in the intervening time, I've found a number of people who have played with this sort of toy successfully. My primary use of these units is for intimidation play. Sort of a "show but don't touch" rule. However, I have felt the output of several stun guns without ill effect, and I have known a number of submissives who have enjoyed this level of intensity. It's not for everyone, but I'm not going to insist on a blanket condemnation any more.

Obviously, with any toy you are going to use, electrical play is one area where a dominant is required to test any stimulation on himself or herself prior to using it on a submissive. This doesn't mean you are expected to enjoy the experience, but it tells you better than anything else what the sensation is and where it ranks among other toys. This axiom also serves as a valuable check against over-enthusiastic tops.

Suggested Reading
Toybag Guide to High-Tech Toys, John Warren, Greenery Press

Catheterization

Catheters have been used by human beings for centuries. Some ancient Chinese carvings even indicate that they may have been first used as sexual toys. Ah, the infinite ingeniousness of humanity in getting its collective rocks off sometimes awes me.

However, this particular trick seems to have suffered a well deserved decline until recently when some BDSM practitioners, principally gay, made it part of their repertoire.

Simply put, catheterization, as it applies to BDSM play, is to insert a specially-made soft-rubber tube into a man's cock or a woman's urethra, and letting urine escape and/or filling the bladder with another fluid.

If your reaction is, "That doesn't turn me on," I'm overjoyed. Make no mistake about it, catheterization is dangerous. If it were less known, I would gladly have left any mention of it from this book. However, given that I was relatively sure you would hear mentions of it, with reluctance, I will try to tear away the confusion surrounding the technique.

There are two principal dangers. The urethral tube into the bladder isn't designed to handle anything except a warm liquid under slight pressure. If you doubt this, think about the agony from passing a kidney stone. That can be an educational experience.

In a woman's body the urethral tube may bend a bit on its way to the bladder. However, in a man's body, the route might be described as a prostate roller-coaster ride. Combine the tube's fragile nature with its less-than-straight course and you have a situation fraught with peril. While stories abound of people shoving swizzle sticks, pipe cleaners and even pencils up the urethra, most of these are just that, stories. The rest had their end in an emergency room.

The second danger is infection. While many people consider urine "dirty," it is almost sterile. It is the rest of the world that is dirty.

The major trick in using a catheter is to keep the rest of the world's dirt out of the urinary tract. Failing to do this can lead to a world of hurt.

First, if you are bound and determined to do this, try to find someone to instruct you. A book is a poor place to learn what is essentially a motor-skills task.

Second, let me give you some serious warnings. Use only medical urethral catheterization kits. An amateur may be able to make rubber and plastic hose that look like what comes in the kits, but they are rarely as soft or as smoothly cut, and they are probably not sterile.

Do not use naso-gastric catheters that are sometimes available in leather stores. A rose may be a rose be a rose, etcetera, but a catheter is not necessarily a catheter. There are several reasons for avoiding them, but the best is simply that they aren't as flexible as urinary catheters. Remember that roller-coaster ride?

While doctors use solid rods called sounds to work in the urethra, in untrained hands they can be extremely dangerous. If you must play in this area, I recommend passing up anything except the basic urinary catheter kits.

Finally, if your submissive has a history of bladder infections, of venereal diseases like gonorrhea which affect the urethra, or of kidney stones, catheterization is not for the two of you.

You will need the following equipment: sterile gloves, Betadine solution, sterile water, catheter kit with a 5-cc syringe, paper tape and a small sterile packet of KY jelly. Some of these items will come in the catheter kit; some you will have to find on your own. You should check if your submissive has any allergic reaction from the paper tape by having him or her wear it next to the skin for a few hours.

First, you must open the catheter kit and open the package of KY jelly and drop a large dab onto a one of the gauze squares in the kit. Do not let the outside of the KY package touch anything in the kit.

Next, you must put sterile gloves on and take the folded, sterile, paper towel from the kit and put it at a convenient place so that there is enough room to put the catheter on it. With a female submissive, it is best to have her legs spread widely and work between them. With a male, work from one side with the toweling next to the hip.

Next, it's time to sterilize the area. This means, with a man, grab the cock. Remember that the hand you do this with is now not sterile, and it shouldn't touch anything that is sterile throughout the rest of the procedure. Wipe the entire length of the cock, paying particular attention to the tip, with gauze soaked in Betadine. Spread the lips of the urethra and wipe inside. Do not force the gauze into the opening, just clean the area. Then, repeat the whole process with another gauze soaked in sterile water.

With a woman, it means spreading the labia with one hand, which is now not sterile, and keep it open. With the Betadine-soaked gauze, you must first wipe one side of the clitoris and urethra, then wipe the other side and then wipe the center. You need to repeat this procedure with another gauze soaked in sterile water.

The remainder applies to working with both sexes. With your sterile hand, take the catheter and hold it about one inch from the opening of the urethra. Make sure you have found the opening of the urethra. You do want to go into the right hole. With your non-sterile hand holding the outside of the KY packet, generously lubricate the tip of the catheter. You should use lots of KY. It's cheap.

Now you can gently begin to insert the tip into the urethra. Your submissive will feel a slight stinging feeling at this point. That is normal. Continue to insert it until you see drops of urine coming out the end; that indicates the catheter is in the bladder. Next you must take the 5-cc syringe and place it in the special tubing for the balloon on the end of the catheter and inject 5 cc of sterile water. This will inflate a tiny bulb on the end to hold it in place.

You can remove the tube by deflating the bulb and sliding it out.

Generally, people use catheters to drain bladders for golden-shower-type activities. However, some use the catheter to put fluid into the bladder. Obviously, this fluid must not interfere with the bladder's normal function and must be completely sterile.

The best material, I am advised, is an isotonic solution, such as normal saline, which can be purchased at a drug store. You should not open the bottle until you are ready to use it. The contents must remain sterile. I once heard about a less than attentive dominant who put ordinary ice cubes into the solution to chill it. Obviously, it never occurred to her that the ice cubes were not made with sterile water. If you want a chill solution, chill the whole, unopened bottle in the refrigerator.

To transfer the solution into the bladder, you will need to get a "Tomey" syringe. It looks like a huge hypodermic needle, but the opening at the top is wide enough to fit snugly on the end of the catheter.

Gray's Anatomy reports that a healthy bladder should be able to hold a pint of fluid and that women have slightly larger bladders than men. However, I wouldn't want to push things past a cup or so.

You must allow the existing store of urine to drain out, attach the Tomey syringe to the catheter and slowly and inject the solution. If there is cramping, stop and wait until it subsides. If it does not, you have reached the limit.

A word of warning, while an occasional inflation may not be dangerous, if it is done often, the submissive may develop a flaccid bladder which could require medical intervention. Moderation, as with all else, is the keyword here.

Branding

If you ask most people who have seen or read *The Story of O* for a list of the hottest scenes, and most of their lists will include the branding scene at Anne-Marie's. The slow buildup, the glowing coals, the white hot iron and the agonizing scream all combine for an over-whelmingly erotic effect.

However, in real-world BDSM, branding is an exotic subspeciality rarely practiced outside a relatively small group. It is both dangerous and permanent. While it is difficult and expensive to remove a tattoo, it is almost impossible to remove a brand. Much of the material in this section comes from Raelyn Gallina of Oakland, California, who is an expert at branding and piercing.

When most people think of branding irons, they visualize those heavy, cast-iron monsters used by cowboys on non-consenting cattle. Human brands are more delicate. They are made of sheet metal, such as coffee cans and heating duct material, and they are something like cookie cutters. The iron doesn't have to be very thick because the brand spreads over a period of months and will eventually be four or five times the thickness of the metal.

If a burn goes completely around a piece of skin, the entire surface will turn to scar tissue because the encircling burn cauterizes all the capillaries feeding that section of skin. Therefore, the branding irons should be made without closed loops. For example, Q's and O's should have openings at either the top or the bottom, and the vertical part of B's and P's should be separated from the curved part by a strip of heathy skin.

While your submissive may desire to wear your initials as a gesture of subservience, it is incumbent upon you to overcome the, admittedly intoxicating, feeling of power, and refuse. There is no guarantee that this relationship will last forever. Because submissives give us their power, it is our duty to look out for them and protect them from their own folly. A geometric or symbolic symbol may be more appropriate in the long run.

Brands should never be placed on any part of the body where major blood vessels, bones or nerve clusters approach the skin. Nor should they be where the skin is being constantly bent or where clothing is going to rub against the brand. Remember, this is a burn. It is going to take several weeks or several months to heal. A moment of pain is exciting, but three weeks of it can become tedious. If it stretches to a couple of months of pain, well, nobody can stay hard for that long.

Curved areas should be avoided for aesthetic, rather than physiological, reasons. It is difficult to apply a brand properly on, for example, an upper arm. While highly experienced branders can roll the brand so that it is a consistent depth throughout, even they occasionally find that, after they have done a brand on curved skin, the middle has gone too deep while the edges have barely touched the skin.

The first stage in making a brand is to draw the design on a piece of graph paper exactly as you want it on the submissive's body. Don't forget that the branded lines will spread. A delicate precise design with a lot of narrowly spaced lines will most likely end up as an ugly lump of scar tissue.

The branding iron is made from that design. Because of the necessary breaks to avoid enclosing an area of skin, it is not unusual for a single brand to be made from a number of small irons.

There is no need for a complex branding iron with an attached handle. The most common approach is to use a pair of a locking pliers as a detachable handle. Hemostats are not recommended because their tiny grasping areas preclude a good grip on the hot metal and because they tend to conduct heat too well. The idea is to brand the submissive's body, not the dominant's fingers.

Once the set of irons is finished, branders should practice in exactly the place where they are planning to do the actual branding with exactly the same equipment. A professional should be adaptable, but the middle of a branding scene is no place to have to be dealing with surprises. They may use wet leather, potatoes or a notepad of paper. The notepad has the advantage of allowing them to check precisely how deep the brand has penetrated.

Because branders are not dealing with a thousand pounds of steak tartare on the hoof, they only need to go in about 1/16th of an inch to make a very permanent scar. Holding the iron against the skin for one second is often enough.

Before having the brand done, you must draw the design and transfer it to the submissive's skin.

First, you can trace the design you made on the graph paper onto a piece of tracing paper.

Second, you should turn the tracing paper over and put it on a blank piece of white paper so you can see your original tracing clearly.

Third, you can retrace the design (now reversed) on the back of the tracing paper with a transfer pencil like an ink pencil.

If the area to be branded is hair-covered, you should shave it or have it shaved. Then, have your submissive stand so that the skin will be "hanging" properly. A person wears his or her skin differently when sitting, standing and lying down because of the pull of gravity and the tension on various muscles. You can put a coat of Mennen stick deodorant on the area to be branded, and place the tracing paper on the coated skin with the negative side down and press along on each line with your finger.

Most branders recommend having a few assistants present at the scene itself. The submissive should be held down as well as tied. Not only are people more adaptable in restraining a struggling figure but the touch of humanity has a soothing effect that no leather cuff can match. The brander may also have someone heating up the next part of the set of irons while he or she is making a part of the brand.

The submissive should be secured horizontally. Each component part of the set of irons needs to be heated red hot just before it is used. The person doing the heating should aim a propane torch so that the metal heats from the gripper outward to the branding edge.

Healing will be a lengthy process. Each brander has his or her favorite technique to make the burn heal safely. You should make sure that your submissive follows it to the letter.

A branding iron is almost guaranteed to be completely sterile. However, the wound can become infected later. If cloudy pus comes from the wound, redness or black marks appear, or if the skin becomes hot, a doctor should be contacted immediately.

As I have written, a branding is a serious, serious piece of business, and it should be done only be trained, experienced people. However, I offer the following as an example of how you might be able to satisfy the need in a safe and sensible way.

A number of years ago, a submissive begged me for a branding. At that time, I had never even seen a real branding, and I was certain that I had neither the skills nor the interest to make such an experience work.

Consensuality is a two-way street, and I firmly refused. However, she was lovely and quite persuasive. I was beginning to appreciate the feelings of Adam when he entered the first not-guilty-by-reason-of-insanity plea, "Lord, the woman tempted me."

I never agreed to do the branding, but one day after she had been firmly tied to the bondage table, I brought out a small hibachi. On it was a branding iron with my initial "W." I had borrowed the branding iron from a set used for branding steaks as rare, medium and well-done.

As the iron heated, I played with her a bit with various toys, but whatever I did, her eyes rarely strayed far from the red-hot iron. Occasionally, I took it from the fire and held it close to her thigh while I pretended to evaluate whether the temperature was suitable.

She could not take her widened eyes off the steel block and the colors that chased themselves along its surface in response to the heat-roiled air. Time after time, as the tiny hairs on her skin writhed in the radiated heat, I pronounced, "Not yet, let's let it get a bit hotter."

Finally, when it was almost white hot, I said, "I think it is ready. Do you really want to go through with this?"

She gulped, speechless, but nodded vigorously.

I blindfolded her and then washed her thigh with some very hot water. When she felt the touch of the washcloth she arched and hissed through her teeth, but I said, "I have to make sure it is completely clean; we don't want any infection."

With that, she laid back, but every muscle in her body was standing out in sharp relief.

Then I took the branding iron and held it close to her thigh so she could feel the intense radiated heat. As the skin below the iron became a brighter and brighter shade of red, I asked, "For the last time, do you want to go through with this?"

Again, she nodded.

With one smooth motion, I put aside the branding iron and pressed hard on the reddened, heat-sensitized skin with an ice cube I had concealed in my other hand. Her scream was ear-splitting. She completely lost control of her bowels and bladder and passed out cold.

When she recovered consciousness, I had draped a white cloth over her body (and cleaned up most of the mess). She was almost incoherent in thanking me for what she called the most intense experience of her life. However, when I released her hands and she lifted the sheet, she was completely dumbfounded. I explained what had happened and pointed out that I had never promised to brand her.

Her reaction was a mixture of relief and resentment. I did notice, however, that for the next few days, she would gingerly touch her thigh with a hand as if to check that, indeed, she was not branded.

Some Special Relationship Issues

Contracts of submission

While a contract isn't exactly what we generally call a toy, drawing up, signing and living under a contract of submission can be an exciting experience. While they are obviously not enforceable in court, contracts do have a very practical function: they clearly spell out various rights and responsibilities of each member in the relationship and require both individuals to think about them. They also allow you to define the universe in which you want to live, a created reality.

Clauses usually include:

- The duration of the contract
- Restrictions on where and with whom the submissive (or either) can play
- Limitations on the forms of bondage and discipline used
- Sexual activities permitted
- Types of behavior required for, conduct of and/or work to be done by the submissive
- Safewords
- How the contract may be terminated or modified

Most sample contracts like those in *The Leatherman's Handbook II* and *The Lesbian S&M Safety Manual* strike me as a bit too one-sided. They certainly spell out what the submissive owes to the dominant, but the dominant's duties are considerably more vague. Part of this, I suspect, is because these are sample contracts and, as such, contain more than a bit of fantasy. To give you some fair and realistic models

I am reprinting, in the appendices, two actual contracts between couples, who are active in the BDSM scene. I think you will see the degree of give and take that was necessary to work out these agreements.

Polyamorous play

"Polyamorous" is another of those cloudy words whose meaning seems to change depending upon whom you are speaking. In the simplest form, it means having several partners for sensual play, and as such, it really doesn't fall under the BDSM umbrella with the same certainty as, let's say, flogging or bondage, but I'm including this section for two reasons.

First, successful polyamory shares a number of precepts with BDSM including consensuality and open communications. Second, there is a persistent belief that almost everyone in BDSM is polyamorous. I'll address the second one first.

After many years in the public and private BDSM scene, it's my firm belief that the majority of people who practice BDSM do so in the confines of a monogamous relationship. There are two facets of BDSM culture that tend to obscure this.

First, polyamory is relatively accepted in this subculture. No one raises an eyebrow when a domme arrives at a party with two slaves on a leash or when a dominant invites a submissive to join him and his partner in a three-person scene. It's accepted as part of life, and for that reason, it's done openly and above the board. To people arriving from the vanilla world where such liaisons are generally condemned and therefore conducted covertly, it seems that "these people are everywhere."

When I hear that, I give a little shrug and respond, "They are also everywhere in the vanilla world. You just don't see them." When I was active in the academic and business world, there was rarely a time when someone wasn't speculating if A and B weren't spending too much time together and did A's wife or B's husband "know about it." Parties spawned rumors like leaves falling from oak trees in the fall, and a giggle behind a hand served as an updated version of a scarlet "A" sewn on a Puritan's dress.

Are there more "unconventional linkages" in the scene than in vanilla society? I can't really say, but I do know that the ones in the scene are generally open to "public" view, while those in vanilla society usually lock the doors before locking lips. Because of the bias that multiple partners is somehow unusual, these relationships tend to stand out and seem to be "everywhere." However, many, many couples are quite happy being monogamous.

Polyamory shares the same relationship with "cheating" as BDSM does with abuse. In both cases, the key differences are consent and how the partners feel about the situation.

For a polyamorous relationship to really work, all parties must be aware of what is going on and benefit from it. One of the great myths that dominants fall prey to is "I'm the dominant; what I want is what happens." This ignores the fact that submissives are neither cartoon characters nor legal chattel (although the latter can be a hot fantasy). As I've written before, a dominant who fails to take into account his or her partner's needs eventually ends up partnerless. Many doms have fallen on their faces, when they allow fantasy to write checks their skills can't cash.

Because of the observation that "everyone else has multiple partners" or because it's just a hot fantasy, many novice dominants feel that they need multiple submissives to be properly validated. First, nothing could be further from the truth. The quality of one's dominance comes from one's soul, not from counting the bodies one is surrounded by, and more importantly, like a desire for BDSM, a desire for a polyamorous lifestyle should come from the soul and not be created by an ego-driven need to look good to one's contemporaries. As with BDSM, you should take a long hard look at what you really want as opposed to what you think is expected. Intellectual honesty is important in both realms.

You should also consider what you can really handle, because polyamory is hard work. It's like single-tail play. You may really, really want to give a single-tail whipping (or, less nobly, be seen giving a single-tail whipping), but you can't even think about applying a single-tail to human flesh until you have developed the appropriate skills. There is no equivalent of a pillow target for polyamorous skills; however, you can exercise moderation at first. For example, the two of you can try some casual play with a third party. Afterwards, sit down and talk about how it felt. Did new fantasies appear or did insecurities cloud the fun? Building slowly and limiting your expectations won't guarantee a smooth transition but it is certainly better than running full speed into the psychological reefs.

In managing a polyamorous combination, you have to keep in mind a pair of interrelated fantasies, limits, realities and a multitude of other factors. One relationship coach wrote that, for a relationship to be really successful, each partner has to compromise seventy percent of the time. It may not make good math, but as a piece of practical empiricism, it seems to be pretty accurate. That's just with two people. I have no idea what the percentage needs to be with three... or four... but it surely doesn't get smaller.

To make things even more complex, there are a number of ways people approach polyamory. One of the tricks to making it work is finding a pattern that pleases both you and your partner. Some couples include intercourse in their relationships, while others limit sexual contact to oral play. With others, there is no genital sexual component. Some couples will only play with another as a couple, while each member of another couple is free to play alone.

There will be problems. Accept that up front. Such are inevitable. If you treat them as failures on the part of your partner or of yourself, you will be wearing away the core of the relationships. Problems are opportunities for change. Here, again, communication is the key.

Jealousy is almost impossible to avoid, so an admission of that early on can go a long way in limiting the power of the green-eyed goddess. Also, jealousy isn't limited to submissives. It's not unknown for a dominant to feel a little put out when submissives begin to discover pleasures that don't entirely include us. What's the best way to minimize it? It's communications, again. It's easy and more comfortable simply to create an environment where your partners feel uncomfortable in expressing jealousy and other insecurities. It's so easy, in fact, that many people do it unconsciously. This is the emotional equivalent of putting a book on top of a pressure cooker because the noise of escaping steam annoys you. It's a workable short term solution, but you end up with a big explosion down the line.

A better approach is to search out to just what is making any of you insecure and see if it can be dealt with. Sometimes the solution is as simple as just letting A know when you are going to be playing with B so he or she isn't surprised. For example, Libby and I have a rule that anyone who wants to play with either of us, negotiates it with the other. That way each of us knows what and where the other is.

Dealing with expectations upfront is another way of keeping jealousy under control. As with one-on-one scene negotiations, knowing what each party wants out of the relationship lets you either craft a mutually rewarding situation or recognize "this ain't gonna work." Just as before, recognizing the unworkability of a connection isn't a judgment on any individual. It's just an acceptance of the complexity of this world and how difficult it is to match needs and expectations.

Generally, I find those who seek polyamorous relationships are often disappointed, generally by this very complexity. It seems the best approach is to be open to a polyamorous approach if the situation presents itself, but not to be forced into what may turn out to be an unsatisfactory situation because of perceived outside pressures or unrealistic expectations.

Suggested Reading
The Ethical Slut: A Guide to Infinite Sexual Possibilities, Dossie Easton & Catherine A. Liszt, Greenery Press

Protocol

In the world of BDSM, "protocol" is a word that has many meanings. Protocol, as in the vanilla world, can be the lubricant that allows disparate individuals to work together with a minimum of friction. As outlined in the chapter on party behavior, these rules are pretty much common sense and probably wouldn't even be needed if individuals remembered the behavior they had been taught at their mother's knee still applies, even in what seems like a no-holds-barred atmosphere of a play party.

What I'm writing about here is more like the created protocol of the military, the sign and countersign of Masons, the salute and pass-in-review of a regiment, the kneeling or prostration of a slave when his or her master enters the room, using both hands to pass anything to an honored guest, or even a submissive using third person to refer to himself or herself. Viewed from a lofty detachment, these protocols have no obvious utility, but they can touch deeply into the soul of both the dominant and the submissive.

We do not live in a slave-holding society. In fact, the real world where all but the most favored of kinky people live is one of transcendent egalitarianism. We need the symbols to remind ourselves that the world within is strikingly different from the world without.

For example, most slaves and submissives are out in the professional and work world where they are often required to take on the mantle of control and order others about, when their soul yearns for the different world with very different duties. As simple an act as touching a collar disguised as a necklace, or a bracelet camouflaging a cuff, can be immensely reassuring that his or her secret world exists.

Just as an astronaut has to pass through an airlock to go from the incredibly hostile world of space into the comfortable confines of the shuttle, some kinky people need a tangible transition as they move into their personal world. One couple I know of has the slave, each evening upon returning from work, kneel before her master and take her oath of obedience. Others reserve a special collar to symbolize that now they have moved from an inner, thought-driven BDSM to one of touch and action.

Groups also have protocol. These can be valuable in reminding the members of their special status. One of the things that I loved about the Marines was knowing I was part of something bigger than I was, both in size and time. When we did a pass in review on the drill field at Quantico, we were going through the same ceremony that warriors had been doing in precisely the same way back to the time that Queen Anne's muster masters used it to assure themselves that a unit could march in formation and the officers could use their swords with skill and precision. That sort of thing touches the soul.

Sadly, BDSM doesn't have that sort of history to fall back upon. The earliest still-existent organization is TES (The Eulenspiegel Society), and it dates only to the 1970s. Those that went before, like the loose confederation of gay motorcycle clubs that has become known as "The Old Guard" and social/sexual groups like Hellfire, weren't big on producing policies and procedures manuals. People can guess, but often the guesses seem to be more based on wish fulfillment and projection rather than objective research. I'm so much more comfortable being told that, "These are our protocols, and we're comfortable with them," than, "This is going to be a genuine old guard induction ceremony." But then, that's just me.

Protocol doesn't have to have the weight of history behind it. It needs only to touch the souls of those involved and speak to their needs.

13 Saving the Scene on Film

Head back, mouth open, every muscle standing out in bold relief, few things in this world are more beautiful than a submissive in the middle of a session. It is little wonder that most of us have dabbled in photography to make some of their beauty ours forever. The sad truth is we often manage to capture little of the reality and none of the fantasy. The pictures come out stiff and unreal or technically flawed, and they serve only as souvenirs to jog our memories.

What went wrong? Probably several things.

The most common errors start with too little preparation and expecting too much. We accept that the keys to a good BDSM session are preparation and control. Nothing will break a mood faster than the dominant digging through a set of drawers muttering imprecations while searching for a riding crop or discovering that *that* chain won't reach *this* hook.

If you simply pick up a camera for a grab shot, that is what you will get – a grab shot with little to redeem it. Surprisingly for some, the more expensive the camera the more likely this will be true. Expensive camera are considerably more versatile than cheap ones, but they are more demanding and less tolerant of sloppy technique. My Nikon F has literally thousands of possibilities for wrong settings on the controls.

The key to good photos is planning.

You should set aside a session for photography, arrange the room for it and decide the activities that will yield the most photogenic results. Choreograph the activities so you know everything that will be happening when you take the picture. Photographers call this process pre-visualization.

Check what will be in the background. Remember you are creating a mood and don't want distractions. I remember one shot a friend took showing his wife in full suspension. Truly lovely, except, in the background was a crayon sketch their child had made at school that they had stuck on the bedroom wall. It was so incongruous that, instead of appreciation, the picture produced giggles. Digital cameras are superior to conventional cameras in preventing this sort of thing because, presenting the image on a screen instead of a viewfinder, they invite you to look at the image as a whole rather than what you are focusing upon.

One of my pictures has a shelf that seems to be growing out of the side of the subject's head. The impact of a picture can be spoiled by such a little thing as clutter on a bedside table. Even professionals forget to check the background in the heat of the moment, and we do expect these moments to be heated. This sort of thing can be dealt with using a program like PhotoShop, but how much easier it is to simply not to make the mistake in the first place?

After you have gotten rid of the distractions, consider what kind of background props you could use to enhance the mood. Whips and chains on the walls are nice, of course, but don't forget the power of symbolism. One of my favorite shots shows one of my submissives, arms spread wide and chained to rings in opposite walls with horizontal chains. Her back is toward the camera, and she is facing a blank wall on which a crucifix hangs.

I have a strong prejudice toward faces. My greatest turnon is to watch the expression on my submissive's face. Therefore my camera tends to dwell on that part of the anatomy rather than "where the action is."

Don't overlook lighting. It can add immensely to the impact. It helps a lot to have a good camera with manual controls or at least a manual override. However, good results can be had with automatic cameras if you put a little effort into tricking them. You don't need an expensive set of lights, but it helps. You can get clip-on reflectors at the local discount store and photoflood bulbs at a photographic supply store. A note of warning: make sure the reflectors are solid metal. Photofloods are hot, and silver-coated plastic won't stand it. For the same reason, handle them with care.

Silhouettes are dramatic, and thanks to apartment owners insisting on white walls, they are easy to obtain. Simply put the lights so they shine on the walls instead of the submissive. If you don't have a white wall, tacking up a white sheet will do. Try putting a bare bulb, just an ordinary lamp without the shade, behind the subject. This will create a glow around the darkened body and highlight the hair.

Dramatic, contrasted lighting really sets the mood for bondage. Put your lights at right angles to the camera and outside the camera's field of view. If you are using an automatic camera, put something between the lights and the camera. Some of the light sensors on automatics have a wider angle than the camera lens and can be confused by an off-camera "hot spot." You can also get really dramatic lighting effects by using a focused source of light like a slide projector.

Another source of contrasted light is candles. Although they are relatively dim, you can use a tripod and the bulb setting on a manual camera to keep the shutter open. This takes experimentation, but it is well worth it. An advantage of bondage is, if you do it right, the subject isn't going to move during the exposure.

To soften the effect of candle light without overpowering it completely, use an electronic flash and a slow shutter speed. By keeping the shutter open for a relatively long time, you capture the image of the candle flame, and the instantaneous blast of light from the flash fills in the shadows. Again, a bit of experimentation is needed, but the effects are well worth it.

Another interesting source of light is a strobe. I don't mean the electronic flash unit that has replaced flashbulbs. I'm talking about the blink, blink, blink flasher that was made popular in the '60s that is still sold by places like Radio Shack.

The beauty of this kind of dramatic lighting is that the flashes are so short that it is virtually impossible for the individual pictures to be blurred. Unlike candlelight, strobe light is most dramatic when the subject is in violent motion because one exposure can capture a number of images depending on how often the light flashes. Care should be used when employing strobe lights, although. They have been known to cause seizures.

We all want to be part of the action, but leaving the camera and entering the picture has its own set of problems. Ideally, you can leave the camera in another's hands. This will yield incalculably better pictures as the camera is being controlled by a conscious eye and an aware brain. Unfortunately, this isn't the kind of thing you can ask of the helpful next-door neighbor (unless your neighbor is infinitely more fun than mine). Lacking a third body, most people turn to some sort of remote triggering device, and they are deeply disappointed in the results.

It seems too simple to set the camera on a tripod, step into the action, and produce an erotic masterpiece. In reality, using a remote-triggered camera for anything more complex than a simple, "OK, everybody, look at the camera and scream" calls for considerable thought and planning if the result is even to approach acceptable standards. While it is difficult to mix a real BDSM session with photography, it is almost impossible to mix a session with remote photography. If you want to use a remote camera, plan a photo session which will include BDSM rather than a BDSM session which will include photography.

There are several ways to trigger a camera indirectly, like self-timers, air releases and wireless releases. The self-timer is the most common and the most difficult to get good pictures with. You set the timer, actuate it, run around into the action and wait for the timer to run out. This is a bigger mood wrecker than dead batteries in a vibrator.

There is simply no way to maintain the rhythm of a session while fiddling with a camera, running around and posing. To make this worse, you can't really know when the timer will run out. This makes shooting anything other than a frozen tableau an exercise in frustration. Take a whipping; out of the five seconds it takes to take a stroke, only one shot or less is of any photographic value. Factor in Murphy's Law, and you might as well be playing poker with a guy named "Doc."

An air release is a squeeze bulb connected by a thin, flexible tube to a plunger on the camera. Squeezing the bulb causes the plunger to trigger the camera. Some electronic cameras have replaced the air-operated plunger with a solenoid fired by a button you can hold in your hand, but the principle is the same. This has the advantage that you know exactly when the camera is going to go off. The disadvantage is that the tube or wire may show up in the picture. Wireless releases work in a similar fashion, except that radio waves or infrared light replace the wire.

As important as planning is in a conventional photo session, it is an order of magnitude more important when you are using a remote camera. One of the most common errors is to cut your own head off or lose an arm to a picture border.

Use the submissive as a registration point and plan what you are going to do around that point. Don't forget to allow for perspective. If you are going to be in front of the registration point, you will be larger and more likely to be cut off. This problem is heightened if you are using a wide angle lens, which amplifies perspective. The easiest thing is to stay in the same plane, the same distance from the camera, as the submissive or to get behind him or her.

I also block out the frame. Before the session I set up several camera locations and mark where the tripod touches the floor with masking tape. Then, sighting through the camera, I have the submissive mark the floor at the edges of the camera's frame (what it can "see") with strips of tape. That way, when I have set up the camera at one of the marked locations, I can just look down at the floor to see if I am in the horizontal part of the frame.

Blocking the vertical parts are more difficult. This is why I suggest you remain in the same plane with the submissive. By remembering where his or her head is in reference to the edge of the frame, you can judge how you are fitting. I also use a spare light stand. By putting it where I intend to stand with the top of the lamp where my head will be, I can adjust the camera so I will be completely in the frame when I take my position replacing the light stand.

Whether we are part of the picture or our camera dwells on the magnificence of submission, the beauty we create in our submissives can be ours forever. The camera is a natural adjunct to chains, whips and the erotic stimulation we lavish on those we control.

Once the pictures have been taken, there is the temptation to show them around. There is an old saying, "Don't write anything or take a picture of anything you don't want shown in open court." I'm not that paranoid, but I respect the sentiment.

This is where being part of a group can be valuable. You can bring prints to a meeting or a munch (if the rules allow it), pass them around, bask in the admiration and retrieve them for safe storage.

Online is a whole different matter. There is no such thing as "sharing" electronically. It's always "giving away." Once you have sent an electronic image to anyone you have effectively lost all control of it. From a legal point of view, you still retain the copyright and theoretically have complete control over how the picture is used. You also have a complete right to go through an intersection when the light is green, not that it does you much good if the other car doesn't feel like respecting that right. Depending unthinkingly on either right, can leave your life a pile of smoking wreckage.

To make things worse, as I said, in the section about going from online to face-to-face, you don't really know someone until you've met them face-to-face. The "best friend" you have online might be quite different from how you imagine him or her. About the best "bad news" you can get is to discover that your photo is now on someone else's website or in an advertisement with another person's name attached to it.

That's the best news.

What happens if your name is attached to the photo?

Sadly, there isn't much you can do. Oh, you can sue. That's expensive, and worse, it requires an explicit admission from you in public that this, indeed, is your photograph. Newspapers and television news programs provide a valuable service to the community, but they also have a ravenous appetite for trivial scandal. In the late 196/, Andy Warhol promised everyone fifteen minutes of fame. Do you want this to be yours?

The best way to prevent it is to be careful with what you do with photographs, particularly in this digital age.

A graphics designer friend of mine suggested a unique approach that has the added fillip of embarrassing the person who's trying to embarrass you. I'm not certain of how well it would really work, but I'll pass it on with a chuckle. Before she sends out any pictures of herself, she runs them through her computer, carefully cuts off the head and pastes it back on, a pixel or two out of register. It's her plan that, should any of the pictures come back to haunt her, she'll announce it's a fake and point out that the head was "obviously" grafted on from another picture.

Making Leather Toys

Naked, except for leather cuffs and collar, the submissive stands before the master. Clad from head to toe in leather, the mistress enters the dungeon. Cool leather against the throat and the touch of a leather glove sliding possessively along the small of the back.

There is something about leather, its texture, its color, even its smell. It calls to us. Unfortunately, that call has a price tag. Leather goods are not cheap, and the very special items we use in the scene are even more expensive than the semi-vanilla coats, dresses and gloves we admire in the display windows of such paragons of the status quo as Saks and Bergdorf Goodman.

The flip side of this is that somebody did make the whips, cuffs and collars we admire. There is no magic in leather work. A whip need not be made by the dark of the night while obscure odors rise from a bubbling, nearby pot and ancient hags chant in a forgotten language. (It might be fun, but you don't have to do it that way.)

For basic leather work, only a few basic tools and supplies are needed.

- A metal straightedge will allow you to draw straight lines and make straight cuts
- Shears with serrated blades are invaluable when cutting light- and medium-weight leather
- A Strip-Ease draw gauge cuts straps of even widths with a replaceable razor blade
- A mat knife with replaceable blade is useful for general cutting
- A moderately light hammer can be used for setting rivets and other fasteners

- A pounce wheel or space marker is used for indicating evenly spaced marks for hand sewing
- An edge beveler takes a sliver off a thick piece of leather to give a beveled trim along the side
- A rotary punch has tubes of various sizes for punching holes in leather
- A cutting board should be made out of soft wood
- An anvil serves as a backstop for hammering or pounding
- A few heavy needles for sewing the pieces of leather together
- Expendable supplies consist of: leather glue, waxed thread, sharpening stone

First, let's look at some basic techniques.

Perhaps what's most important to recognize is that you are going to make mistakes at first. True, leather is expensive, but it is better to "waste" some leather practicing than to make the mistakes during a major project. Begin by practicing techniques on scrap leather.

There are three basic ways to cut leather: with free-hand knives, with shears and with a draw gauge.

When cutting with a knife, always place the leather flat against a soft wood surface. Press a ruler against the leather and draw the knife along the ruler's edge. There is no need to cut completely through the leather with one stroke. Many strokes will cut even the thickest piece.

Don't hesitate to resharpen the knife frequently. There is no such thing as too sharp a knife. Even replaceable blades can be touched up with the sharpening stone.

Shears can be used to cut both light- and medium-thickness leather and are preferred when there a lot of curves to be cut. However, knives work best on long straight runs.

A draw gauge cuts even strips, and it is invaluable for collars, cuffs and whip lashes. After you make a single, guide cut, it will make another cut a constant distance from the first. It requires a firm grip and a steady pull, but it produces a fine, even cut. One version of the draw gauge, called the Stript-Ease, is inexpensive and uses replaceable razor blades.

Use an edging tool to put a bevel in the edge of the heavy leather you are going to use for a collar or cuff. They come in sizes 1 (smallest) to 5 (largest) and have a U-shaped blade that you push along the edge.

To make the bevel smoother, you can sand it with fine sandpaper or emery paper.

There are several ways to attach two pieces of leather together. The two most common are sewing and gluing. Often they are used in conjunction with each other.

Hand sewing is quite simple because you aren't expected to shove the needle through leather. Use the pounce wheel and a ruler to make a series of evenly spaced marks on the leather and then poke a hole through with a hammer and punch or with what is called a saddler's awl. With the holes already in place, sewing is a cinch.

Two basic stitches are the running stitch and the backstitch. With the running stitch, you simply go down through one hole and up through the next. The backstitch is made after the running stitch is completed. While the running stitch went down through the first hole, with the backstitch, you come up through that hole. This way, thread is on both sides of the leather.

Often, you will want to glue two pieces together before sewing. In fact for some applications, you can just glue and avoid sewing. There are adhesives sold specifically for leather. One of my favorites is Tandy Leathercraft Cement. However, there are many others, and most do a very good job.

The basic process is to coat both pieces of leather with the cement, let them dry and then press the pieces together. They will form a permanent bond almost instantly, but you should tap them with a mallet to assure that the bond is solid.

Because the bond is instantaneous, if you are connecting two pieces that have to be in perfect alignment, use the slip-sheet method. You should prepare the pieces with cement and let them dry. Then you can put a sheet of paper or clear plastic over one piece. The other piece should be placed on top of the paper or plastic. You should make sure that the pieces are in perfect alignment and then slowly pull the paper or plastic from between them, pressing down on each section as the pieces come in contact.

Rivets can be used for decoration or as another method of fastening two or more pieces of leather together. First, you can use your rotary punch to make a hole through the leather, lay the rivet post over the pounding board, and place the punched leather over the post. You should make sure that the pretty side is up. If you are connecting two pieces of leather, make sure that the bottom one has the pretty side down.

You can choose a rivet that is the correct size. This may take a bit of practice. A rivet that is too short will not make a permanent connection, and one that is too long will not make a firm connection. About an eighth of an inch of the male part of the rivet should be showing above the leather after you have inserted in the hole in the leather. Then you can just put the female end of the rivet onto the prong and strike it sharply with the setting tool. The two will be permanently connected.

Snaps are easy to close and easy to take off. For this reason, they aren't really useful for anything that will be used for restraint. However, they are great for decorative collars and cuffs.

There are four parts to a snap. Two go together in one piece and two go together in the other. Each brand is slightly different so you should follow the instructions carefully. As with rivets, practice is essential before you attempt to set a snap in a for-real project.

For items you will use for restraint, buckles are effective fasteners. Generally, the simplest, a single-bar buckle, is best. The oblong slot for the prong can be cut away with your mat knife, but special oblong punches are also available. You can expect your buckles to be taking a lot of pressure so it is wise to glue, sew and rivet them in place.

Black leather is traditional for scene activities, and while any color is acceptable, many people like the look of black. This means your leather will have to be dyed. Fortunately, dyeing is quite easy.

The basic rule is that the leather must be clean and dry before you begin. If the leather has grease or oil on it, you should get some leather cleaning solution. Do not use saddle soap for cleaning at this point because that is for cleaning finished projects.

Dyes are available in both oil- and water-based formulas. Since scene gear is often worn close to the skin, and during a scene sweating is not uncommon, so I recommend an oil-based dye.

Dye can be applied in several ways. For large areas, you can use a soft cloth or piece of woolskin you can buy at leather craft stores. If you use woolskin, soak it in mineral oil to keep it from absorbing too much of the dye. The dye should be in a shallow pan. Pouring it out from the bottle onto the applicator takes too much time, and it is likely to result in an uneven application. You should apply the dye with broad, smooth strokes. Once you start, do not stop. Going back once the dye has dried never gives a good result.

For smaller areas, the use of a dauber is best. You can make one with a bit of cotton waste or woolskin on a piece of wire. It looks like the dauber in a shoe polish bottle.

Once the dye is dry, you should rub the are with a soft cloth to remove the excess dye. Finally, for a glossy, water resistant finish, you can use Omega Finish Coat or Fieding Tan-Kote.

Omega Carnauba Creme gives a soft, lustrous finish. However, saddle soap, or even Vaseline petroleum jelly, will do the job quite well.

Some leatherwork projects

Now, let's look at three simple projects you can do, a whip, a blindfold and a pair of wrist cuffs.

For the whip, you need an eight-inch by 22-inch rectangular piece of leather and a six-inch-long dowel. You must draw a line six inches from one end of the piece of leather and then cut a series of strips, 1/2 inch wide, from the other end to this line. This should give you a fringe-like affair of about 16 strips, 1/2 inch wide and 16 inches long.

Next you can put the wooden dowel against one side of the un-cut part of the leather and roll the leather around it. You now have a workable cat. All you need to do is nail the leather against the dowel, and you are ready to whip.

Of course, you may want to fancy up the whip by dyeing it or putting rivets or studs in the handle. However, for all practical purposes, you are finished

6 INCHES

6 INCHES

22 INCHES

Making a blindfold is a bit more complex. You will need two circular pieces of leather and two circular pieces of rabbit fur or lamb's wool three inches across, one piece of leather 33 inches long by half an inch across, and a metal buckle.

You can cut two three-inch-long pieces off the 33-inch strip. One of these should be riveted to the good side of each circular piece of leather. Each strip should have two rivets one inch in from the side. This will leave one inch between each pair.

Next you can glue the fur circles to the opposite side of each piece of leather and attach the buckle with a rivet to the end of the long strip of leather, which should be 27 inches long now. Finally, you must slide the strap under the leather strips on the circular pieces.

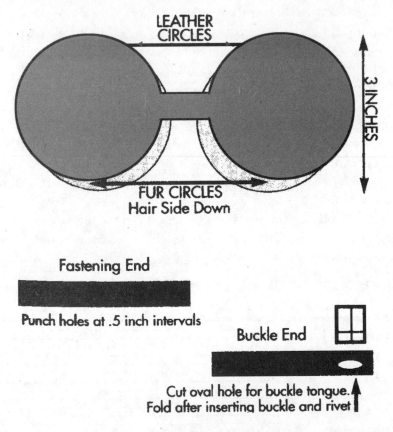

LEATHER CIRCLES

3 INCHES

FUR CIRCLES
Hair Side Down

Fastening End

Punch holes at .5 inch intervals

Buckle End

Cut oval hole for buckle tongue.
Fold after inserting buckle and rivet

The most complex project I'm going to get into is a leather cuff. This kind of cuff can be used either on wrists or ankles but cannot be used for suspension.One cuff requires:

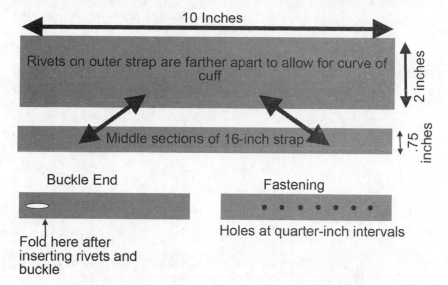

10 Inches

Rivets on outer strap are farther apart to allow for curve of cuff

2 inches

Middle sections of 16-inch strap

.75 inches

Buckle End

Fastening

Holes at quarter-inch intervals

Fold here after inserting rivets and buckle

- A ten-inch by two-inch rectangle of heavy leather
- A ten-inch by two-inch rectangle of heavy rabbit fur or lamb's wool
- A 16-inch by 3/4 inch strap of leather
- A belt-type buckle

To start, you should cut an oblong hole in one end of the 16-inch strap to let the tongue of the buckle go through and move. Then, you must glue and rivet the buckle in place by cutting the other end into a "V" and putting holes for the buckle's tongue not more than 1/4 inch apart for at least eight inches.

The next step is to put the assembled "belt" on the leather rectangle. The end of the buckle should be about a 1/2 inch from one end. You can rivet the belt to the rectangle four inches from that end of the rectangle and put a D-ring over the far end of the belt before sliding it up against the rivet.

This next is important. You must bend the incomplete cuff around an object until you can fasten the belt as tightly as could you ever expect to do it. Now, you need to mark the position for the next rivet on both the strap and on the leather rectangle. It should go seven inches further along the strap than the first rivet. You can now unbuckle the belt and set the rivet. The belt should be buckling out from the leather rectangle if the rivet is set in the right place. If it is tight against the leather, you will not be able to curve the cuff to put it on.

If you expect your submissive to enjoy struggling, you might add another pair of rivets halfway between the two you have set, with the D-ring between them. It isn't necessary, but it holds a bit more securely. The final step is to glue the fur on the inside of the cuff.

Suggested Reading
21st Century Kinkycrafts, Janet W. Hardy (ed), Greenery Press

Your Secret Dungeon

A while back I visited a personal dungeon belonging to some members of Black Rose, the Washington, D.C., BDSM group. Located in a finished basement, it was a fantasy paradise. The walls and ceiling were painted black and decorated with a profusion of straps, paddles, ropes and whips. Wall-to-wall red carpeting covered the floor, and the place was lit with a number of aimed, colored accent lights on the ceiling. The equipment included a suspension frame made of heavy timbers, a leather-covered spanking bench and a barred jail cell.

Not all of us are lucky enough to have a space that we can set aside for such a room. In fact, this particular dungeon was almost as large as many New York apartments. However, with a little imagination, we can put together a room suitable for entertaining vanilla friends which can be quickly converted to more energetic activities. The key to this decorating is a term I borrowed from friends in the intelligence community: plausible deniability. This means that every item has a plausible vanilla use, so you can answer any suspicion with an innocent blank stare.

The centerpiece of such a room is a table suitable for bondage. If you look at the coffee tables in a furniture store, you will find that some of them are too delicate for such activities, but others are quite firmly put together. You should seek one at least four feet long. This length will support any head and torso combination. The legs can be allowed to bend at the knees and hang over. However, my feeling is, the longer the better. There is something delicious about a submissive spread out and available like a buffet.

When you get it home, put a series of attachment points about six inches to a foot underneath the overhang of the top. Of course, if you really want to generate curious questions, you can put them along the edge. Screw eyes are acceptable, but I prefer cleats from a marine supply store. These are used to attach boats to piers and look like squashed H's resting on their side. Their advantage is that ropes attached to them can be untied quickly and easily.

If your submissive enjoys a bit of additional stimulation while tied up, get a non-skid chair-pad from an office supply store, and trim it so it fits the top of the table. The little plastic spikes on the bottom of the pad provide an interesting surface for any submissive to lie on. You should provide padding or make a cutout in the pad so the submissive's head and, if appropriate, knees or elbows are protected from the bed-of-nails effect. The pad can easily be stored out of sight when not in use.

As I noted in the "Cutting" section of the *Fun and Games* chapter, a futon, with or without its pad, is the perfect bondage frame. However, most are put together too delicately to restrain an enthusiastic submissive. You need to drill a few pilot holes and reinforce where each slat is connected to its brace. The original screw and a three-inch reinforcing screw will withstand almost any conceivable stress that a submissive bound in place on the frame could produce. Naturally, this is another place where the reversed office mat can find an application.

By throwing the futon's padded mat over the raised back, you have a perfect surface for spanking or cropping. You can have the submissive stand behind the futon and bend forward so his or her hands are touching the seat and tie the hands to the crossbars at the front of the seat with the legs tied to the vertical braces on either end of the end. This provides a beautiful, spread target. If, despite the pad, the submissive is uncomfortable, try doubling up the pad to cut down on the pressure on his or her stomach.

Another piece of Asian furniture that lends itself to bondage is a Korean Papa San chair. The basic configuration is a bowl made of heavy pieces of curved bamboo with a circular pad that fits inside the bowl. The whole thing rests on something that looks like a giant egg-holder. This chair can be used for bondage in its "normal" configuration with the submissive either sitting with feet on the floor and hands and knees tied to the rim, or it can be used with the submissive sitting in the lotus position with his or her hands and knees tied to the rim.

However, if you put the bamboo-frame bowl upside down on the floor, its real potential for bondage comes out. Here we have a dome-shaped frame on which a submissive can be tied in a multitude of ways while arched to receive stimulation. Simply as an objet d'art, such a combination of bamboo and flesh is a prize to be cherished.

If you enjoy spanking, a heavily padded loveseat (what an appropriate name) or an antique cobbler's bench provide a perfect surface, while not exciting any comments at all from vanilla visitors.

If you have exposed beams, you have an ideal place to put a few screw eyes. Paint them black or the same color as the beams, and most people won't notice them. Few of us ever look up unless something catches our eye. Further camouflage can be provided by a hanging plant or two.

For the floor, I've seen some plate-and-ring units that fit right into the floor and, when not in use, lie perfectly flat. Of course, they require that you use a chisel or router to make an appropriately sized hole in the floor, but once in place they are almost unnoticeable. The people who had them said that they were purchased at a marine supply store.

If you don't want to put in permanent eyebolts, get a pair of heavy carpentry clamps and fasten them to the top of a door. You can then put someone in standing bondage against the door. Exercise stores also sell removable chinning bars that provide an attachment point that should be fairly secure.

While it wouldn't be appropriate for the living room, a free-standing swing set would not be out of place in a playroom or in the cellar, and it provides a perfect brace for standing bondage or even a bit of suspension. If you don't have children, you can deflect suspicion with a casual comments such as, "The last tenants left this, and we haven't gotten around to taking it down," or, "Isn't it cute? We got it to try to recapture some of the memories of our youth."

Even more discreet is a simple ladder. After all, everyone needs to change light bulbs or dust for cobwebs. Even an ordinary ladder provides a multitude of attachment points for naughty submissives, and modern technology has made the ladder even better. A neighbor has a Rube-Goldberg-type ladder, called a MultiMatic™, that is jointed so that it can be converted into a conventional straight ladder, a step-ladder, a scaffolding or into a number of other forms. Occasionally,

I borrow the ladder with an appropriately vague excuse. If only he knew.

In the bedroom, a four-poster or a Shaker-style pencil-post bed fits right in. However, you should make your attachments as close as possible to the frame. A friend literally pulled her pencil-post bed apart when her lover tied the ropes from her legs to the top of the posts. The combination of her orgasm, the strength in her legs and the leverage provided by the long post was too much for the antique. The bed was repaired, but the relationship did not fare as well.

Antique brass beds provide a multitude of attachment points. Modern beds, particularly water beds or those designed like water beds, are less congenial. However, a series of marine cleats or screw eyes along the base of the bed, under the mattress overhang, increase the utility of these beds from a bondage point of view. If you have a waterbed, make sure that the attaching screws have not penetrated the wood to rest against the mattress material. This kind of oversight could give a whole new meaning to the term "water sports."

Modern beds can be turned into an exceptionally versatile bondage surface by adding Sportsheets. These are described in more detail in the *Opening the Toybox* chapter.

Lighting is important in setting the scene. In most cases, this is as simple as unscrewing the white bulbs in a few selected sockets and replacing them with colored lights. However, anyone who has watched late-night movies knows dungeons often have flickering torches. Unfortunately for the modern dungeon master, the old dungeons also had stone walls. Romantic torches are not kind to wallboard walls and ceilings. However, I've found electric lights that flicker just like candle flames. A cluster of these gives an impression of a torch (if you squint really hard).

With a little work and a bit of imagination, you can have it all, kinky dungeon and vanilla home.

Party Manners

Being invited to your first scene party can be a great thrill, but at the same time, it can be a nervewracking experience. However, if you're reasonably able to deal with people as people, have been housebroken to the point that you won't embarrass yourself and others in a well-run mall and have a bit of common sense, you shouldn't have any problems.

Of course, the rules among groups vary. Some groups, like Threshold on the West Coast, won't even let you attend one of their parties until you have attended an orientation meeting. Most, however, assume that you are sufficiently intelligent to ask if you're uncertain. The problem lies with knowing what to ask about.

Clothing

Most scene people are casual about clothing, but at the same time, a Lacoste shirt and Eddie Bauer jeans can "suck energy" from a scene. This doesn't mean you have to invest two months of pay in a leather outfit complete with codpiece. Basic black is always acceptable. Ladies can let their imagination run wild. I've never seen an outfit too extreme for a scene party.

However, and this is a big however, when the party is held in a private home the hosts may not want to advertise their orientation to the entire neighborhood. It might be a good idea to slip on something over the outfit or carry it in a paper bag.

Punctuality

In much of the vanilla world, an 8 p.m. party invitation means showing up sometime after 8:30. If you are going to a scene party, arriving at 8:45 may mean facing darkened windows and locked doors.

Both for security (imagine a neighbor coming over for a cup of sugar) and to prevent the rhythm of the scenes from being broken, many parties lock the doors after the action begins.

Parking

You may be told to park in a particular place. Do it. Many people don't want to advertise the party with cars lining the street outside their house.

Tag-along guests

Even more than at a sit-down dinner for a head of state, unwanted and unknown guests are a no-no at a scene party. It is all right to ask, once, but if the answer is "No," drop it right there.

Anonymity

Expect to cultivate a selective amnesia about people. At the party, they are who they say they are. You might make a hit by saying, "Gee, I recognize you. I loved your last picture," but it is more likely you'll find yourself shunned as a barbarian. After the party, forget who you met until the next party. You may think you are being cute by saying, "Remember me? We met at Irene's party," to a familiar face, but a more likely result is no more invitations. If you see someone, a shy smile indicating vague recognition is about as far as you can go unless they respond.

If you really want to meet that little red-headed submissive you played with last night, it is permissible to call the host and give him or her your phone number to pass on if possible. It is the height of bad manners to ask for anyone else's phone number, except from the person in question.

To make this easier, I keep some small printed cards in my toy belt. They have my name, post office box address and telephone number. It is a lot easier to give someone a card like this than to try to make out a phone number scribbled on the back of a matchbook the next day.

Dungeon masters or dungeon monitors

At large parties, there are often experienced players who are in charge of keeping order and making sure people play safe. They are usually very polite, but their word is law. If one of them says something like, "I don't think it is safe to do that," stop it immediately. The reasonable tone is not an invitation to a debate.

Scene behavior

Usually, there will be one or more areas set aside for scenes. While you are in these areas, keep the casual chitchat to a minimum. It can be very distracting to both the submissive and the dominant in the midst of a scene to overhear someone discussing the stock market. Even if your broker is E.F. Hutton, take the discussion out into a social area.

Give people room to play. By the same token, if you are playing, keep your play reasonable for the space available. You may be proud of your ability to use a bullwhip, but a 10' by 12' scene room during a party is no place to demonstrate it.

If you want to ask someone who is in the middle of a scene a question, ask it after the scene is over. Breaking into a scene is always disruptive and can be dangerous. In some scenes, concentration is vital. In all of them, it is part of the pleasure.

If your scene is messy, clean up after yourself or have your submissive do it. A thoughtful dominant who brings a sheet to catch bits of wax or shaving cream is much more likely to be invited back than one who leaves a pile of litter behind.

If you think someone's scene is dangerous, you can seek out a dungeon master or the host to draw it to his or her attention. Again, debate is not an option. Accept the master's opinion. What you cannot do is stop it yourself or criticize it.

If you simply find a scene distasteful, go somewhere else. No one is making you watch. As an extension of this, displays of homophobia (or for that matter, heterophobia) are in the worst possible taste.

Intoxication

This varies a lot according to the group, but most BDSM groups are pretty straitlaced when it comes to drugs and booze. Some forbid it entirely, while others expect you to limit yourself to a single beer. Drunkenness is a sure ticket to the door. Remember, under the present laws, if you are caught with drugs by the police, the party giver could have his or her house confiscated. That is not good manners.

Party Manners

Some people feel that if they wear their whip on the left side it somehow excuses them from conventional manners. Actually, the opposite is true. Manners didn't arise from the lower classes. They were developed by a bunch of very dominant individuals to keep them from cutting each others' throats at the slightest jostle. Saying "please" and "thank you" to the serving submissives doesn't weaken your air of dominance; it enhances it. The same goes for cleaning up after yourself.

Never use or even touch another person's toys without asking. Most people are proud of their collection and enjoy showing it off. If you damage a toy, offer to replace or pay for it. These things can be very expensive. Assume the first refusal is a courtesy. I would recommend asking three times to show you are serious.

As in the public clubs, submissives are to be looked at but not touched or used in any way unless you are given specific permission. There may be submissives serving the food. Unless you have been told that it is desired, do not attempt to humiliate them in any way.

Safewords

You may assign or have your submissive choose a safeword. However, some parties have a house safeword. This is usually something common like "red light." This assures that the dungeon masters can check on the consensuality of the scene and that any "pick-up" scenes are fully consensual.

Even more than at public clubs, your behavior at private parties can make or break your reputation. You want to make sure that everything you do enhances the reputation that is your most important scene possession. Sending a short note thanking the hosts is always appropriate.

First Aid for The Scene

Just because we are playing does not mean that our submissive won't get hurt at one time or another. We are playing, but we often are playing rough. People get hurt riding bicycles, skating, jogging. My local newspaper carried an item about an elderly lady who, excited about winning at bingo, stood up too quickly, fell back over her chair and broke her collarbone.

This does not mean that we should accept any injuries as part of the game. After everything has returned to normal, it is incumbent upon both of you to sit down and try to prevent whatever happened from happening again. There is nothing contradictory between playing hot and playing safe.

This section is far from a complete first aid guide. I strongly recommend that you supplement it with a conventional first-aid manual. Read them before something happens. When someone is bleeding it is no time to try to assemble a medical education. Many dominants know more about taking care of their toys than their submissives. If I were licensing dominants, I would make a basic first-aid course including CPR one of the minimum requirements.

As the prices drop from four figures to three, I'm becoming a big fan of automatic defibrillators. Defibrillators used to be usable only by highly skilled technicians, if they were to do more good than harm. This new generation has hardwired most of the skills needed right into the machine. Slap on the pads, press the button and the machine will decide what's needed and go ahead and do it while you wait for the EMTs, that you've already called, to arrive.

Make sure your submissive has read this section. While most injuries do happen to submissives, dominants have been known to fall, set themselves on fire during a waxing, or cut themselves with straight razors. I use the word "submissive" throughout for consistency, but don't assume you are somehow bullet-proof.

Both of you should also practice emergency procedures. When things go wrong, sometimes people panic and take refuge in the familiar. One woman vacuumed her carpet while waiting for the paramedics to arrive when her husband had a heart attack. Make the emergency procedures familiar and commonplace, and you'll be much better off when all hell breaks loose.

Cuts and bruises

The most common injuries in the scene, as almost everywhere else, are cuts and bruises. Bruises are unsightly, except to those who wear them as badges of pride, but they generally will disappear after a while. You can speed up healing by putting ice packs on them for no more than a half hour. Hot water will only increase the size and discoloration, and because the skin is not broken, antiseptic or astringent solutions are useless.

You should already have asked if your submissive has a clotting disorder or takes any kind of anticoagulant drug like Coumadin. This will make him or her bruise much more easily.

The greatest danger from cuts is infection. Clean the area with warm water and a mild soap. Then sterilize it with Betadine or alcohol and have the submissive hold a bit of clean gauze against the cut until the bleeding stops. Hydrogen peroxide, recommended by some first-aid books, doesn't sterilize as well and, with repeated use, may actually retard healing. If you think you may have gotten any blood on you, wash carefully with soap and hot water. A Band-Aid can be used to keep the injury clean after the bleeding has stopped.

If, later, the cut gets red and swells, you see red-purple streaks under the skin or it is sensitive to a light touch, it is probably infected. Go to a doctor. Aside from simply being dangerous, an infection greatly increase the chances that a scar will form.

If the bleeding is severe or if it spurts, apply tight pressure with your hand or elastic bandage over the site of the bleeding and call 911. A person can die from a severed artery in seconds. Do not attempt to use a tourniquet unless you have been trained in how to apply one. A poorly applied tourniquet can cause much more damage than you realize.

Unconsciousness

Simply because of the excitement of the scene, because their air supply has been inadvertently cut off or because they have been standing in one place too long, submissives occasionally faint. Some people have the habit of holding their breath during orgasms which causes them to pass out. It is called orgasmic syncope. Diabetics may faint if violent activity causes their blood-sugar level to drop. As I noted in an earlier chapter, you should know your submissive's medical history before you begin to play.

Immediately remove all bondage. If it won't come off fast, cut it off. This is where the EMT scissors or bolt cutters come in handy. The submissive should be on his or her back without anything under the head, with the legs elevated slightly. Smelling salts can be used, carefully ,to awaken the submissive. Do not attempt to do CPR unless the submissive has stopped breathing and you know how. CPR is a wonderful technique but its application is limited to very specific circumstances.

If the submissive remains unconscious for more than a couple of minutes, seek medical help. However, if the submissive recovers and seems all right, you should still keep him or her lying down for at least a half hour. If he or she is a diabetic, offer some food.

Severe chest pains spreading to the shoulder, neck or arm and/or a crushing feeling in the chest accompanying a shortness of breath might mean a heart attack. Call 911 immediately before you do anything else.

If it turns out your submissive was using drugs or alcohol, you have some soul-searching to do. First, why didn't you notice before this? Second, do you want to continue to play with a person who would do such a stupid thing? Obviously, many people will disagree with me, but my basic rule is that drugs and the scene do not mix.

Stroke

A stroke is caused by a leaking blood vessel in the brain. Among the causes is great excitement or agitation (you know, the things we try for in the dungeon). The symptoms include sudden numbness or weakness of the face, arm or leg, especially on one side of the body, sudden confusion, trouble speaking or understanding, sudden trouble seeing in one or both eyes, sudden trouble walking, dizziness, loss of balance or coordination and sudden, severe headache with no known cause.

This condition, more than most others, calls for an immediate 911 call and transportation to the nearest emergency room because the quicker treatment is begun the better the chances of recovery. For example, there is a medication called a "clot buster" that can work wonders in the event of a stroke. However, it must be administered within three hours of the initial attack.

Convulsions

A more frightening experience is if the submissive goes into a convulsion. Remove any bondage immediately, and place a loop of rope or a piece of soft leather in his or her mouth to protect the tongue. Do not use something hard like a whip handle or something vulnerable like your fingers. The first may cause damage to the teeth; the second will be damaged.

Any clothing around the neck and waist should be loosened, and you should place pillows, cushions or rolled blankets around the body. Unless you have reason to believe that these convulsions are not significant (or example, if you know the submissive is epileptic), call for medical assistance.

Head injuries

Head injuries can be time bombs. Television and detective fiction have made people casual about blows to the head. The truth is any blow to the head severe enough to cause unconsciousness is cause for a trip to the hospital. If the membrane covering the brain inside the skull is bruised, a dural hematoma can slowly form over a period of hours, eventually causing unconsciousness and, possibly, death.

At the very least, the injured party should be under observation for a full day following the injury and regular follow up for a few days after that.

Symptoms of serious injury include returning unconsciousness, nausea and or vomiting, swelling, severe headache, stumbling or knocking things over, and confusion. One check for the last is to ask three questions, called "Orientation times three:" "What is your name?" "Where are you?" "What is today's date?" Any errors indicate possible serious problems.

"Misplaced" toys

What do you do when you "lose something inside?" If it is in the vagina and is doesn't have any sharp edges or points, relax. There isn't any place for it to go. Like Mary's lamb, it will soon be back. Losing something in the rectum is more of a problem. Do not try to get it out with an enema. You also shouldn't try to reach in and get it. I know one panicked individual who tried to use what looked like salad tongs. Don't do it!

Lubricate the anus and go sit on the toilet. Bring a good book – this one, maybe. Wait, don't force it. After all, your body wants to get rid of it as much as you do. If it doesn't come out in a few hours or if there is severe pain, go to an emergency room and next time don't use something that can slide all the way in.

Heat-related injuries

Certain kinds of mummification, bondage or vigorous scenes in hot weather can lead to heat cramps, heat exhaustion or heat stroke. Because the human body uses the head to get rid of almost half of the body's heat, a hood by itself can lead to a dangerous increase in body temperature. While none of the injuries in this chapter are limited to submissives, heat-related conditions are a particular threat to dominants who do scenes in hot weather. We tend to pay so much attention to the submissive that we tend to neglect our own needs.

Heat cramps are painful muscle spasms caused by excessive sweating and the loss of salt. This can be treated simply by consuming food or liquid containing salt.

Heat exhaustion is indicated by nausea, faintness, dizziness, excessive sweating and weakness. The individual's skin is pale and clammy, and he or she has a weak pulse and may show signs of shock. The affected person should lie flat with the head down and take drinks of a cool, slightly salty liquids every few minutes. However, you should never offer food or drink to anyone unless he or she can speak and hold up his or her head.

Heat stroke is potentially lethal. Initial symptoms begin like those of heat exhaustion, but soon, the individual develops a fever of more than 104 degrees and may experience convulsions or become unconscious. Cool him or her immediately. Packing in ice or snow is not too extreme, but a more common treatment is wet towels or sheets and a fan. You should call 911. While waiting, check his or her temperature often to make sure you don't overdo the cooling. You want to reduce the temperature, not chill the victim.

Burns

Burns sometimes occur during waxings when a beeswax candle is used or if you are too busy watching where the wax is falling that you don't notice where the flame is going. Electricity can also cause burns.

Reddened skin is the sign of a first-degree burn. Immerse the area in cold water or cool with an ice pack and apply a used tea bag that has been allowed to cool. Aloe vera gel will moderate the pain. Commercial burn ointments are made for this kind of burn. Do not use petroleum jelly or butter.

If blisters form, it is a second-degree burn. Again, the initial treatment is cold water. Then, you must cover the blister with a sterile gauze pad. If the blisters fill with a clear fluid, leave them alone; do not open them. If the fluid is cloudy, they may be infected; this calls for a trip to the doctor.

Third-degree burns are very serious. The injury may, at first, resemble a second-degree burn but quickly progresses to a charred or whitish color, and the surface may be warm and dry. Interestingly enough, it may not be painful at first. This is not because the injury is not serious; it is because the pain nerves have been damaged. This kind of injury is beyond first aid. If you are not trained and equipped to handle this kind of burn, get the submissive to a doctor. Do not use cold water or burn ointment. You can, however, cover it with a sterile dressing.

Bone and muscle injuries

Occasionally, something goes wrong and a submissive takes a severe fall or crashes against something. In most cases, these accidents were caused by simple carelessness – to be precise, *your* carelessness. A common cause of falls is a littered play room, one with wires or ropes scattered about, or one with an ultra-shag carpet that acts as a trap for high heels.

In any case, if there is serious damage, such as broken bones or torn ligaments, you need immediate medical assistance. If you suspect a break, immobilize the limb by tying a rolled-up magazine or ruler to it with a bandage or scarf, and get the person to a doctor.

If the muscle is only strained, the treatment is exactly the opposite as with bruises. You should apply warmth. I tend to lean toward fluffy towels soaked in hot water, which should get the blood flowing again. Then you can wrap it with an Ace bandage and elevate it on a stool or a few pillows.

If a muscle has a minor tear, you will see a large bruise where you should apply an ice pack. Over-the-counter painkillers will help. If the pain continues, go to a doctor.

Dungeon first-aid kit

A good dungeon first-aid kit includes many of the same items as a good home first-aid kit – with two additions. If you do handcuff or chain bondage, it should contain a pair of bolt cutters and an extra set of keys.

I would recommend at a minimum:

- 4x4 sterile dressings
- Ace Bandages
- Adhesive tape
- Aloe vera gel
- Anesthetic spray
- Antibiotic ointment
- Band-aids
- Betadine and/or rubbing alcohol
- Burn ointment
- EMT scissors
- Ice pack
- KY Jelly
- Sling bandage (triangular)
- Smelling salts
- Splint
- Sterile cotton
- Sterile bandage roll
- Tweezers

A final note

I've written several times, "go to a doctor" or "call 911." In the middle of a scene, you, and probably your submissive, are going to be reluctant to climb out of the closet this way. First, medical professionals have seen it before. One of my friends, a lovely dominant and a New York City EMT, was confronted by a man who admitted sticking a gerbil in his wife, where it had, "passed to its reward," and was now stuck. My friend, without looking up from her notepad, said, "Vagina or anus?" They have seen it all before. You probably won't even make the top 100.

Second, but more important, it is your responsibility to care for another individual. You have accepted responsibility for another. To allow, him or her to be put in danger simply because you are embarrassed is irresponsible. You have a duty in these cases to seek medical aid.

To minimize embarrassment, if there is time, change into vanilla clothing. Medical people do tend to give a bit more respect to those who look "normal." If there isn't, grab something out of the closet. If the ER is anything like most, you will have long enough to make a complete outfit from bolt fabric before they get around to you. You can easily change clothes in the rest room. Another thing to bring along is a note pad. Keep track of those who have talked with you. You may want to hand out condemnations or compliments later. In any case, the sight of someone politely taking notes does tend to make people behave.

You don't have to tell the complete story of the scene. If, for example, your submissive fell from a suspension frame and broke her leg, a simple, "she fell," should be sufficient. Male dominants are especially at risk in this area. In today's political-medical environment, if there is a suspicion of "abuse," the less on the chart the better. However, you should never withhold information that could be necessary to the treatment.

Suggested Reading

Toybag Guide to Dungeon Emergencies and Supplies, Jay Wiseman, Greenery Press

Sex Disasters... And How To Survive Them, Charles Moser, Ph.D., M.D., and Janet W. Hardy, Greenery Press

Appendix: Reading Resources

21st Century Kinkycrafts , Janet W. Hardy (ed), Greenery Press

Becoming a Slave, Jack Rinella

The Compleat Spanker, Lady Green, Greenery Press

Consensual Sadomasochism: How to talk about it and how to do it safely, William A. Henkin & Sybil Holiday, Daedalus

Erotic Slavehood: a Miss Abernathy Omnibus, Christina Abernathy, Greenery Press

The Ethical Slut: A Guide to Infinite Sexual Possibilities, Dossie Easton & Catherine A. Liszt, Greenery Press

Exhibitionism for the Shy, Carol Queen, Cleis Press

Family Jewels: A Guide to Male Genital Play and Torment, Hardy Haberman, Greenery Press

Fantasy Made Flesh: The Essential Guide to Erotic Roleplay, Deborah Addington, Greenery Press

The Finer Points of Pain and Pleasure, FifthAngel, Self published [note: FifthAngel is the handsome devil on the front cover of this book – I'm the handsomer devil on the back cover]

Flames of Passion: Handbook of Erotic Fire Play, David Walker & Robert J. Rubel, Power Exchange Books

Flogging, Joseph Bean, Greenery Press

A Hand in the Bush: The Fine Art of Vaginal Fisting, Deborah Addington, Greenery Press

How to Capture a Mistress, Karen Martin, Power Exchange Books

The Human Pony, Rebecca Wilcox, Greenery Press

Intimate Invasions: The Erotic Ins and Outs of Enema Play, M.R. Strict, Greenery Press

Jay Wiseman's Erotic Bondage Handbook, Jay Wiseman, Greenery Press

Leatherfolk, Mark Thompson (ed), Alyson Press

The Leatherman's Handbook: Silver Jubilee Edition, Larry Townsend, L. T. Publications

Leathersex: A Guide for the Curious Outsider and the Serious Player, Joseph W. Bean, Daedalus Press

Master/Slave Relations, Bob Rubel, Power Exchange Books

The Mistress Manual, Mistress Lorelei, Greenery Press

The New Bottoming Book, Dossie Easton & Janet W. Hardy, Greenery Press

The New Topping Book, Dossie Easton & Janet W. Hardy, Greenery Press

Partners in Power: Living In Kinky Relationships, Jack Rinella, Greenery Press

Photography for Perverts, Charles Gatewood, Greenery Press

Play Piercing , Deborah Addington, Greenery Press

Protocols for the Leather Slave, Power Exchange Books

Radical Ecstasy: SM Journeys to Transcendence, Dossie Easton & Janet W. Hardy, Greenery Press

The Seductive Art of Japanese Bondage, Midori, Greenery Press

Sex Disasters... And How To Survive Them, Charles Moser, Ph.D., M.D., and Janet W. Hardy, Greenery Press

The Sexually Dominant Woman: A Workbook for Nervous Beginners, Lady Green, Greenery Press

Slavecraft: Roadmaps for Erotic Servitude, Guy Baldwin

SM 101: A Realistic Introduction, Jay Wiseman, Greenery Press

Ties That Bind, Guy Baldwin

Toybag Guide to Canes and Caning, Janet Hardy, Greenery Press

Toybag Guide to Clips and Clamps, Jack Rinella, Greenery Press

Toybag Guide to Dungeon Emergencies and Supplies, Jay Wiseman, Greenery Press

Toybag Guide to Erotic Knifeplay, Miranda Austin & Sam Atwood, Greenery Press

Toybag Guide to Foot and Shoe Worship, Midori, Greenery Press

Toybag Guide to High-Tech Toys, John Warren, Greenery Press

Toybag Guide to Hot Wax and Temperature Play, Spectrum, Greenery Press

Toybag Guide to Medical Play, Tempest, Greenery Press

Trust, the Hand Book: A Guide to the Sensual and Spiritual Art of Handballing, Bert Herrman, Alamo Square Distributors

When Someone You Love Is Kinky, Dossie Easton & Catherine A. Liszt, Greenery Press

Appendix: Scrubbing Up Afterwards

Cleaning up after a scene can present some interesting problems that are often not completely covered in Good Housekeeping books. While you may delegate the actual clean-up to your submissive, it is, after all, your property, and you will probably want to supervise, with or without a riding crop.

When speaking about cleaning, in most cases, the goal is disinfection rather than sterility. Disinfection is the removal or killing of pathogenic (sickness-causing) organisms. Sterility means there is no life. While sterility is the aim with toys like needles which break the skin, it is difficult to obtain and even more difficult to maintain. With most toys, our aim is purely not to transfer any "bad stuff" from one submissive to another.

Cooled wax from your submissive's skin can easily be vacuumed up if this is done before it is ground into a carpet or into the cracks in a wood floor. Hot wax that falls on fabric is more difficult to remove. However, if you put a soft, absorbent cloth over the cooled wax and then heat the cloth with an iron, the wax will melt and be absorbed into the cloth. I have had particularly good luck with using this technique on a black, velvet-covered chair I occasionally use for waxing.

Leather hoods, straps and clothing can be cleaned with commercial leather cleaner. In the previous edition I recommended saddle soap, but so many expert leather workers have told me I was wrong that I'll concede error and go with their recommendation. Every six months or so, leather articles should be treated with neat's foot oil. You should use several light coats and finish by polishing with a soft cloth, while being careful not to use too much. You want to oil it, not drown it. If leather has to be stored, simply hang it up. Do not seal it in plastic, because it needs air.

Because leather whips come in such intimate, and forceful, contact with the submissive's skin, there is a chance that they could pick up a bit of blood. For this reason, first, wipe them with a rag soaked in hot, soapy water; then, with an alcohol-dampened rag and, finally, with a rag soaked in hot clean water. After the whips have been allowed to dry, they should be lubricated to prevent them from becoming stiff.

I use a thin layer of butter to soften whip tails. It is a natural lubricant that contains little to irritate or inflame sensitive or broken skin. I just stroke it on and rub the surface dry. Some other dominants use mink oil for the softening agent. Saddle soap can also be used, but because it contains chemicals that could cause an allergic reaction, I tend to avoid it.

Toys like dildos, douche nozzles, or knives should be washed in hot, soapy water wiped with a mixture of one part household bleach and nine parts water. I strongly recommend that you not use the same toy on different submissives. Dildos can be made easier to clean by covering them before use with a condom.

Vibrators should be wiped with a rag soaked in hot, soapy water and another with ten percent bleach. However, because of the construction of most vibrators, they cannot be soaked. Instead, they should be covered with a condom before use. For those too large to cover with a condom (although you will be surprised how much one stretches), use a surgical glove. Some vibrators like the Hitachi Magic Wand and the Oster Stick Massager have attachments that can be soaked in water-bleach mixture. Another approach is to use a laboratory sanitizer like Hibiclens, letting it sit for about ten minutes and wiping with warm water.

Rope and nylon strapping can be washed in an ordinary washing machine. However, you should first put them into a bag to minimize knotting and to prevent them from becoming tangled in the agitator. A mesh bag like those used to wash delicate fabrics is ideal. However, a pillow case will do.

TENS accessories combine a number of cleaning problems. The insertable toys have internal contacts that can be hard to reach and may react badly to immersion in a bleach solution, and condoms aren't useful because they are insulators. About the only way to be confident of disinfection is to use an autoclave or pressure cooker for at least a half hour. Another approach is a spray with a laboratory sanitizer using the approach mentioned above. Some external contacts made from rubber can be cleaned with a bleach solution, but the leather ones should be cleaned like any other leather toy.

Condoms, dental dams, finger cots and latex gloves should be sealed in a plastic bag with a bit of alcohol and disposed of in the trash. Ideally, they should be treated like biohazard materials and incinerated in a sanitary manner, but sometimes the principal way to make sure that the wrong thing is done is to make the right thing too complex to do. Let's just keep it simple, and dispose of them in a sealed container full of alcohol fumes.

Appendix: Contracts

Here are the contracts entered into by two dominant/submissive couples. The styles are quite different, but the basic features remain constant.

Master Morgan's and Leah's contract:

1. Leah agrees to place control of her body, thoughts, and behaviors in the hands of Master Morgan while they are in direct contact. She will follow all commands that fit within the limits of this contract completely, faithfully, and with immediate speed. She will answer all questions honestly and completely. She agrees to receive punishment if she fails to comply with the above.

2. Master Morgan accepts the responsibility for leading Leah in the exploration of her sexuality. Morgan agrees to protect Leah's sense of internal self-worth while removing ego barriers that have prohibited her from exploring these areas on her own. Morgan agrees to a long-term goal that Leah will become comfortable in the knowledge of her sexual desires, as expanded by this training. She shall achieve her "graduation" when she is able to control her own sexuality because her restructured sexual ego and sense of self-esteem are in harmony.

3. The choice of behaviors, sexual partners, physical devices, and punishments is determined by Master Morgan, with the following exceptions:

a.   Leah may stop any activity at any time by the clear use of her safeword;

b.   Leah and Morgan may leave this agreement temporarily and return to the outside world at any time simply by requesting it;

c.   While the level of acceptable force will be learned by mutual exploration and may change with time, nothing will be done to cause physical injury to Leah. Nor will she be exposed to risks of pregnancy, arrest, or disease.

d.   Verbal humiliation will be used only as it affects Leah's preconceived notions about sexual morality. It will never be used to describe her general worth as a human being nor her non-sexual behaviors, except her unwillingness to follow orders.

4.   This contract expires immediately upon clear notice by either party that the contract is terminated.

Sir Spencer's and M's contract:

That the two of us have become united as closely as we have in our lives, I now unite and align myself with you in the signing of this agreement and state as carefully my own additional commitment to the strength and assurance of our relationship. We thus compose and provide this document as our original "Agreement of Submission," as a statement of our devotion to our continued relationship and to provide the sense of solidity that we both so very much want.

Of my own free will, as of (date), I, (M's name here), hereby submit to you as my master, and grant you full ownership and use of my body and mind from now until (date about six months later). I further understand and agree to the conditions of the sharing of my body, mind, heart, and soul which I desire to give over to you, and submission as you have detailed herein.

I will strive diligently to acquaint my personal self, my habits, and my attitudes with those that are in that are in keeping with your particular interests and desires for me as your submissive. I will thus always seek to discover new ways of pleasing you and will be observant that I always do those things that you have already indicated that you enjoy. I will gracefully accept any criticism you may choose to inform me of.

For example, when deciding modes of dress, rather than dictating what they should be in this document, to maintain a more flexible position, I am allowed by you here to assist in the planning and negotiation of what forms and fashions of apparel are to be worn by me.

As another example, I will gladly honor at your desire and request, to undertake the public display and to exhibit the exact condition of the state of my submission through the symbols we have chosen and will choose in the future.

I will not conceal or hold private from you, any aspects of this component of my life and existence. I will advise you immediately and without hesitation of all events and occurrences in this and related aspects of my life. Especially, of anything which may affect our special relationship and the condition and status of my ownership and submission.

Thus to this end, I will always look toward and seek your kind assistance. I will be firm in my assurance with conviction and understanding, that you do hold with love and concern, my best and highest interests. I will try to please you and thus achieve any rewards you may so kindly deign to give me. I will obey you at all times and will wholeheartedly seek your pleasure and well-being above all other considerations.

Accordingly, I know that you sincerely have my own safety and hopes at heart and will thus ensure that my obedience is complete and I thus may safely entrust myself to your exacting care and attention with no fears or apprehensions on my part.

I am aware that this agreement is not to be considered as being synonymous with a slave contract. In the main intent and context of our agreement, I will obey you at all times during the period of this agreement.

Again, in keeping with the context and intent of this document, I thus give over to you the direction of my own privileges to my own pleasure, comfort, or gratification insofar as you desire or permit them. Or in this aspect I will, at all times, first ask you for your kind permission, before I may be allowed to enjoy my own pleasure in some particular manner or way. This would be any type of activity at all beyond routine sexual "self-pleasure," which use and frequency, you have allowed me to negotiate with you.

In keeping with the intent of this agreement, I will answer any question posed by you immediately and without hesitation, fully and truthfully. As a counterpoint to this, and as you have expressly wished, I will understand that you want me to feel free to express, also without hesitation any question, interest, desire or need, in keeping with the nature and condition of my submission and my desire for your pleasure; knowing that you do insist upon this questioning. However, I am first to ask permission in any case that I may desire to do something or to ask you a question.

In regard to the conditions of my ownership I agree to the following. I freely offer to you, in this aspect, the full and sole possession of my self; and that with the addition of the special clauses detailed herein, the condition of my ownership shall be fully determined by you.

As to exclusivity: As we have discussed and agreed; in addition to the condition of ownership, you have hereby allowed me to share time and activity in submitting to J.W. as my Mentor, just as you are my Master. For this additional consideration, I am very grateful to you and to J.W., as I know it will please both you and he, to allow for this arrangement.

In regard to the giving of myself to any other Masters, Mistresses, or any Dominants of any design, I hereby renounce any rights or privileges to do so; unless by special arrangement discussed with you directly, on an exception basis, and which may also include a three-way discussion between you, myself and Mentor J.W.

Also in connection with the conditions of my submission and ownership, I will also be responsible to maintain myself in condition pleasing to you. I will heed your wishes as regards to during which portions of my day to day existence you wish me to be fully aware of the condition of my ownership and submission, and during what times of day and night these requirements are to be in force.

I also understand that you will determine any occurrences of our encounters, but that also during times in between our personal encounters, in order to please you, I may be also required to engage in my own remote training at your direction.

I understand that I need to maintain my own personal diary of events and emotions that I have had and felt since the very moment that I began to embark on this unique life adventure. Therefore I know that it is my responsibility to dutifully maintain my diary, and from time to time read to you from it, upon your request.

I understand that my failure to comply in any way with the intent, or with the clauses and conditions of this contract will constitute sufficient cause for me to face possible punishment of your sole determination.

Accordingly, I have humbly and at your instigation asked for the single "safe" word of "Prodigy," should I need to plea for a cessation of some treatment. You have assured me here and now that we may discuss and agree to any future change or addition to safety signal.

You have further assured me herein that you may give audience to my pleas in regards to some particular method or treatment that you may desire to place me under. I am assured and trusting, that you will always consider the current state of my limitations in making any determination and imposition of any treatments I am to receive or endure. I am fully aware with my entire conscious being that your treatments of me, my body, flesh, mind, and spirit will be imposed always with your care and love.

Beyond these requests and considerations, I graciously allow and submit myself to receive any nature of treatment that you so desire to give me.

At my request, I gratefully understand that a minimum of one weekend a month will be set aside for my personal attention and further training.

Due to the unique nature of our relationship, the duration of the agreement (contract) of this relationship has been determined as stated at the top of this document. At a time approaching the termination of this agreement, you have assured me that you and I will discuss its renewal.

Also at that time any planning for modifications or updating of the terms and clauses of the agreement may be discussed. As that time I understand, as you have told me, that we may discuss some sort of award based on my successful and pleasing completion of the terms of this agreement. The nature of this award may take the form of some type of emblem or insignia, or even some adornment, be it of a temporary or permanent nature, to mark the end of this first period of my grateful submission. Future emblematic awards may be further granted at the ends of each subsequent passing period of renewal as representative of the continuation and deepening of our relationship.

<<the following added at a later date, as negotiated>>

I, (Spencer's name here), vow to keep myself only unto you, in these things which we share and enjoy with each other, and participate with no others, except those which we have already discussed with other. This would include the clause in our main agreement document for Mentor, and now in this addendum for myself, to participate on occasion with KT and AI. I will hereby also vow that I will not engage in, nor seek to engage in any new activities with any parties, unless you, and I have thoroughly and completely assessed and discussed the particulars of the situation with each other, and are both in complete agreement and anticipation of such outside activity.

Excluding the exceptions already stated, we will not engage in any of these pursuits without the presence of the other. As our two rings which we will always wear have become symbols of our relationship.

Appendix: What color is *your* handkerchief?

Almost everyone who has come in contact with the scene has heard about "the handkerchief code"; even the title of this section was taken from a well-respected, although out-of-publication, book by the lesbian BDSM group, Samois. However, to most people, the signals remain a mystery. There is a good reason for this: There is no consistent nationwide, mutually agreed upon set of signals. Each city and group has some local or personal variation from a ambiguous and nebulous norm. Handkerchief codes are most common in gay and lesbian circles, but some hetero groups have adopted them.

The closest thing to a norm is a vague agreement that right side display indicates submissive and left dominant, but in the real world, a handkerchief in the left pocket or a set of keys on the left side of the pants may simply indicate a left handed person.

Some of the more common colors are:

Black = Heavy into the scene
Gray = Bondage
Red = Fistfucker
Dark blue = Anal sex
Light blue = Oral sex
Purple = Into piercing
Green = Wants money or is willing to pay
Brown = Shit scenes (Scat)
Yellow = Piss scenes (Golden Showers)
Pink = Breast fondler

Orange = Anything goes

White = Wants or is novice

White Lace = Victorian scenes (lesbian or CD)

Maroon = Likes menstruating women or is menstruating (lesbian)

Unfortunately, to make things even more complex, headbangers and other fringe groups have adopted wearing handkerchiefs in their belts or carrying them in their pockets recognizing only that they indicate some sort of socially forbidden behavior.

Once, at an TES meeting, Lenny, the owner of The Vault and a large, imposing gentleman who clearly has had more than a passing acquaintance with leather and motorcycles, told with glee about approaching two youngsters who were defiantly sporting brightly colored handkerchiefs in their pockets. As he told it, he walked up to them, pointedly looked at their handkerchiefs while they tried to decide whether to run or to stand their ground and said, "So, you want to get your asses fucked and drink some piss." That persuaded them. They ran.

Appendix: Spencer's Questionnaire

The following is a questionnaire that a colleague, Master Spencer, developed for delving into the fantasies of submissives.

A. Preliminary Idea/Format: Do you like something that is highly planned, or spontaneous, unplanned and unstructured? Or perhaps something with elements of both?

    Do you like the planning and negotiating to be verbal or written or a little bit of both? Do you prefer knowing what will happen:

        * completely
        * mostly
        * somewhat
        * very little
        * not at all

B. Roles and Fantasies (Those that you like to be doing as the Bottom):

    a.   A role which is set in the present, the here and now, and you are "yourself," and "getting it" just as you are. For example just because you "like to" or to "atone" for certain emotions present or past.

    b.   A role which is set in the present, and you are being "yourself," but some "fantasy" becomes more involved in these roles. For example, you are "in role" as a type of person who has certain faults and failings for which you need to atone, be corrected, or punished for. In these types of roles you may either "remember" and describe the things you need correction for, or

may maintain an "imaginary" or real "Log Book" or "Diary."
Common imaginary or real failings are such things as:

* Assignments and things not carried out.
* "Faults" of timeliness: late to work, for appointments or not calling when coming home late.
* Making a clutter, failing to clean the kitchen or the windows, failing to vacuuming or dust or do other assigned tasks.
* Causing loss and breakage, auto fender benders, personal possessions of yourself or your Top, housewares, small collectibles, large or valuable collectibles and possessions.
* Behaving in a naughty way like being argumentative, pouty, bored, and moody, in a foul, nasty mood or aloof, sassy, sarcastic and teasing, "flirtatious," other scandalous or exhibitionistic behavior.
* Money things. Spending too much on big items, or too much on small items, forgetting items you were told to buy.
* Appearance, not dressed to please deliberately, accidentally, or dressed entirely inappropriately for the occasion.

c. Fantasy roles where you may be "being" someone other than yourself, either in cast in present day circumstances, or in times and places past.

These types of fantasy roles can be sort of grouped into several different types of circumstances. In a sense these tend to gradually increase the level of the (Bottom) player's role.

(1) Fantasy roles in which the "victim"/Bottom/submissive is involuntarily "captured" and/or kidnapped and either "dealt with" randomly without any reason, or as a symbol of some oppressed cause:

* In the present time: by terrorists, mercenary soldiers, as "westernized" women in Islamic states, Western women by Islamic courts, by bikers, a liberal woman by a community of reactionary "survivalists", (UK) "skinheads" vs. the wealthy class, a socialite kidnapped for ransom.
* Set in the past: a "heretic" by the Inquisition, the noble classes of old France and Russia, the village girl cap-

tured by de Sade, the Indian girl by cowboys or western pioneers.

(2) In a very servile, subservient, even "slavelike" situation, often "punished" for very little provocation, these settings seem to be mostly in the "past":

* The heroine of the Science Fantasy/Sword and Sorcerer/ Sword and Sandal epic stories; Norman, S. Greene, Gene Wolf's "Shadow of the Torturer"
* A slavegirl in the secret Seraglio in the Topkapi Palace of Suleiman the Magnificent in Istanbul
* Girl on a plantation ruled by a tyrannical owner/ overseer
* Girl in an English women's reformatory about the 1880s
* a young hooker being "disciplined" by her pimp

(3) In a community where breaches of "standards" are dealt with most harshly by ritualistically inflicted corporal punishments:

* In colonial American jails for theft
* The frontier "schoolmarm" by locals
* On the English country estate by the lordly masterly owner, the girl in the employ for offenses of "manor" or "manner"
* Lady in her late teens or early twenties who is still receiving punishment from a stern "parental/guardian" figure.

(4) In circumstances "sort of" semiforced into accepting corporal punishment when some wrong has occurred or been committed:

* A modern British (or even American) woman being disciplined by her partner for something, and who both happen to have lurid BDSM lifestyle passions
* Lady working in a bookstore, for being too inquisitive into subjects of sexual deviation
* A store employee, where some error or pilferage is suspected
* A member of a conservative/Bible-oriented secret community who punish the women for sinful thoughts or behavior.

(5) An accepted submissive who is actively involved in the "lifestyle":

* Assigned to go out to a "dangerous" S/M bar, and "pick up" a dominant; she is to be the "feature exhibition" at a display/exhibition at a B&D party, or a B&D club.
* An actress/model in B&D flicks being done, post filming by a dominant who is getting "carried away"
* A lady in a B&D parlor/salon in the US, Amsterdam, or Bangkok or simply rented out to a dominant.

Roles you like or prefer your Top to appear in/as:

* Alternating between punishing, soothing, praising, comforting
* Straightforward no-nonsense, silent, impassive, punisher
* Any kind of "humiliation" dominance, or degradation
* Mostly just himself/(or herself), with a touch of some of the above in it.

Play and Treatments:

* Are there any particular types of treatments you like?
* What are your "turn ons"?
* Any particular parts of yourself you like or prefer being "treated"?
* Are there any particular types of treatments you don't like, won't do or try, or can't handle?
* What are your "turn offs"?
* Any parts of yourself you do NOT like or want to be "treated"?

Anything you haven't tried yet, but might want to or would like to consider? Or do you like to have things suggested and talk about them with your Top, to get some ideas about what you might like to try as things develop?

What particular safety or code words or signals do you like or have?

One idea for determining to particular discipline to be appropriate for certain circumstances, is the "punishments jar" or "punishments box." Or even better, three each of these "punishments jars." One for light punishments, medium punishments, and heavy punishments. Then each type of failure, problem, or offense in the "Log Book" is accorded its own appropriate "level" of punishment to "choose" from that particular "punishments jar," Then one merely fills up the jar with little bits of paper upon which are written various punishments of the level indicated on the jar. If, for example the Bottom has recorded certain things in her "Log Book" which indicate that a punishment from the "medium" level jar is to be dealt, she gets to reach in that jar and pick one out at random, not knowing what it will be until, of course, she opens it up and reads it (aloud of course).

D. Scene, Setup, Costume, Dress:

* What sort of costumes do you like to "dress up" in? Or do you like to tailor the costume to the developing scene?
* What sort of costumes do you like your Top to "dress up" in? Or likewise do you like him/her to also tailor the fashion to the scene?
* Do you like any music, or do you prefer silence, or should the scene fantasy be considered?
* Do you like to view appropriate B&D videos preparatory or during and in context with the scene, or while "relaxing"?
* Do you like any refreshments to be available?

Appendix: A Highly Idiosyncratic Glossary

I've tried to find definitions that reflect a kind of consensus among the people to whom I've talked over these many years. However, there is hardly a term or phrase applying to BDSM over which there hasn't been some sort of flaming argument. The reader is urged to remember words are maps in a way; they guide and suggest but they aren't the territory being described. In a very real way, they are like newspaper photographs. They give a certain amount of information, but when you put them under a magnifying glass, you get less... rather than more... information. Often, a word is enough, but usually a sentence is better, a paragraph better still and some concepts demand volumes. If someone comes up to me and says, "I'm a slave." I'll smile and nod. If she says, "I want to be your slave," I'm going to want a hell of a lot more information.

Age Play – A role play where one or both partners take personas of people older or younger than they really are. Common examples are Teacher/Schoolgirl, Babysitter/Naughty child.

Animal Play – The assumption of the persona of an animal by the submissive, usually in conjunction with some sort of use or training by the dominant. See Pony Play.

Alternate lifestyle – An umbrella term for those whose sexuality is not in the common mold. Includes BDSM, swingers, gays.

Auction – An activity that often takes place in BDSM clubs where dominants and submissives are put on auction. Usually, the rules require that any resulting scene take place in the club during the evening the event took place. Further restrictions are common.

B&D – Bondage and Discipline. A subgroup within BDSM which is largely involved in making the submissive physically helpless and applying stimuli which outside of a scene would be painful. See Bondage. See Discipline

Bastinado – Striking or whipping the feet with a cane or rod.

Ball dancing – Using temporary piercings as attachment points for balls, bells and other small weights and then moving in such a way as to make them swing and ring.

Birching – Striking with single birch rods or bundles of birch twigs. Often causes minor scratches and is considered a mild form of blood play.

Black snake – Single tail whip that is flexible throughout its entire length, including where the user's hand rests.

Blood sports – A group of techniques in which the submissive's skin is broken and blood is allowed to escape. Since the advent of AIDS and the spread of hepatitis, those who practice blood sports have developed techniques to protect themselves. The most common blood sport is cutting. See Cutting.

Bondage – A group of techniques for rendering a submissive physically helpless. These include rope ties, handcuffs and manacles, wrapping and mummification. See B&D. See Mummification. See Decorative binding. See Immobilization.

Bottom – Someone who engages in stimulation play as the receiver of the stimulation but who does create a semblance of submission as part of his or her play.

Bottom drop – A kind of seeming depression that may follow scenes. It is hypothesized that the body interprets the return to normal sensation levels as a depression and the mind creates a further downward spiral in attempting to explain the perceived depression.

Boundaries – Limits agreed to during negotiation.

Branding – Burning the skin with a piece of hot metal, usually to create a design.

Breath control – A form of play where the dominant controls the breathing of the submissive. This may be through air-tight masks, strangulation, drowning or other techniques. The safety of this activity is the subject of major debate within the BDSM community, with many holding that it is impossible to do with reliable safety. The majority of BDSM related deaths (solo or partner play) have come from breath control play.

Brown showers – Defecation upon a submissive.

Canes – Not the type used by people to walk with. In BDSM, they are thin and flexible. Traditional ones are rattan. Recently, space age materials have been used with great success. Avoid bamboo canes as they have a tendency to split and produce edges that can cut the skin.

Cat – A multitailed whip. For purists, the only true cat is made from unwinding a thick rope in the naval tradition.

Catheterization – Inserting a sterile tube into the urethra for the purpose of controlling urination.

CBT – Cock and ball torture.

Cicatrization – Scarification. Making cuts in the skin for the purpose of creating a pattern of scars.

Code words – Another term for safeword used by some dominants and submissives

Collared – To have accepted a collar from a dominant. This presumes a certain degree of continued submission the degree of which is up to the individuals involved and may range from highly dedicated to extremely casual.

Consensual – Agreed to. Most people feel that informed consent is necessary during all BDSM play. This means that both parties are aware of the inherent risks and accept them.

Crashing – See Bottom drop.

Cupping – Use of a vacuum device to stimulate the submissive's skin, often the nipples. The vacuum can be created by suction cups, vacuum pumps or heating the air in a rigid container and allowing it to cool.

Cutting – A technique in which cuts are carefully made in the submissive's skin to produce an aesthetically pleasing pattern and stimulation to the submissive. The cuts are sometimes made into permanent markings by placing sterile foreign substances in them before they heal. See Blood sports.

Decorative binding – Using rope or cord to compress or tie a portion of the body where struggle will not cause it to tighten or cut into the submissive. See Immobilization.

Discipline – The application of stimuli which, outside of a scene, would be considered painful. Common discipline techniques are whipping, spanking and strapping. See B&D.

Do-me queen – (derogatory) A person of either gender whose entire involvement in the scene is totally for his or her pleasure. Usually these people take a pseudo-submissive orientation, and being involved with one can be very frustrating and draining for the dominant.

Dominant – An individual who accepts the submissive's power and uses it for their mutual pleasure. See Sadist.

Edgeplay – These are particularly dangerous BDSM that are looked upon with some trepidation. Because there is no formal "ruling body" in BDSM, what is called edgeplay is up to the individual. Therefore, something that to one person might be considered edgeplay might not be edgeplay to another.

Edgeplayer – A person takes part in edgeplay. Example: "The guy is a real edgeplayer; he's into heavy bloodsports and asphyxia."

Electro-play / Electro-torture – Using electricity in one or more of its many guises to create intense stimulation during a scene.

Encasement – Sealing the male genitals in a sack or ball to prevent them from being stimulated in any way.

Endorphins – Chemicals similar to opiates created by the body to deal with stress and pain. "Runner's High" is due to these. Much of scene play, particularly intense stimulation, is aimed at producing the release of endorphins.

English / English Arts – Spanking and caning.

Erotic embarrassment – "Forcing" a submissive to dress, speak or perform acts that he or she actually desires but has been restrained by societal pressures.

Fetish – In psychological terms, one has a fetish when an article, action or sensation replaces a human being as the primary stimulus for arousal. In the scene, it is more liberally interpreted and often simply means an intense desire for as in "I have a fetish for leather."

Fireplay – Either caressing another with a flame or creating a burst of flame on his or her body. This can be done quite safely and need not even be slightly painful.

Flogger – A multitailed whip usually with flat tresses. Generally a thud toy.

German/German Arts – Sadomasochist play.

Go word – A signal by the submissive that everything is all right and you can continue with or increase the present level of stimulation. See Safeword, Stop word, Slow word.

Golden showers – A humiliation technique where the dominant urinates on the submissive. Consumption of the urine may be part of this scene.

Heavy play – Intense but like so much in the scene, subjective. What is heavy play for one is a light warm-up for another.

Humiliation – In this book, I try to differentiate humiliation from erotic embarrassment. Humiliation is to express hurtful words or force a submissive into acts designed to reduce his or her self-esteem.

Immobilization – Using rope or other bondage tools to render a submissive relatively helpless despite his or her struggles. See Decorative binding.

Infantilism – Roleplay where the submissive partner assumes the behavior and dress of an infant. Pure fantasy, as all children are actually nonconsensual dominants.

Kajira – A sex/pleasure slave taken from the Gor series. This fantasy is seen much more in the on-line world than in extended face to face play, since it is generally a cartoon of BDSM life.

Knife play – Using a knife as part of a scene. Often does not involve cutting, but is used it to gently scratch the surface of the skin, threaten, stimulate.

Knout – A very vicious single tailed whip from Russia. It can be highly dangerous since a single blow has been known to kill.

Lacing – Connecting temporary piercings with thread or light chain. The piercings may be connected to each other or to a framework.

Masochism – The ability to derive pleasure from pain. Derives from the writings of Leopold von Sacher-Masoch. See S&M.

OTK – Over the knee. A form of spanking.

Pain slut – (NOT derogatory) Someone who glories in receiving what most would call intense pain.

Panic snap – A linking device used with cable and chain that allows two lengths to be disconnected even when there is tension in the system. A safety device.

Player – A great example why no one should feel shy about asking "What do you mean by this." There are two antithetical definitions. One, most often seen in the online world and in certain subcultures holds that a person so named "plays" people and therefore is not to be trusted. Another definition from the intelligence, law enforcement and gambling communities is that the person is skilled at "playing the game" and therefore is to be taken seriously.

Play piercing – see Temporary Piercing.

Pony play – Pony play combines elements of bondage, display, control and service to create a unique kink that is enjoyed by a very active subgroup within the BDSM community. Basically, in pony play, the submissive takes the role of a pony and is used and presented as such. Pony play can include sophisticated, lovely and expensive "rigs" including harnesses, saddles, bridles and even carts. The pony can carry or pull the dominant or can be put through elaborate dressage movements guided by the signals of either a mounted rider or dismounted trainer. See Animal Play

Pushing limits – The gradual expansion of a dominant's and a submissive repertoire as he or she gains confidence and seeks new challenges. A wise axiom is "Never say, "I'll never'."

Queening – A dominant woman sitting on a submissive person's face for the purposes of breath control. Purists insist that cunnilingus should not take place, but it often does.

Roman showers – Vomiting upon a submissive.

S&M – Sadism and Masochism – A term often used to describe the BDSM scene; however, it is falling into disrepute because it is both inaccurate (dominants are not sadists) and overly limited (all submissives are not masochists). See Sadism. See Masochism.

Sadist – An individual who enjoys causing pain in a non-consensual manner or regardless of the presence of absence of consent.

Derives from the writings of the Marquis de Sade. See S&M.

Safe, Sane and Consensual – A slogan popular in the scene defining the components of proper play. Like any slogan, it is oversimplified and the topic of much debate, but it does get its point across.

Safeword – A word or phrase which permits the submissive to withdraw consent and terminate the scene at any point without endangering the illusion that the dominant is in complete control. See Slow word. See Go word.

Saint Catherine's wheel – A vertical wheel to which a submissive can be strapped and spun around.

Saint Andrew's cross – An X-shaped cross.

SAM – Smart Assed Masochist. A pseudo-submissive who attempts to control everything the dominant does. A term of contempt. Example: "She's cute and willing, but she's a real SAM; you will spend most of your time trying to keep her from telling you which whip to use and how to swing it." See "Topping From the Bottom."

Scat – A slang term for scatophilia, taking pleasure in playing with and sometimes eating feces. While this is occasionally used as a means of humiliation, it presents a relatively severe health risk, not limited to AIDS and hepatitis.

Scene (A) – An individual session of whatever duration where the participants are in their BDSM roles. Example: "It was a tremendously hot scene last night when Master Carl waxed Linda at The Vault."

Scene (The) – The gamut of BDSM activities and people considered as a whole. Example: "The scene contains some of the nicest people I have ever met." It's an umbrella word that covers a lot.

Scrotal expansion – Injecting sterile saline into the male ball sack, causing it to expand significantly.

Sensory deprivation – A form of restraint where all sensory input is systematically cut off through blindfolds, ear plugs or earphones and secure but non-painful bondage

Slave – Often used interchangeably with submissive. However, generally reflecting a more intense level of submission or non-sexual or sexual-plus submission. For example, a slave might be someone who remains in a 24-hour-per-day submission and cooks, cleans and, otherwise, takes care of a dominant's house. See submissive.

Slow word – A signal by the submissive that things are getting too intense and you should change or decrease the stimulation. See Safeword. See Go word.

Sound – A medical device shaped like a curved rod that is inserted into the uretha

Squick – A cyber term that has moved into the off-line world. Coined by STella of ASB, it means, essentially, "This disgusts me."

Stapling – Temporary piercing and lacing done with a surgical stapler and sterile medical staples.

Strapple – An elongated paddle with a bit more flex so that is something intermediate between a strap and a paddle.

Sting – A sensation from a toy that is "stingy," as distinguished from "thud." Intense surface sensation.

Submissive – An individual who gives up power in a BDSM relationship for the mutual pleasure of those involved.

Suspension – A set of techniques for suspending a submissive using ropes, webbing or chain so that no part of the body touches the floor. This is a highly specialized technique and great care must be used to prevent damage.

Switch (Switchable) – A person who enjoys both the dominant/top and submissive/bottom roles. A switch may be dominant to one person and submissive with another or may be dominant or submissive with the same person at different times.

Sub drop – See Bottom drop.

Temporary piercing – Using a sterile needle to penetrate the skin as a stimulation rather than to produce a hole to be used for jewelry as in conventional piercing. See Lacing and Ball dancing.

Thud – Sensation from a toy that is largely impact and felt deeply in the body, often moving the body itself. Distinguished from "sting."

Top – A person who in play delivers the stimulation but does not require the submission of his or her partner.

Top drop – See Bottom drop.

Topping from the bottom – (derogatory) For a submissive to dictate the precise action in a scene. A term of contempt. Example: "She's cute and willing, but she's always topping from the bottom; you will spend most of your time trying to keep her from telling you which whip to use and how to swing it." See "SAM.'

Top's disease – A condition where a top or dominant projects the fantasy role into the real world with an assumption of superiority. This kind of person can be a real pain in the ass.

True – A term when used in conjunction with "master," "dominant," "slave" or similar term rates, at best, a snicker. As a putdown to others, it says much more about the one who is using it than the one who is being put down.

TT – Tit torture. The term applies to both males and females.

Urtication – Using stinging nettles in scene play. They can be simply pressed into the skin or used as a whip.

Vanilla – Not in the scene. A term used to describe ordinary, conventional life both sexual and otherwise. While it can be used in a pejorative sense, it is more often used to distinguish between scene and non-scene activities and people. Example: "I have to be careful in my vanilla life that people don't find out that I'm a dominant."

Violet wand – An antique medical device still being manufactured that creates a large, but harmless, spark and is used extensively in electro play scenes.

YKINMK-BYKIOK – A mantra by many in the scene. Your Kink Is Not My Kink, But Your Kink Is OK. Intended to point out that our desires and needs do not define the scene for others.

Wrapping – Allowing the ends of a whip to go around the target's body rather than hit cleanly in the target zone. When done unintentionally, it is a mark of a careless or inexperienced whipper and is usually caused by standing too close to the subject. The intensity of the stroke is magnified several times wrapping.

Wartenburg wheel – A spiked pinwheel intended for use by neurologists but taken up and used for play by ingenious scene players. The sensation looks intense but is generally perceived as pleasurable.

Index

U

Ullerstam, Lars 13
unconsciousness 223

V

vagina, toy lost in 225
vanilla 24, 63, 65
Velcro 122
Venus in Furs 11, 42
vibrator 108, 109, 110, 111, 234
violet wand 179
von Krafft-Ebing, D.R 10
von Sacher-Masoch, Leopold 11

W

wax 13, 30, 31, 135, 152-158, 226, 233
webbing 121
websearch 46
websites 46
whip 16, 30, 32, 37, 50, 62, 83, 88, 125, 135, 137-141, 156, 162, 205, 209
    whip, selecting a 137

Y

Yahoo 46

Z

zipper 102

BDSM/KINK

The Artisan's Book of Fetishcraft: Patterns and Instructions for Creating Professional Fetishwear, Restraints & Equipment
John Huxley — $27.95

At Her Feet: Powering Your Femdom Relationship
TammyJo Eckhart and Fox — $14.95

... But I Know What You Want: 25 Sex Tales for the Different
James Williams — $13.95

The Compleat Spanker
Lady Green — $12.95

Conquer Me: girl-to-girl wisdom about fulfilling your submissive desires
Kacie Cunningham — $13.95

Family Jewels: A Guide to Male Genital Play and Torment
Hardy Haberman — $12.95

Flogging
Joseph Bean — $11.95

The Human Pony: A Guide for Owners, Trainers and Admirers
Rebecca Wilcox — $27.95

Intimate Invasions: The Ins and Outs of Erotic Enema Play
M.R. Strict — $13.95

Jay Wiseman's Erotic Bondage Handbook
Jay Wiseman — $16.95

The Kinky Girl's Guide to Dating
Luna Grey — $16.95

The Mistress Manual: A Good Girl's Guide to Female Dominance
Mistress Lorelei — $16.95

The New Bottoming Book
The New Topping Book
Dossie Easton & Janet W. Hardy — $14.95 ea.

Playing Well With Others: Your Field Guide to Discovering, Exploring and Navigating the Kink, Leather and BDSM Communities
Lee Harrington & Mollena Williams — $19.95

Play Piercing
Deborah Addington — $13.95

Radical Ecstasy: SM Journeys to Transcendence
Dossie Easton & Janet W. Hardy — $16.95

The Seductive Art of Japanese Bondage
Midori, photographs by Craig Morey — $27.95

The Sexually Dominant Woman: A Workbook for Nervous Beginners
Lady Green — $11.95

SM 101: A Realistic Introduction
Jay Wiseman — $24.95

GENERAL SEXUALITY

A Hand in the Bush: The Fine Art of Vaginal Fisting
Deborah Addington — $13.95

The Jealousy Workbook: Exercises and Insights for Managing Open Relationships
Kathy Labriola — $19.95

Love In Abundance: A Counselor's Advice on Open Relationships
Kathy Labriola — $15.95

Phone Sex: Oral Skills and Aural Thrills
Miranda Austin — $15.95

Sex Disasters... And How to Survive Them
C. Moser, Ph.D., M.D. & Janet W. Hardy — $16.95

Tricks... To Please a Man
Tricks... To Please a Woman
both by Jay Wiseman — $13.95 ea.

When Someone You Love Is Kinky
Dossie Easton & Catherine A. Liszt — $15.95

TOYBAG GUIDES:
A Workshop In A Book — $9.95 each

Age Play, by Lee "Bridgett" Harrington

Basic Rope Bondage, by Jay Wiseman

Canes and Caning, by Janet W. Hardy

Chastity Play, by Miss Simone *(spring 2014)*

Clips and Clamps, by Jack Rinella

Dungeon Emergencies & Supplies, by Jay Wiseman

Erotic Knifeplay, by Miranda Austin & Sam Atwood

Foot and Shoe Worship, by Midori

High-Tech Toys, by John Warren

Hot Wax and Temperature Play, by Spectrum

Medical Play, by Tempest

Playing With Taboo, by Mollena Williams

Greenery Press books are available from your favorite on-line or brick-and-mortar bookstore or erotic boutique, or direct from Revel Books, www.revelbooks.com.
These and other Greenery Press books are also available in ebook format from all major ebook retailers.